Who's Who in American Quilting

American Quilter's Society

P. O. Box 3290 • Paducah, KY 42002-3290

Located in Paducah, Kentucky, the American Quilter's Society (AQS), is dedicated to promoting the accomplishments of today's quilters. Through its publications and events, AQS strives to honor today's quiltmakers and their work – and inspire future creativity and innovation in quiltmaking.

Editor: Bonnie Browning
Book Designer: Lanette Ballard

Library of Congress Cataloging-in-Publication Data

Who's who in American quilting.
      p.   cm.
    ISBN 0-89145-886-7
      1. Quiltmakers--United States--Biography. 2. Quilts--United
States--History--20th century.   I. American Quilter's Society.
NK9112.W52   1996
746.46 ' 092 ' 273--dc20
[B]   96-44771
                                        CIP

Additional copies of this book may be ordered from: American Quilter's Society, P.O. Box 3290, Paducah, KY 42002-3290 @ $49.95. Add $5.00 for postage & handling.

Meredith Schroeder
President – American Quilter's Society

Publisher's Message

This book is dedicated to all quiltmakers, past and present, who have preserved the art of quilt-making by sharing their quilts and the techniques for making them.

The American Quilter's Society (AQS) is dedicated to promoting the accomplishments of today's quilters. Since AQS began in 1984, we have been able to feature the work of thousands of quiltmakers in the AQS Quilt Show & Contest, the *American Quilter* magazine, the Museum of the American Quilter's Society, and in quilting books.

We are now pleased to be able to present the first *Who's Who in American Quilting*. This book records the contributions of more than 500 people involved in quilting today.

An old Chinese proverb states: "Preserve the old but know the new." As you read the biographies of these quilters, you will see that the old traditional quiltmaking techniques are still being utilized. Yet, some quilters are using new methods in their quiltmaking brought about by technology, such as the rotary cutter for faster cutting, computers for designing, and computerized sewing machines for accurate repetitive stitching and quilting.

Quilters make quilts for a variety of reasons. In 1907, Eliza Calvert Hall wrote in *Aunt Jane of Kentucky*: "I looked again at the heap of quilts. An hour ago they had been patchwork and nothing more. But now! The old woman's words had wrought a transportation in the homely mass of calico and silk and worsted. Patchwork? Ah, no! It was memory, imagination, history, biography, joy, sorrow, philosophy, religion, romance, realism, life, love, and death; and over all like a halo, the love of the artist for his work and the soul's longing for earthly immortality." This statement is just as true today as it was in 1907; quilters continue to document their lives in their quilts.

Finally, special appreciation goes out to everyone who submitted biographies, memorable experiences, and photography of their involvement in the world of quilting. It is our sincere hope that this book will serve as a vehicle through which future generations will remember you as quilters and the legacy that you will leave – your quilts.

Meredith Schroeder

Meredith Schroeder
President, American Quilter's Society

Rebecca Abell, Spokane, Washington

Born March 15, 1949 in Kansas to a dairy farmer. Educated as an RN and proud mother of two daughters. Became disabled in 1988 but continues to pursue quilting goals.

Quilting has played a central role in my life since 1976. I design and execute my own one-of-a-kind quilts. I have done some writing on the subject.

Three time exhibitor at AQS and many other juried shows. Member of Without Borders, a contemporary fiber group, dedicated to promoting quilts as art.

Barbara Hendrick Abrelat, Decatur, Georgia

Designer, quiltmaker, and writer. Quiltmaking combines my love for fabric, texture, and color with the design skills I've developed in my life-long career as an illustrator. Quilts have always been a part of my life. Growing up in Mobile, AL, I watched my grandmother and great-aunt make functional quilts. Sharing my enthusiasm by teaching enhanced my appreciation for the many individual expressions quiltmaking inspires. The excitement of creating unique pieces continues to lead me in new directions.

Created quilt top for "A Quilt of Leaves," the official "Look of the Games" for the 1996 Olympic summer games in Atlanta, GA.

Clara Baker Adams, Cave City, Kentucky

My name is Clara Baker Adams. A lover of quilts since making my first one at age 15, a Sunbonnet Baby. Since then I have made around 75 quilts. Some I have designed myself. I have won many ribbons and awards. I give each niece and nephew one for a wedding gift. My very special project was a quilt I made for my pastor, Rev. David

Thomas. In recognition of his first two churches I appliquéd the two churches on the quilt, you could open the doors and see him in the pulpit. Nothing is more satisfying than making a quilt. I plan on making many more. I have been married to Thomas J. Adams for 38 years. We have no children.

Mildred Adams, Birmingham, Alabama

My quilting began in 1982 after watching Georgia Bonesteel's "Lap Quilting" on TV. I quilt every night and find it very relaxing. The pattern chosen, the fabric bought, and no more decisions to make. Just enjoy the quilting and watching a beautiful quilt emerge. My Christmas tree quilt just "grew." My dahlia blocks in red and green looked like poinsettias, so I set them together to form a tree. Angels and stars are quilted in the background top and a train, teddy bear, and sailboat are quilted under the tree. This quilt received blue ribbons at the Alabama State Fair and local quilt shows.

Jean S. Adkins, Fayetteville, North Carolina

I am a self taught quilter of 35 years and an inventor and manufacturer of four quilting/sewing products. These items include the Hand-held Thimble, the Adhesive Seam Gauge, the "Stick to It" Adhesive Pin Cushion, and Finger Savers. Having taught quilting since 1979, I have heard every excuse why my students could not wear a thimble, therefore I invented one you can hold instead of wear. Quilters have always told me they needed "something" for sore fingers, thus came the Finger Savers. All of these products have made my dreams of traveling a reality, I have now become a world-wide traveler while demonstrating my products. The Lord has blessed me in many ways. In addition, I own a quilt shop where quilting is still being taught.

Allyson Allen, California

Recently granted residency by the Cal Arts Council, I'm a self-taught quilter/self-defined "resource artist," i.e. I attempt to

incorporate handmade, organic, or recycled materials in each project, whether I'm making quilts, soap, or paper. A world traveler, I've had invaluable exposure to numerous art disciplines and my work is influenced by each. I try never to use existing patterns and enjoy appliqué and dimensional embellishing most. About a third of my work reflects ethnic themes as I love to use exotic fabrics and beads. Most of the year I teach school in a southern California desert community. Summers I direct a western-style camp for inner-city kids established by my sister and her actor/director husband, Glynn Turman.

abroad and has won numerous awards and prizes for her work. Her quilts are about endangered wildlife, the environment, and current social issues. As a teacher she is best known for machine appliqué and embroidery and the mysteries of color theory. Marta is on the Wyoming Arts in Education Roster, Arts Across Wyoming, and is a Wyoming Arts Consultant. She has been the recipient of three Art in Public Building Awards and two state grants. She is an active member of the Front Range Contemporary Quilters in Boulder, CO, and AQS.

Mary Emma Allen, Plymouth, New Hampshire

Author, collector, designer, quiltmaker, teacher, lecturer, and judge. Mary Emma Allen, born October 27, 1938, in Dutchess County, NY, currently resides in Plymouth, NH. She graduated from New Paltz (NY) State Teachers College in 1960. For many years, Mary operated a quilting business, Mea's Quilts, in her home and sold patchwork and quilted items by mail order and in shops. One of her specialties was appliquéd vests for children. Mary made her first quilts with her grandmother when she was 8 years old. She is carrying on that tradition by creating quilts with her 4-year-old granddaughter, Karalynn. Mary and her daughter, Beth Mastin, collect old quilts. They've also been restoring old family quilts as well as preserving them in hangings and framed pictures. Mary wrote "The Business of Patchwork" columns for *Quilt World Omnibook*, "Work Patch" columns for *Traditional Quilter*, and writes other quilting articles. She has published a book, *The Magic of Patchwork*. In addition, Mary gives talks on quilt history, has taught quilting workshops, and judged at quilt shows.

My quiltmaking business (Mea's Quilts) was written up in Yankee magazine and brought me a great deal of contact with other quilters.

Marta Amundson, Riverton, Wyoming

Martha Amundson was born February 26, 1955, in Los Angeles, CA. She attended University of Stockholm in Sweden and graduated magna cum laude from Albion College in Michigan. She has lived in Riverton, Wyoming, for the last 19 years with her husband, Larry. Marta is a professional quiltmaker and travels throughout the United States, Sweden, Brazil, and Great Britain giving workshops and lectures for quilt groups, conferences, and art schools. She has exhibited widely throughout the U.S. and

Charlotte Warr Andersen, Salt Lake City, Utah

Fiber artist, designer, author of *Faces & Places – Images In Appliqué*.

A quilter since 1974, I specialize in making one-of-a-kind, pictorial quilts in both appliqué and piecing techniques. I also lecture and teach nationally and internationally and design wearable art.

Second place winner in first Great American Quilt Contest (Statue of Liberty), 2 Best of Shows – Houston International Quilt Festival; 2 Best of Shows – Silver Dollar City; 4 1st places – AQS Quilt Show; 1st and 2nd places – AQS/Hobbs Bonded Fibers Fashion Show; 5 time Fairfield Fashion Show designer.

Marita Anderson, Rolla, Missouri

I am a 42 year old quiltmaker. Dave and I have been married for 20 years and have four teenagers whom we've educated at home. We are Christians and active in our church. I lead an informal church quilt group. I have been quilting nearly every day with my morning coffee since 1990. My horizons, skills, and love of the quilting process have widened steadily. My favorite quilting love is appliquéd landscapes. A special quilt memory is of the time I made an intricate, heavily quilted, queen-size Missouri Chain as a Christmas gift for my husband's mother. She was the perfect recipient, awed and breathless with appreciation. I cherish her reaction because she passed away last year, and I'm glad to have given her joy.

Charlotte Angotti, Virginia Beach, Virginia

Author, designer, teacher, motivator, and quilt shop owner. Began quiltmaking in 1977 and still learning. Teaching and motivating techniques have always included humor and fun.

Published author, 1994, *Still Crazy After All These Quilts.* Has taught at Quilt Festival and Quilt Market, Houston, TX, since 1989 and other large shows plus at quilt guilds and clubs throughout the U.S. Since 1992 she has worked with Alexander Henry Fabrics, designing quilts using their fabrics to be displayed by the company in shows and exhibits. Opened her shop, Quilt Works, in 1981 where she still works, teaches, and motivates others to quilt. Charlotte has also given a better home to old quilts and has a large collection of new and old quilts she takes along with her on her many trips teaching and lecturing.

Cynthia G. Applegate, Montrose, Pennsylvania

Quiltmaker, designer, and quilt teacher. First grade teacher; former vegetable gardener now perennial gardener; cross-country skier, country-western dancer.

Completing/selling Liberty Legacy (Pennsylvania), Rose Basket I (West Virginia), Rose Basket II (Sweden), Viewers Choice Award for Liberty Legacy at Totem Pole Quilt Show (Athens, PA).

Corinne Appleton, Jacksonville, Florida

Corinne Appleton was born July 29, 1963, in Ottawa, Canada. She began quilting in 1991, a year after moving to Jacksonville. In 1994 a PR firm with international clients commissioned Corinne and a friend to make a quilt to be used for their annual signed-and-numbered Christmas poster which is sent to clients in lieu of a card. A 1995 All-Star Quilter's Guild project led and designed by Corinne resulted in a cheerful wall quilt for the cancer unit at Nemours Children's Clinic; she has made several small quilts for charitable groups. Her nieces and nephew are "quilt literate" and friends and family members are often recipients of her quilts. Both the ribbons and remarks she received in 1993 after entering her first show encouraged Corinne to pursue her obsession; incidents involving the cats in her life have been fodder for her most popular and successful quilts, including her first entry juried into the 1995 AQS Show. As a member of AIQA her quilts will be seen at International Quilt Festival. Much of Corinne's work, which is almost entirely by machine, is original or her interpretation of a design or traditional pattern; her greatest joy in quiltmaking is the ongoing process of discovery and growth.

Connie E. Ark, Enon, Ohio

Appraiser, author/journalist, curator, designer, editor, educational library media specialist, historian, judge, lecturer, photographer (freelance), quiltmaker, researcher, restorer, show producer, teacher.

Maternal grandmother taught me to sew on a machine by age 11. Played with fabric, thread, needles & scissors. By age 12 made doll quilts with grandmother. Member of 4-H sewing clubs for 7 years. B.S. in education from Wright State Univ. (Dayton, OH) 1975. Educational library media specialist for 20 years. Quilter for 32 years. Quilting mentor & only person from whom I've taken a quilting class, Mary Ann Schmid (Enon, OH). Member of NQA, AQS, Ohio Educational Library Media Assoc. Charter member & one of the founders of the Remembrance Quilt Guild (Springfield, OH). Curator of 5 annual month long Amish quilt shows at the Daisy Barrel (Fairborn, OH). Continues to research traditional Amish quilts still made today. Plans to concentrate on writing about Amish quilts and possibly publish a book based on collected research. Plans to continue judging, appraising & teaching. Would like to help develop research databases & a quilting library.

Memorable experiences: (1) Learning to quilt from my grandmother at age 11. (2) 1989 – 1991 local quilting competitions, 2 Best of Show; 14, 1st places; 7, 2nd places; 2 honorable mentions (open class); 2nd & 4th place antique quilts. (3) Curator of 5 quilt shows featuring newly made traditional Amish quilts from Ohio, 1990 – 1994. (4) 1993 research grant from NQA/1994 research grant from Glass City Quilt Commission (Toledo, OH). (5) 1985 to present/research, study, collecting survey data about Ohio's Amish quilters; hope to publish book about traditional Amish quilts made today in Ohio. (6) Charter member & one of the founders of Remembrance Quilt Guild (Springfield, OH). (7) Writing articles about Amish quilting in Ohio; designing & publishing quilt patterns based on original, unusual & antique quilts; and researching & writing about the imported quilt controversy. (8) Traveling around to give quilting lecturers (have lecture, will travel just about anywhere). (9) Completing unfinished antique quilting projects I've inherited & collected. (10) Making quilts for each of my nieces & nephews. (11) Traveling to Australia to learn about their quilting & share information about Amish & American quilting.

Jane Marie Aruns, Franklin, Tennessee

Jane Marie Aruns was born in Ohio in 1948, and now resides in central Missouri. She holds a B.A. from the State University College at Oswego and an M.A. in art from the University of Dallas. Jane learned quilting basics from her mother in 1962 and became a professional in 1988. She designs, teaches, lectures, and judges quilts. She enjoys traditional quilting and loves seeing a quilt top blossom under beautiful hand quilting. Since 1989 her innovative work has run concurrent with the traditional. Her expressive side explores color, form, and fabric. Jane exhibits nationally including the AQS annual show. She has won numerous awards including purchase awards from the Museum of American Folk Art in NYC (1991) and MSC Publishing (Creative Traditional Design 1991 & 1994). She is a member of AQS, NQA, and local guilds. She can also be found in her garden or creating cloth character dolls.

Virginia Avery, Port Chester, New York

Active professionally in the quilting field since the late 60's Virginia has been featured as teacher, lecturer, and judge at major quilt conferences, guilds and art museums throughout the world. Her international credits include Australia, New Zealand, Canada, France, Switzerland, and others. She has twice represented the U.S. at International Quilt Conferences in Salzburg, Austria; and Karlsruhe, Germany. She is known especially as a leader in the wearable art movement, and her award-winning work is in both private and public collections. She has had numerous one-woman shows, and continues to exhibit widely. She received the Distinguished Alumnus citation from her alma mater, is listed by *Mirabella* magazine as one of the thousand most influential women of the 90's, and is featured in Nihon Vogue's new book, *88 Leaders in the Quilt World Today*. She writes for many quilt, sewing, and needlework magazines. Virginia is also the author of *The Big Book of Appliqué, Quilts to Wear, Wonderful Wearables: A Celebration of Creative Clothing, Hats: A Heady Affair,* and *Nifty Neck Wear.* For R & R, Virginia plays piano for 8 men in a Dixieland Jazz band.

Audre J. Avilla, Glendive, Montana

I've always been interested in quilting and the first quilt I made was in 1976 for the U.S. Bicentennial contest, sponsored by the Laura Ashley Corporation. Joined the Guild Quilters of Contra Costa County (California) in 1987 after attending their quilt show. In 1992 I retired and moved to Montana. There seemed to be a great deal of interest in quilting in this area but no guild, so I helped form Patches on the Prairie Quilters Guild in January 1995 and now serve as the president. Also a member of the Badland Quilters Guild (Dickinson, ND). As a member of the Prairie Creative Arts, Wibaux, Montana, I participated in making blocks for a quilt they designed in 1993 which depicted historical local scenes of Wibaux and eastern Montana. My prime interest at this time is hand appliqué.

Mimi Ayars, Ph.D., Bedford, TX

Native Delawarean and hardy Texas transplant; sociologist; quiltmaker; founder of Brunswick Star Quilters (NJ); officer of Trinity Valley Quilters' Guild (TX); AQSG, AQS, NQA member; teacher; speaker; author of numerous articles, and with Patricia B. Campbell, four books: *Jacobean Appliqué: Exotica* (AQS, 1993) & *Romantica* (AQS, 1995), and *Theorem Appliqué: Abundant Harvest* (Chitra, 1994) & *Summer Splendor* (Chitra, 1995). Her "Stars and Stripes" was selected by the MAQS to hang in

their "Fifteen Years Later: Bicentennial Quilts" exhibition in 1992. Quiltmaking is her art form, therapy, recreation, introduction to America's incredible maternal ancestors, inspiration for talks to community groups, and material for books and articles.

Ruth Cattles Cottrell accepting the 1st place trophy from the President of the British Quilters' Guild for the bed quilt, "Rosehurst," at Quilts UK, 1995, Malvern, England.

Barbara Hendrick Abrelat (left), Sammie Smith (right). Makers of a "Quilt of Leaves" the official look of the games for the 1996 Olympic Summer Games in Atlanta, GA.

Catherine Elizabeth Knotek Bahnsen, Columbus, Indiana

Catherine Elizabeth Knotek Bahnsen was born August 6, 1949, in Defiance, Ohio, graduated from Defiance College in 1971 with a degree in biology. Cathy and her husband, Willis, and son, Matthew, live in Columbus, IN.

She learned her needlework skills from her mother, Fany Knotek, and made her first quilt at the age of 16. After learning with traditional patterns, Cathy now designs her own patterns for quilts using native art, art deco, and nature as sources of inspiration for her designs. She also lectures, teaches, and judges local quilt shows.

Cathy is a member of AQS, Indiana State Quilt Guild, and a charter member of Columbus Star Quilters. Her quilts have won awards in both local and national shows. A Best of Show at NQA in 1992 for her wall quilt "Mother Earth Spirit" and a ribbon at AQS were very exciting. Her quilts have been pictured in quilt magazines since 1984, the latest in the June 1995 issue of *Quilter's Newsletter* magazine.

Paula Amelia Baimbridge, Corpus Christi, Texas

Designer, quiltmaker. Started quilting in 1971; won second place at Texas State Fair with crazy quilt in 1985; won 2nd place with Baby "Maypole" quilt at Georgetown, in 1986.

Won honorable mention at the Houston International 1991 (Innovative Appliqué – "Reflection of Eagles," published in *Treasures From Yesteryear* by Sharon Newman, That Patchwork Place, pg. 66. Second place "Reflection of Eagles," in San Angelo, TX, 1992. Second place "Reflection of Eagles," in Victoria, TX, 1992. Won all the awards while a member of the Midland Quilt Guild. Moved to Corpus Christi October 16, 1994, now a member of the Coastal Bend Quilt & Needlework Guild.

Courtney Linn Jackson Bain, Benton, Illinois

Look out quilters here she comes. The quilting queen of the 90's. She is four year old Courtney Linn Jackson Bain. Born May 11,

1990. Mother is Lana Kay Linn Bain, grandmother is Jeanine Page Linn, and great-grandmother is Mary Gustin Page. She was three when this picture was taken with her great-aunt Cherita Shorty Page Walker. Courtney begged to quilt so Aunt Shorty is teaching her. After threading the needle Courtney would say, "up down up down goes the needle." I still have her first stitches in that quilt, which won a First Place Ribbon at the Duquoin, IL, State Fair. She and I are piecing her a cat quilt. Courtney learned to use the scissors to cut thread at age 2.

Lana Kay Linn Bain, Benton, Illinois

Quiltmaker and collector of family quilts. Lana Kay (Linn) Bain, born December 3, 1960, in Benton, IL. Graduated from Benton High School. Attended Rend Lake College. Owner and operator of Coldwell Banker Team Realty in Benton, IL. Lana has two children, Charles, and Courtney. At an early age, Lana's mother, Jeanine (Page) Linn, taught her to knit and sew. At age nine, home from school with pneumonia, her grandmother Mary (Gustin) Page taught her to piece and quilt a doll quilt. She designed and quilted a Teddy Bear Coal Miner quilt that won First Place at Duquoin State Fair. She has quilted for her family and friends.

My grandmother teaching me to make a doll quilt at age 9 is my most memorable quilting experience.

Susan Damone Balch, Reading, Vermont

Susan is a professional quiltmaker living in Reading, Vermont. Her mother taught her to use a sewing machine when she was only 5 years old. She always enjoyed making things and learned very early in life to knit (from her mother), crochet (from her aunt), and embroider (by herself).

She began making quilts in 1978 when she was 21 years old and had her first very own sewing machine. Reading in a book about quilts is what got her started, and she fell in love with color, design, and machine techniques.

Susan's first judged quilt, inspired by Native American rugs, won an award at the Vermont Quilt Festival in 1984. Since then, she has exhibited throughout the United States receiving many awards including the Governor's Award at the Vermont Quilt Festival in 1989 and 1995. Up until 1984 she was mostly self-taught, completing over a hundred quilts and wallhangings, when she began taking a few workshops with some of the nation's most noted quiltmakers including Nancy Crow and Michael James. She is an active member in several regional quilt guilds, has curated several exhibits, and had her quilts published in national and international publications.

In recent years, Susan has been designing and producing quilts mostly for the wall as art, including a commission in 1989 for the Psychiatric Hospital in Concord, New Hampshire, that consisted of ten wall quilts. Her current work includes a series of machine pieced pictorials depicting anadromous fish and their environs. Being an enthusiastic fly fisher gives her much of her inspiration for these pieces, some of which were exhibited in the winter of 1994 – 95 at the American Museum of Fly Fishing in Manchester, Vermont.

In 1991, she began teaching at Fletcher Farm School for the Arts and Crafts in Ludlow, Vermont, where she still teaches every summer. She also teaches around New England. Her workshops are designed to inspire creativity in her students and to help them develop their skills.

Andrea Balosky, Camp Sherman, Oregon

Quiltmaker. Self-taught; now and then quiltmaker since 1964; committed quiltmaker since 1991. Makes quilts amid the ponderosa; listens to opera incessantly.

Author: *Working in a Series*, published by That Patchwork Place, Inc.; current and active member of the East of the Cascade Quilters, Sisters, Oregon; among the original founding members of The Association of Pacific Northwest Quilters, Seattle, Washington.

Quilt National, 1983; Finalist, Labor of Love, Houston, 1992; Sisters Outdoor Quilt Show, 1992 – 1995. Design Contest Winner, Quiltmaker, 1995. White House Christmas Ornament Project, American Artisans Invitational, 1993.

Shirley M. Bangma, Uxbridge, Massachusetts

Member of NEQG, Eastcoast Quilters Alliance, and AQS. Taught adult education quilting for 3 years in late 70's and taught two granddaughters to quilt for five years. Winner, 1979 Mountain Mist "Nursery Rhyme" quilt square contest. 3rd place, 1979 and 1st place and honorable mention 1994 Craft Adventure, Big "E," Springfield, MA. Best of show ribbon, fall 1991 meeting of NEQG and same published in *QNM*, Dec. 1992.

Mary Banks, Woodstock, Illinois

Hello fellow quilters! My name is Mary Banks and I love to quilt. I live in Woodstock, IL, and I work as a medical technologist. I enjoy quilting because it has a lot of challenges and it connects us with people. The traditional quilt patterns are my favorites, but I like to experiment with trying to make the pattern look more "modern." The new fabrics make quilting a dream. I love to make quilts for friends and for family for the special events in our lives. The McHenry Country Quilters guild I belong to makes quilting exciting and fun with all the new ideas and friends I have made. My all time favorite block is the Nine Patch. My three kitties enjoy my quilts the most.

Barbara Barber, Andover, Hants

Daughter of Alfred and Dorothy Ploug, was born in Kingsville, Texas, in 1954. She went to England in 1974 and married an Englishman in 1979, and has been living there in rural southwest ever since. They have two children. Barbara started quilting in May 1991 and is self taught. Her awards include Best of Show in all three of the major shows in England and 1st place Traditional Pieced, Professional at the 1995 AQS show. Quilting is a much loved, full-time occupation for her and her time is divided between teaching and personal work.

Eugenia A. Barnes, Marcellus, New York

Eugenia A. Barnes is a quiltmaker, teacher, lecturer, and appraiser certified by AQS. Genie has been teaching quiltmaking since 1974 in local shops, two Community Colleges as well as joining the national circuit in 1979. Genie has taught in most of the U.S. as well as Canada, the Caribbean, and South Africa. Genie founded the first quilt guild in Central New York, has a quilt included in the National Archive Project. Assisted with the NY project, served as an advisor to the state of Connecticut project, and is presently serving on the advisory board for the MA project. Genie served as a member of the Appraiser Certification Committee for seven years assisting in developing a syllabus for the Appraiser's Skills Course as well as the written and practical exams. Genie has contributed to *American Quilter* as well as a number of topic specific books and co-authored *Protecting Your Quilt*. Genie has been awarded, published, exhibited and has judged a number of shows for guilds, conferences and art centers.

Jayne Barstow, Austin, Texas

Born July 10, 1949, wife of Bill, mother of two spoiled puppies, Prissy and Scruffy. Senior vice president of the Alliance Flexible Benefits Group, plan to attend law school in Sept. 1996. Avid reader, enjoy traveling, and visiting quilt stores. I love anitques and handmade linens, especially quilts and embroidered pillow cases. I always have several things in process and never enough time to finish them. I am totally addicted to the how-to quilt and home improvement shows on cable. I think they should have a 24 hour quilting channel.

Elizabeth Barton, Athens, Georgia

Patchwork in the U.K. in the 60's. American style traditional quilts 1984 – 1993 when I met and was converted by Nancy Crow – now my focus is art quilts.

I teach beginners at the University of Georgia; design and sell or display art quilts.

Book: *No Quilt Quilt* 1986. Georgia Council for the Arts grant 1994 – 1995. Quilt National and AQS, 1995.

Linda Adams Barton, El Paso, Texas

As a child, I entertained myself for hours with Mama's scrap bag. As I sorted the pieces into rows, I savored the colors, textures, and combinations. Logically, I progressed as a textile design major at the University of Texas; but quilting was not a part of my life until 1982 when Mama, a friend, and I pieced a Log Cabin. The next year I lost my job as an editor and became a passionate full-time quilting student.

Constance E. Bastille, Peterborough, New Hampshire

Particularly interested in antique quilts, tops, and fabrics, and history of quilts and their makers. Was a founder Monadnock Quilter's Guild. V.P. first year, president next nine years.

Member New England Quilter's Guild, New England Quilt Museum, American Quilt Study Group, and National Quilting Association. Also two local quilt guilds, Monadnock and Cheshire, and American Quilter's Society. Was on site search panel for proposed New England Quilt Museum. Past board member New England Quilt Museum. Now on museum library committee. Dedicated museum volunteer. On core committee for ongoing NH quilt documentation project. Involved with Vermont Quilt Festival.

Worked on both bicentennial and 250th anniversary quilts of Peterborough. Also NH Quilter's Guilds quilt, and raffle quilts

for local groups and quilter's guilds. Enjoys planning quilts. Collects books on all aspects of quilts and quilting.

Amelia S. Beadle, Convent, Louisiana

Shop owner of Quilts and Country Treasures, located in Gonzales, LA. I particularly enjoy machine piecing traditional blocks in traditional settings. Although my interest in the history of quilts and quilting has been piqued, my true interest is the preservation and continuing education of current and future quilts and quilters. Seminar director of Gulf States Quilting Association, a four state quilt guild encompassing Louisiana, Mississippi, Alabama, and the Florida panhandle with a membership of over 800. I am responsible for coordinating an annual four-day seminar that brings in nationally recognized teachers. Member of several quilt guilds including River City Quilt Guild and Remember Me Quilt Guild in Baton Rouge, LA. Charter member of Embroiderers' Guild of America, Baton Rouge Chapter, and Threadbenders' Anonymous of Gonzales, LA. Chairman of the volunteer docents committee for the 1993 Gulf States Quilting Association, "Heart of Quilting" quilt show.

Jean Ann Dusil Bean, Cambridge, Iowa

Staff R.N. in the PACU (Post Anesthetic Care Unit) at Mary Greeley Medical Center, Ames, Iowa. Charter member and past state treasurer of ISPAN (Iowa Society of Post Anesthesia Nurses). Married 27 years to Brent, P.E., sons: Eric, R.N.; and Adam, accountant.

Member of Iowa Quilt Guild, Des Moines Area Quilters Guild, and charter member and VP of Mary Greely's Healing Stitchers. Volunteer at Iowa Historical Bldg. working on the preservation of Mary Barton's quilt collection. Home business: Jean's Quilts and Designs. Contribute quilt for the annual church bazaar. Designed "Pinwheels-Plus-Nine Fantasy" featured in pattern form in the *Quilting Today* issue 44, October 1994. Follow-up profile article and picture in the *Ames Daily Tribune*.

Joyce R. Becker, Kent, Washington

Joyce has been a quiltmaker for 13 years and has attended workshops and lectures by many nationally acclaimed quilt personalities. Many articles written by Joyce have appeared in national quilt magazines, featuring Northwest quilting events and artists. Currently, Joyce is under contract with The Quilt Digest Press recently procured by NTC Publishing Group for a book called *Quilts Alive! Inspirations From Nature*. Featuring 23 artists, this title includes scenic Northwest photography, 30 nature inspired quilts, in-depth profiles on the artists, and some directions.

Author and quiltmaker. A founding member of the Association of Pacific Northwest Quilters (APNQ) presenting the First Great Pacific Northwest Quilt show in July of 1994 and every two years thereafter. Staff writer and correspondence secretary for APNQ 1992 – 1994. Currently, APNQ board member/features editor for newsletter. Being published and producing the first non-profit, regional, juried, and judged quilt show in the Northwest are two memorable experiences.

J. Richard Becker, Jr., Terre Haute, Indiana

J. Richard Becker, Jr., AQS member from Terre Haute, IN, was born December 24, 1925, in Auglaize County, OH. He retired from teaching at Indiana State University in 1988, and now keeps busy doing volunteer work. His quilting dates from about 1978. Since 1984 he has pieced over 90 quilt tops for the local church women who tie the quilts and give them to the Red Cross for disaster victims. Most of his quilt work is done on an old treadle-model Singer using a variety of materials donated by the church women. Quilts for family use or gifts are machine quilted. His quilts have received awards at the county and state fairs. He also has given quilts to organizations for fund-raising activities.

Judy Becker, Newton, Massachusetts

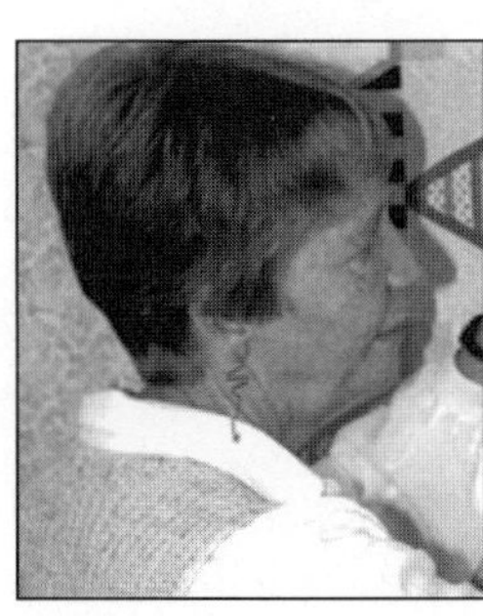

Judy Becker began quilting in 1972 because it was not as messy as paints or clay. After teaching herself to sew by following traditional patterns, she started to design contemporary wall-hangings with bold color contrast, asymmetrical geometry, and strong linear elements. She enjoys doing large commissioned work for both public and private spaces and smaller pieces for galleries and homes. But she is still waiting to make a baby quilt for a first grandchild.

Quiltmaker, designer, judge, teacher, and lecturer. Judy's quilts have been juried into Quilt National '89, '91, '93, '95.

Jean Lenon Beckon, Okemos, Michigan

Jean Lenon Beckon was born March 7, 1942, in Mason, MI. She now lives in Okemos, MI, with her husband, Larry. Jean began

quilting in 1979 after many years of embroidery, needlepoint, and other crafts. She works on her own and loves the solitude which quilting brings. Most of Jean's quilts are traditional, hand pieced, and hand quilted. She is now beginning to learn machine piecing and quilting. Jean has exhibited her quilts in numerous fairs and shows in Michigan, including the Michigan State Fair. Jean created quilts for each of the three children of her younger sister, presenting the quilts upon their graduation from high school, all as valedictorians. Larry and Jean enjoy going to quilt shows and shops all over the United States and Canada. Jean is a charter friend of MAQS in Paducah, KY.

Norma Jean McKee Behnken, Brookville, Ohio

Norma Jean McKee Behnken was born in 1934, in Preble Co., Ohio. She married Glen in 1954. She has one daughter, Nancy, married to Dennis, with two children; Ashleigh who loves quilts, school, and outdoors; and Amanda, who loves cats, worms, and butterflies. She has a son, Bill, married to Rhonda, with two children; Curtis who just loves to play outside, and a baby, Jacob. I have always loved fabric. I have sewn clothes and have done all needlework arts. Made my first quilt in 1956 for my first child.

I have won ribbons at small, local fairs for needlework and quilts. I am thankful to Ohio Valley Quilters Guild for their seminars and their help with trips to Paducah, KY, AQS. I am a member of Towne Square Quilt Club, Greenville, OH, and local Brookville club. I just love quilts. I have so many ideas in mind, I'll quilt forever. I am also a charter member of AQS and support NQA also.

JoAnn Belling, Des Moines, Iowa

JoAnn has enjoyed the sewing machine since she began producing her own clothes at age 12. In 1965 she began quilting with heavy polyester fabrics and no formal instruction. Encouraged by a friend, she enrolled in classes in 1977, and has designed numerous quilts and wallhangings. She has taught a variety of classes in Iowa, Washington, Oregon, Georgia, and Texas. Her influence in quilting has been felt from coast to coast.

The Belling household has hosted a number of quilt groups for lectures and tours. Her finest work has been reproduced in national publications. Concepts of color and composition which JoAnn

uses in her photographic art are applied to the designing of quilts, borders, and quilt back art. All phases of quilting are enjoyed by JoAnn but of greatest interest are the color and design portion. Planning and short cut methods are discussed. Organization in her dream sewing room gives you an insight to the reason JoAnn is able to create a number of quilt works each year.

Bonnie Belshe, Normal, Illinois

Researcher, designer, and maker of Hawaiian quilts. Bonnie Belshe, born Mar. 1, 1920, has been a quilter since her childhood in Missouri. In the 50's she began writing research papers on quilt patterns and began the extensive quilt book collection she now owns. In the 70's she organized the Bicentennial Quilt Show for the Illinois State University Gallery which was juried by Myron and Patsy Orlofsky. As a demonstration for that show she began her first Hawaiian quilt. Since then, she has concentrated on researching, designing, and making Hawaiian quilts as a hobby.

A charter member of the Hands All Around Quilt Guild of Central, IL, she also belongs to AQS and NQA.

"Mainland Flowers" Hawaiian quilt shown in AQS show in 1995. "Flowers of Hawaii" Hawaiian quilt featured in *Great American Quilts*, 1994. "Illinois Corn," first, 1979 Illinois Quilt Block Contest sponsored by The Folklore Archive at Southern Illinois University at Edwardsville. "Hawaiian Butterfly," best of show, local quilt shop block contest, 1977.

Patricia Bennett, Cornish, New Hampshire

Native of New Hampshire. Busy raising kids, Cardigan Welch corgis, bunnies, gardens – and squeezing in quilting time too!

Quilting is my creative outlet. I'm never happier than when I am planning and making a quilt, or sharing quilts with others. We Cornish ladies made a raffle quilt recently, and I am now teaching a quilting "Exploratory" with some sixth graders.

Being able to sell a few of my quilts has been exciting. There is a county fair in my town, and I often help with the quilt exhibit, show my latest quilt, and give a quilting demonstration. I have also joined a newly formed quilt guild of Cornish and Plainfield ladies, and I enjoy their friendship immensely.

Regina Beno, New York, New York

Regina Beno was born February 20, 1956, and calls St. Louis, MO, her "hometown." She currently lives in New York City. She is a graduate of Washington University in English. As an artist she is self-taught. She made her first quilt of various gingham checks at the age of eleven, using her grandmother's treadle sewing machine. She has created craft patterns and books for Simplicity and Better Homes and Gardens' *American Patchwork & Quilting*. Her articles and quilts have been featured in *International Quilting* and *Forum*. Most recently she has shown her art quilts in New York, Switzerland, and Italy.

She is a member of the American Quilter's Society, The American Craft Council, The American Museum of Folk Art, and Empire Quilters. She divides her time between her studio and work at the Metropolitan Museum of Art. Her quilts often explore intercultural and historical themes and incorporate vintage textiles. Her designs travel across time and between cultures.

Janice Elia Berkley, Arlington Heights, Illinois

My interest in the needle was ignited by my mother, who always made my exquisite clothes. My parents bought a Bernina sewing machine for me in 1970, everyone received homemade presents that year. I expanded this basic knowledge of fabric and thread to express my creative and artistic qualities through quilting. My mom has the first patchwork pillow I made. The fabrics were quite loud, quilters today have better fabric to choose from.

While at a quilt show with my mom, she pointed to a Dresden Plate antique quilt and told me how she used to have a quilt like this that my grandmother made. I discovered I had quilting in my genes!

Joining the Northwest Suburban Quilters Guild was an exciting time. I found myself program chairman for two years and then president. Many friendships were made from this experience. I normally quilt only for my family, they are my biggest fans. However, my first commissioned quilt was a pyramid design with an outer shape of an elongated hexagon. It was made with a multitude of plaids, corduroy, pinstripes, etc. that uniforms are made of. The second quilt was an elongated star design with the uniform plaids as the center of each star. The quilts are hanging in the corporate office of a uniform company in Chicago.

Joan Biasucci, Cedar Creek, Nebraska

My responsibilities as special events coordinator for Anna's

Restaurant, Cedar Creek, NE, require discipline and organization. Quilting allows me to be unstructured and creative.

1. Curator of "Quiltin' at the Creek," a regional exhibit held annually during the month of June at Anna's Restaurant, Cedar Creek, NE. 2. Designer and creator of "Night Flight," an opportunity quilt to benefit AirLifeLine, a nationwide volunteer organization of pilots who donate their time and aircraft to assist those in need of medical attention. 3. Instrumental in organizing local residents in our small community for the purpose of making crib quilts for the Cass County Foster Children's Association. The participants annually make in excess of 75 quilts for the organization.

1. Recipient of Variable Star Award from the Nebraska State Quilt Guild. 2. Sharing with cancer survivors the concept of quilting as part of the healing process. 3. Attending the recent AQS show and learning that my entry in the 1995 Hoffman Challenge was on exhibit!

Nancy Billings, Miami, Florida

Designer, teacher, quiltmaker. After graduation from Pratt Institute in fashion design I taught fiber art at the junior high through college levels. Quilting has been my passionate hobby for the last 22 years, and a business for the last four. Hurricane Andrew's wrath seemed to guide me toward a new artistic course. Shortly after my husband and I rebuilt our home, I attended QSDS to gain a new direction and a freedom to let go. Most recently, I have been exploring dye painting and other surface design techniques, while juxtaposing pattern, color, and texture in each of my works. With every creation I find myself growing artistically, intellectually, and emotionally, creating pieces that are an extension of myself. Thank you Andrew!

Member of South Florida Fiber Artists and of Florida Craftsmen. Volunteer with Temple Beth Am Day School classes to make class theme quilts; acceptance in Coconut Grove Arts Festival.

Ann Bird, Ottawa, Canada

Born in Vancouver, BC, currently reside in Ottawa. Formal education: BScN, McGill University, Montreal. I design and sew in my studio using machine techniques for piecing and reverse appliqué. My images range from landscapes, abstract or figurative graphics to geometric patterns. Most are machine quilted. Each year I make a star mandala, inspired by a favorite color or print. All are hand quilted and I consider them as my visual diary and connection to the traditions of quiltmaking processes. Professional quilter for 20 years. Quilt artist, teacher, lecturer,

judge, author of publication articles. Authority on Canadian contemporary quilts and activities, and the quilts and practices of Canada's native women. 1989 Canadian Quilters Association Dorothy McMurdie Award for contributions to quilting in Canada. Co-founder of Ottawa Valley Quilters Guild 1981 and charter member of CQA/ACC, AQS, CQSG. Other memberships include AIQA, NQA, AQSG.

Wanda Marie Black, Indianapolis, Indiana

Wanda Marie Roeschlein Black was born in Indianapolis, IN, on April 5, 1959. Along with her husband, Kevin, and their two sons, Dustin and Joshua, she currently lives on the southeast side of the city. She and her husband graduated from Lawrence Central High School where they were high school sweethearts. Before her first son was born, she taught herself to quilt and has not stopped since! Twelve years and over 85 quilted projects later, she shows no signs of slowing down! Serving on various committees has exposed her to a lot of responsibilities and created wonderful, lifetime friendships. These committees include two years as president of Quilt Connection Guild of Greenwood, IN. She is also an active member of the Quilters Guild of Indianapolis, and the Indiana State Guild.

Her favorite quilting is Crazy Patch. This is one of her favorite classes to teach, although she teaches all kinds of classes. Sharing the joy of quilting has kept her enthusiasm high which spreads to all her activities. In fact in her classes if you aren't laughing and having a good time she'll refund your money. "We do quilting for fun and enjoyment, not to increase your stress levels!" Her teaching ranges from quilt bees to local fabric shops to guilds on the local and state levels. She also writes articles for quilting newsletters and is currently working on her first book.

Edna Miner Blunck, Tucson, Arizona

Quiltmaker, designer, and instructor. Born: Maynard, Iowa, 1934. Made my first quilt from new and used clothing scraps in 1964. Unable to pursue the craft further until 1985. I have been enjoying a passionate interest since. Making all sizes of traditional, contemporary, and artistic styles.

Sale of my first original design Christmas wallhanging is my most memorable quilting experience.

Arthur A Bluj, Winston-Salem, North Carolina

The first 150 words about quilter Arthur can be found in *Great American Quilt* of 1988 page 63. Since then Arthur has become a member of AQS, NQA, Piedmont Quilters, and Quilters Guild of Dallas. He also completed 6 different large quilts, 4 wall, 1 baby, and 1 challenge. Lucky to be host at Paducah, 1991 – 1995 shows. Luckier to have quilts hang in Paducah 1987, 89, 90, 91. My Aloyse Yorko challenge hung in Paducah 1992. Made a wallhanging, "Kentucky Begins in Paducah," I gave it to tourist bureau. Send my quilts to many shows so judges have lots to say. Have had a couple viewers request patterns. Been to a few workshops to learn more. Love hand appliqué and quilting which keeps me happy leading to a longer life. Eleven quilts on paper and two on way to completion. Over 600 pieces of material upstairs waiting, must get back to fun time quilting.

Vicky Jo Bogart, Fargo, North Dakota

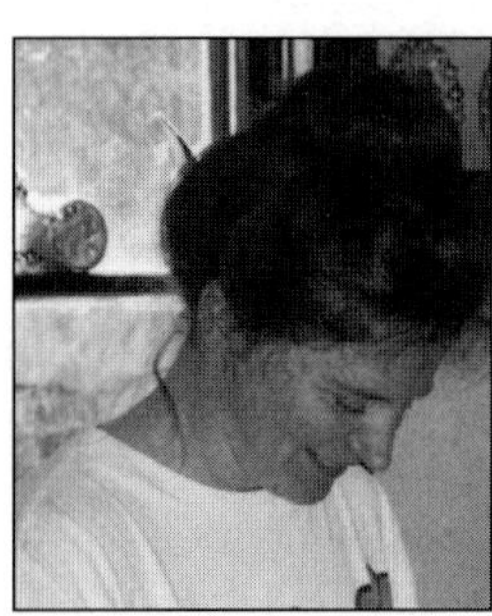

M.S. Textiles and Clothing, North Dakota State University, Fargo, ND. Founder/director of Handworks Cottage Industries, a vocational rehabilitation program for persons with disabilities who are trained in their homes to work as independent contractors in woodworking, weaving, sewing, quilting, dollmaking, knitting, crocheting, needlework, rug braiding, rug hooking, leatherwork, and/or beadwork.

Teaches quilting and related arts and crafts, tap dance and creative movement to persons of all ages. Charter member and past president of the Quilters' Guild of North Dakota, active in planning committees and the Indian Summer Quilt Show and Conference. As part of Designing Quilters, she has exhibited and curated quilt art shows.

Curated and constructed The Great Art Quilt: James O'Rourke @ Sixty, a mixed media presentation quilt of visual art by 63 national artists. Vicky prefers to experience life at the lake, designing and creating, stitching, and gardening.

Ludmila Bokov, New York, New York

Collector, designer, quiltmaker, teacher, and author. Ludmila Bokov was born February 20, 1946, in Moscow, USSR; immigrated to USA in 1975; and lives in New York with her husband and son. Graduated from New York University with MA in Textile/Costume and Certificate in Museum Studies. She began sewing at 8 years of age and quilting in 1990. Ludmila is founder

and president of Cultural Contacts International, a non-profit educational organization. In 1991 she started Friendship Album Program (FAP) that includes making and exhibiting quilts and wearables internationally; quilters' tours to and teaching seminars in Eastern Europe; and world quilters' networking. The culmination of FAP was creating the Friendship Quilt for the United Nations. Truly a world collaboration, this quilt, composed of nearly 180 blocks, each contributed by the U.N. Member Country, is a gift to the U.N. on the 50th Anniversary.

Mae C.H. Bolden, Troutdale, Oregon

Mae C. H. Bolden is a retired reading specialist. She holds a B.S. in Elementary Education and a M.A. in Early Childhood Education and Reading. She lived in the Washington, D.C. area until 1994 when she moved to Troutdale, Oregon. She began quilting in Arlington, Virginia, in 1984. She became an active member of the Daughters of Dorcas and Sons of Washington, D.C., which is Chapter 102 of NQA, Quilters Unlimited, Arlington Chapter, and the Prince George's Historical Quilting Society of Maryland. In 1991 she was commissioned to hand make a queen size Double Wedding Ring quilt. It was a gift given to H.R.H. Princess Haifa Al-Faisal of Riija, Saudi Arabia. February, 1995, she founded and became teacher of the Mt. Olivet Daughters and Sons of Dorcas in Portland, Oregon. This quilt group currently has 35 members.

Gayle Bong, Elkhorn, Wisconsin

Author, designer, quiltmaker, teacher, lecturer. Gayle has been an avid designer and quilter since 1981. In 1988, she began teaching classes on quilting, specializing in adapting the latest rotary-cutting techniques to the 60 degree angle. Her first book, *Infinite Stars*, converts traditional square blocks into dazzling stars. Her second book, *Trouble Free Triangles*, introduces triangular blocks and the endless quilt designs this long neglected shape offers. Gayle also contributes to the "What if? Design Challenge" column, a regular feature in *Traditional Quiltworks* magazine. Gayle continues to develop new concepts and designs for future books in between teaching engagements.

Ruth Bosephflug, West Glendive, Montana

I am one of the two sewers for the Sacred Heart Church quilter's group; finish off all quilts.

Sandy Bosley, Ridgecrest, California

Original quilt/wearable art designer, quiltmaker, lecturer, and teacher. Fabric art is my meaningful form of expression. Began quilting in 1984.

Published: cover of *Traditional Quiltworks*, Aug./Sept. 1991; *Lady's Circle Patchwork Quilts*, July 1993; Quilt "Surf" part of Chitra Publications Nature's Beauty Notecard Collection, 1994/95. AIQA, Innovative, Small Quilt, Honorable Mention Award, 1992.

Rosalie Hierholzer Bourland, Converse, Texas

Quilter as a hobby, volunteer teacher, founder of quilt club in Portland, Oregon. Rosalie Hierholzer Bourland was born Oct. 26, 1925, on a farm in the Black Hill community of south Texas. At age 9, she picked a bale of cotton – because she wanted to – using a sack her mother, Nettie Pearl, had made especially for her. The following year her mother, also a quilter, died. By then, however, creating things from fabric, cotton, wood, and all things natural was already instilled in her. She graduated from Floresville High in 1943, and attended San Antonio College, taking art and creative writing. She and her retired Air Force husband, Les, live in Converse, TX. Their daughter, Linda Keen, and son, Terry and families live in nearby Schertz, TX. A civil service stenographer for 28 years, she retired from the ATC Inspector General's Office, Randolph AFB, TX, in October 1985. She began quilting with the Converse Vol. Fire Dept. Aux. in 1971, and for six years, co-chaired their annual quilt raffle. Evenings she taught quilting in Community Education at Clemens High, Schertz, TX. Also in 1971, her 3' x 5' texture painting, "Shades of Yesterday," took an award at the San Antonio Art League's 41st Annual Artists' Exhibition. The fall 1981 issue of *Quilt* magazine carried one of her quilt designs. Rosalie was also featured in Oxmoor House's publication, *Great American Quilts – 1987*. Her most recent, and proudest, work is "A Journey Remembered," a quilted wallhanging inspired by an entry in her great-great-grandfather, Carl Blumberg's sea journal; "Bremen to Texas, Fall of 1845."

For Converse's 1977 Centennial she co-chaired "Album of Memories," seven appliquéd wallhangings that now hang in city hall, and was instrumental in publishing a historical cookbook, *100 Years of Cooking in Converse*. Because of its historical content, the cookbook is on file in the Library of Congress.

In October 1985, she and Les opened the General Store and Quilt Studio, in an old Texaco station at 305 S. Seguin, Converse, stocking shelves with fabric pack ratted for 20 years. Quilt class income was reinvested continually, until the store now boasts 800 bolts. At one time the Bourlands sold their lap frames to Better Homes and Gardens, and later sold their floor frames at Houston's Intn'l Quilt Festival. She chaired Converse's first quilt exhibit (Oct. 1986) commemorating Texas' Sesquicentennial. Rosalie is a member of the American Quilters' Society and charter member of Greater San Antonio Quilt Guild. She has made 16 quilts for gifts to friends and family and has made many quilt squares for friendship quilts and special projects. In the fall of 1995, she taught quilting, as a volunteer, at Humbolt Elementary School in Portland, Oregon. This replicates the effort in which she was involved in Washington, D.C. before coming to Oregon. Received $3,000 for the hand-pieced and hand-quilted Double Wedding Ring Quilt.

Velma Smallwood Bowden, Ft. Collins, Colorado

Quiltmaker. Velma Smallwood Bowden was born June 14, 1912, in West Plains, MO. She was taught by her mother to quilt during a time and in a place, Newcastle, Wyoming, when quilts were a necessity. It wasn't until later in life that quilting became a joy. She enjoys doing appliqué, embroidered blocks, and any pattern that is patriotic, since she was born on Flag Day. She is a founding member of the Colorado Quilting Council and still participates in their activities whenever possible. She is also a business partner with her granddaughter, Theresa Fleming, for whom she bought a commercial quilting machine for. Most of her quilting is done by Theresa now. Memorable quilting experiences: Having an article plus photos published about her and her Hawaiian MuuMuu quilt in *Old Fashioned Patchwork* magazine. Also having her All State Quilt accepted and shown in the 1995 CQC quilt show in the Colorado state capitol.

Martha Ellen Spencer Bowles, St. James, Missouri

Quiltmaker, designer, collector, and librarian for Piece and Plenty Quilt Guild.

Husband, William G. Bowles Jr.; daughter, Carol. BS 1984 in economics from the University of Missouri. Owner of Bowles Aquarium. Making quilts is a family tradition. As my mother and I would have a quilt in progress on the floor, my daughter Carol, would always take off her shoes and walk across it.

Martha Hoke Bowne, Mercer Island, Washington

Marty was born in Greeley, Colorado, and has also lived in Wisconsin, Indiana, Connecticut, Michigan, Mexico, New York, and now Washington State. Plans to eventually retire to Sandpoint, Idaho. She has been sewing since high school.

After graduating from University of Michigan, taught school in Michigan and New York. Has four children. In 1967 entered sewing field by working and managing a fabric shop to become an owner herself. In 1981 co-founded local Towpath Quilt Guild in Fayetteville, NY. Involvement in quilting since then: 1982 with Mary Lou Schwinn, started Quilting "By-the-Lake" which continues. 1984 to 1995: co-editor of *American Quilter* magazine. 1984 – 1991: Workshop chairman, AQS annual show. 1988 founded Quilting By-the-Sound, which continues. 1993 became owner of Quilter's Quest, producer of videos of today's quilting stars. Consultant to many quilting companies and organizations. Membership in local guilds, National Quilting Association, American Quilt Study Group, and AIQA. Juries, judges, and lectures throughout the U.S. Her quilts are in private collections.

Mary Anne Boyle, Cordova, Tennessee

Widow, three children, and two grandchildren.

Quiltmaker for 22 years. Member of Memphis Cotton Patchers, and Old (cotton) Batts.

Sampler quilt accepted for the 1993 AQS show. It won the Best of Show and Mountain Mist award at Mid-South Fair, 1994.

Vivian Brady, Romeo, Michigan

Quiltmaker for 15 years, collector, quilt show organizer, and guild organizer.

Born 1930 in Jackson, MI. Has lived in Romeo, MI, for 60 years. Six children and 15 grandchildren.

Grandmother taught me to make quilts as a child.

Marcie Brenner, Brooklyn, NY

Born April 17, 1952, Florida, two children. AAS from Fashion Institute of Technology (applied apparel design and patternmaking), B.A Brooklyn College (home economics and women's studies), graduate work Brooklyn College (home

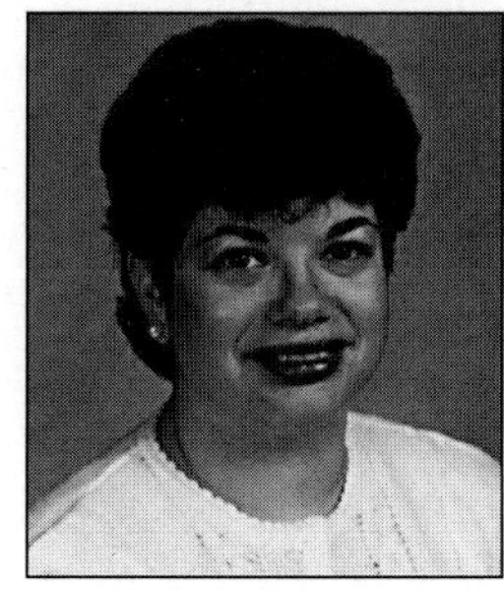

economics education). Teaching sewing, quilting, and needlecrafts since 1981 in adult ed, public school, college, and privately. Designs and writes instructions for a variety of quilting projects. Demonstrates at quilt guild events. Member of AQS, Empire Quilters, and Quilter's Guild of Brooklyn. Opened quilt shop, Sew Beary Special, June 1993.

Invited to conduct workshops at Creative Festival, NJ, 1994, and New York Quilt Festival, 1995.

Mary Bedford Brewer, Lyons, Colorado

Mary Bedford Brewer was born in Oklahoma, December 19, 1935, and grew up with a grandmother who quilted. At age 5 she learned to embroider at Vacation Bible School and still likes the handwork. In an 8th grade sewing class, she learned the basics. That Christmas, her parents gave her a sewing machine when she began making clothing and doing alterations.

Her quilting life began after marriage to husband, James. She made a hand appliquéd and embroidered animal quilt in 1956 for her first daughter, Christal. She machine quilted it and used it for her next two daughters, Jeri and Andrea. Most of the next 19 years were spent employed outside the home when necessary but focused mainly on being a homemaker and sewing all the family clothes from house shoes to hats.

All the many, many special people who came into her life because of quilting. 1969: learned to hand quilt on a frame with local Methodist church ladies in West Los Angeles, CA. 1973: took a pattern drafting and hand piecing class with her first teacher, Charlotte Eckback. 1974: took a pattern drafting and machine piecing class with Glendora Hutson. 1975 – 1995: created and taught quilt classes both nationally and internationally. Mary felt if she knew good basic sewing skills, good basic quilting skills, and could draft all the patterns accurately in Ruby McKim's 101 Patchwork Patterns, she could teach others. 1978: received Lifetime Designated Teacher Credential in Quiltmaking. 1978 – present: participated in the block exchange of numerous friendship quilts. 1981: became National Quilt Association certified teacher. 1985 – present: co-founder of Quilting B's. 1987 received a presentation quilt from Simi Samplers and a friendship quilt from Simi Valley Quilt Guild when moving to Colorado from California. Having Gayle Soles and friends in Simi Valley, CA, put her name on one of the bricks at Museum of American Quilter's Society. 1992 – 93: founding president of the Estes Valley Quilt Guild in Estes Park, CO. 1995: had the presentation quilt from Simi Samplers and a friendship quilt with 8 Hands Round hang at the Colorado State Capitol. Designed and coordinated a biblical autograph quilt for the Second Baptist Church Homecoming celebration. Designed and created the quilt and pattern for the Colorado State Ombudsman project.

Mary's favorite parts of quiltmaking are teaching beginner's classes and participating in friendship block exchanges. She continues to promote the tradition of quiltmaking by marketing her classes and related events in newspapers, leaflets, and charity functions. For her business she repairs and restores quilts; writes, designs, and prints computer quilt story history labels; lectures and teaches on her friendship quilts.

My life has been so rich and full because of family and quilting friends. The Simi Sampler quilt group was started in 1978 with myself as president. We have taken many trips together, made many friendship sampler quilts together. There are approximately 20 members with 5 of us out of the city now and only one is deceased. The group still thrives today with a lot of pictures to show our changes. The second group I belong to is 8 Hands Round which started with 8 members quilting on a frame over 10 years ago.

Betty Higgs Bridges, Webb City, Missouri

A lifetime resident of Southwest, MO and a 4th generation quilter, in 1980 I opened Calico Corner Quilt Shop, in Webb City, MO. I sold fabrics and quilting supplies and taught quilting classes. I continue to teach quilting through local shops, area guilds, and the Continuing Education Dept. at MSSC in Joplin. I was the founding president of the Town and Country Quilters of the Joplin area in 1985. I have also participated in the NQA judges training course and the AQS Appraisal Program. I currently judge area quilt competitions, appraise quilts, and coordinate quilt shows and displays. Dot Willcoxon and I have just completed the eighth annual quilt show jointly held by the Town and Country Quilters and Joplin Historical Society.

I am proud to have a family quilt shown in the Missouri Heritage Quilt Project. Our guild quilt was accepted and shown in the AQS show in 1992. In 1992 I was asked to do some binding repair on an antique appliqué quilt and discovering that it was a Baltimore Album quilt! Having this wonderful quilt in my possession, researching the names, and registering it with the Baltimore Historical Society. Traveling to Baltimore to see the Baltimore Quilt Exhibits at The Historical Society and the Balti-

more Museum of Art; receiving mail in my hometown simply addressed to the "Quilt Lady!"; watching quilting grow into a national and international industry – how it has become such a special part of our lives; and the many friends I've met through quilting – all of these are special memories.

Gail Broadwater, Mammoth Spring, Arkansas

I began machine quilting in 1983. Since that time I have been active in the quilt world. I have placed ribbons in each show entered but mostly enjoy going to the shows without entering a quilt. I also enjoy quilt magazines, new techniques, and old handwork. Accomplishments other than machine quilting are: President, NEA Quilt Arts Guild, 1986 – 87; quilt teacher; 12 first place ribbons; and four patterns for machine quilting currently in circulation. In the future I plan to explore designing quilts.

Susan Anne Hewitt Broussard, Carencro, Louisiana

Susan Broussard, born February 15, 1952, in Lafayette, LA; graduated from Lafayette High School and University of Southwestern Louisianna. Upon reaching adulthood in the early 1970's, I was given many personal items that had once belonged to my deceased mother (1956), one of which was a quilt top in the pattern of Grandmother's Fan. The top was not quilted so I set out to find someone who would teach me to quilt. Many years later, and many quilts later, I still enjoy the art. I have quilted for hire and I have quilted for myself. Quilting unfinished tops for others, seeing the ideas and craftsmanship of others, has given me great joy over the years. My quilts are all over my home and each of my friends has a quilt made by me. I am now helping my friends and relatives make quilts for their grandchildren using the children's clothing. That ought to keep me busy for a while.

Camille Brown, Blythe, California

Born in Carlsbad, New Mexico, August 24, 1939 to John V. & Enid A. Newman. My Newman aunts & grandmother were prodigious quilters. My niece Mary Boyle greatly influenced me in accepting the challenge of quiltmaking.

Started quiltmaking in 1990 and have made quilts & wallhangings, in addition to my sewing business.

I was honored as outstanding quilting student, Palo Verde Community College. Best of Show, Weaver Fever Quilt, Colorado River County Fair. Award of Merit, California State Fair. All these were awarded in 1994. Judge, Wally Byam Carnival, and FFA/4-H craft projects 1992 to present. In 1989 & 1990 I helped my niece quilt a king-size Double Wedding Ring quilt for my daughter's wedding, a true labor of love.

Margaret J. Brown, Gonzales, Louisiana

I am so thankful for the sewing time and effort my mother and grandmother gave to me as a child. Because of their encouragement, I began sewing at an early age. By the time I married and had children of my own I had progressed from making doll clothes to designing and sewing prom dresses and wedding gowns. Now that our four children are grown and gone, I have found I have swung full circle back to sewing doll clothes again, but this time for grandchildren. As you can see, sewing is my life. My husband, who is a dentist in our little town of Gonzales (just outside of New Orleans, Louisiana), has been very "patient" about my disappearing for hours into the sewing room. My mother-in-law, whom I dearly love, also sewed, so he was accustomed to these disappearances. Then it happened. When my 40th birthday popped up, my older sister Bibs treated me to my first quilting class (as if I needed another sewing project!). That was in 1990. My sister Bibs and I had so much fun that we have attended the International Quilt Festival in Houston every year since and taken classes from many accomplished and well-known quilters.

In 1993, eight weeks before Christmas, I received a call from the White House. It was from a friend of Hillary Clinton who wanted to surprise her with very special and unique Christmas gift. I was asked to create a quilted square. It would be part of the tree skirting for the White House Christmas tree that would be placed in the Blue Room of the White House. The square that I was asked to submit would represent the entire state of Louisiana. A quilter from each state was chosen to participate. Each quilter was asked to include as much of their state's history and natural resources as possible then coordinate this into a Christmas theme. I was honored to do the job and quickly visualized an idea that would do Louisiana justice. I created a "Cajun Santa" theme with Santa in a pirogue being pulled by four alligators flying across the state. His large red sack in the back of the boat was spilling over onto the Louisiana Territory with such things as crawfish, crabs, and Mardi Gras masks. I also placed a star where the state capitol and other major cities were located, and naturally Gonzales was one! The tree skirt, although given to the Clintons, will remain a part of the permanent collection of the White House Christmas decorations.

Bonnie Kay Kirkland Browning, Paducah, Kentucky

Quiltmaker, author, editor, teacher, certified quilt judge, and quilt show administrator.

Bonnie Kay Kirkland Browning was born June 18, 1944, in Muscatine, IA; graduated from Muscatine High School; and attended Southeastern Community College. Bonnie and her husband Wayne live in Paducah, KY, where she is employed as the show chairman at AQS.

As a child, Bonnie's mother, Mary Kirkland, Silvis, IL, taught her to sew. Bonnie began quilting in 1979 upon her retirement as executive secretary of Mercy Hospital, Davenport, IA. She taught adult education classes on needlework in 1982 and started teaching quiltmaking in 1985. Today she travels teaching quilting for conferences, and has taught at AQS, Quilt America!, Quilters Unlimited Showcase, NC Quilt Symposium, NQA, and at guilds throughout the country. Bonnie is a certified quilt judge and qualified to judge master quilts. She has served on boards of art councils, local quilt guilds, NQA, and Quilters Unlimited Showcase.

Bonnie is a member of AQS (charter member), the Dubuque Busy Quilters, Easy Pieces, Hill Valley Quilt & Travel Society, Kentucky Heritage Quilt Society, Kentucky Heritage Appliqué Society (charter member), NQA, and the Paducah Quilt & Sew Ons.

In 1995, the book, *A Quilted Christmas*, was edited by Bonnie and published by AQS. Books in process include *Silk Ribbon – Baltimore Style* and *Beautiful Borders*.

Designing and quilting are Bonnie's favorite parts of quiltmaking. She has received numerous awards in local, regional, and national quilt shows. Her quilts are included in the Artists of Iowa Collection, Waterloo, IA; MAQS in Paducah, KY; and private collections.

Ann Brune, Jefferson City, Missouri

Ann Brune, born June 1, 1918, lives in Jefferson City, MO. Learned to quilt from mother, Clara Brune. I started making baby quilts and then larger ones for nieces, nephews, great-nieces, and great-nephews. Have kept a record and pictures of each quilt and of who received them. I do all hand piecing and hand quilting and my favorite is appliqué. I have repaired old quilts and am finishing at least ten quilts that my mother had started.

I belong to the MO River Quilters and quilt every week.

Karen Kay Buckley, Carlisle, Pennsylvania

Graduated Lock Haven University 1979 (B.S. education); owner Country Quilt Shop, Bucks County, PA, 1986 – 1989; full-time teacher, lecturer, designer, 1986 – present.

Author, teacher, designer, quiltmaker, and collector. A quilting class offered through the adult education program at our local high school changed my life. Quilting became an outlet for my then stressful job and I soon became a quilting addict. After three years of part-time quilting, I opened the Country Quilt Shop and later sold the thriving business to devote my time to writing, teaching, and designing. Seeing the excitement and sense of satisfacton in my students has been the most rewarding experience in my quilting career. It is the reason I continue to love what I do. I feel fortunate that my classes and lectures are well received and that my work has been honored both on a local and national level by my peers. Other memorable experiences have been the release of my book, *From Basics to Binding: A Complete Guide to Making Quilts* (AQS 1992), being actively involved with the Letort Quilters, and a founder of the County Line Quilters guild.

Simply being associated with quilters of all ages, sexes, and backgrounds through local and national organizations has been very rewarding.

Charlotte Bull, Cassville, Missouri

Collector, quiltmaker, teacher, reporter, and editor. Charlotte Bull lives in a log cabin near Cassville, MO. She is founder and newsletter editor of her day guild and leads a new night guild. Although no longer traveling as a teacher/speaker, she now devotes her volunteer time to local teaching on a one-on-one basis. Her personal time is divided between designing/quilting and research/writing. She is pleased that all of her daughters and several grandchildren quilt, so that her collection of books, fabrics, and quilts will always be appreciated.

Winner of several national quilt block contests, honored as outstanding program presenter for D.A.R. for trunk show on "150 Years of Quilts."

Shelly Burge, Lincoln, Nebraska

Author, designer, quiltmaker, and quilting instructor. Born April 25, 1954, she and her husband Clint have two children. Shelly started quilting in 1973 and began teaching in 1983. Shows in America, Europe, and Japan have displayed her quilts, where they have won numerous prizes including the NQA Lynn Harris award. *Quilter's Newsletter* selected her quilt as one of the forty finalists in their 1994 International Quilt Contest. Author of the

book: *Terrific Triangles*. Her work has been pictured in *Quilter's Newsletter*, *Traditional Quilter*, *Lady's Circle Patchwork Quilts*, and *Traditional Quiltworks* magazines; along with the AQS Quilt Calendar. Shelly is one of the founding members of the Nebraska State Quilt Guild. In 1992 Shelly received the first Jewel Pearce Patterson Scholarship from the AIQA, she traveled to Quilt Expo Europa in The Netherlands for the award.

Meryl Ann Butler, Virginia Beach, Virginia

Professional artist since 1972, quilt art since 1982. A repeat Fairfield Fashion Show designer, she developed and teaches Glitz Magic prismatic foil techniques. Author, teacher, designer, creates commissioned fiber art and wearable art. Listed in *The World's Who's Who of Women*, 12th ed., and in *2000 Notable American Women*, 6th ed., in recognition of the peace promoting aspects of her quilted art. Her work is in private and corporate collections around the globe, including the University of Peace, Costa Rica; City Hall, Moss, Norway; and in the collection of the Hon. Nelson Mandella. She designed and developed the First U.S. – Soviet Children's peace quilt Exchange Project (1977-88), a historical project chronicled in the media of both countries.

Kathleen Headlee Marra Butts, Pullman, Washington

Quiltmaker, collector, conservator, and teacher of quiltmaking.

Kathleen Headlee Marra Butts was born at Aleppo, Pennsylvania, on December 26, 1924. When she was three, her family moved to Morgantown, West Virginia, where she lived until she and Dr. George G. Marra were married in 1951, and then moved to Pullman, Washington. In 1987, four years after George's death, Kathleen and Dr. William S. Butts were married. They also live in Pullman and Bill is her most supportive quilt fan.

Her degrees included a B.A. in home economics at West Virginia University in 1946, an M.S. in home economics education at Iowa State University in 1948, and a Ph. D. in sociology at Washington State University in 1976.

Kathleen's first project in quiltmaking was a 1930's set of Sunbonnet Sue dime store blocks at the age of eight. During her youth, she was very active in dressmaking in 4-H and later as a homemaker and mother of three daughters. As a college teacher, she taught for more than 20 years in clothing and textile departments at Washington State University and Iowa State University. Courses taught were basic clothing construction, flat pattern design, draping on a dress form, tailoring, and social psychology of clothing. These experiences added much breadth and depth to quiltmaking activities, which first became a full-time passion in 1988. She now gives talks on quilt topics and began teaching quiltmaking classes in 1993. Kathleen has completed and hand quilted four bed-sized quilts. Three were intergenerational quilts as the tops and blocks were made by her mother and aunt in the 1930's – a pieced yellow and orange tulip quilt, a multi-fabric Texas Star, and a multi-fabric Nine-Patch. For her one singly made appliqué bed quilt, "Washington State Centennial Rose," she won the hand quilting award at the Palouse Patcher's quilt show in Moscow, Idaho. Two wall quilts have been published: "Liberty Star" in *Watercolor Quilts* by Pat Magaret and Donna Slusser, and "Passion for Paisley" in *Round Robin Quilts* published by That Patchwork Place, Bothell, Washington.

In addition to quiltmaking, designing, and teaching, Kathleen is an avid fabric collector and maintains swatch catalogs of her fabric collection, has organized an extensive quilt book and magazine library, has an impressive collection of 1860 – 1950 quilts and tops, works on quilt conservation and restoration, and is interested in quilts as history and social documents. Kathleen's prized quilt is the 1930's Wedding Ring utilizing all her childhood dress fabrics and made by her mother and aunt and presented as a wedding gift in 1951.

Her membership in organizations includes: Palouse Patchers of Pullman, Washington; Washington State Quilters; American Quilter's Society; National Quilters Association, American Quilt Study Group; and the Quilt Restoration Society.

Carol E. Butzke, Slinger, Wisconsin

Carol is an NQA certified judge (qualified to judge master

quilts), quilting teacher and artist, registered nurse, wife, and mom. A native Wisconsinite, Carol makes her home there with husband, Bob and sons, Bradley and Ryan.

Her addiction to quilting began in 1980 and has increased continually since. Including the Grand Showcase Award at Quilters Unlimited Showcase, her quilts have received many awards at national, state, and regional shows. In 1986, her quilt, "Bright Hopes, Bright Promise," was the Wisconsin winner in the Great American

Quilt Festival in honor of the Statue of Liberty Centennial. It was one of seven quilts in the contest to receive special recognition and traveled for three years with the Folk Art Museum of New York to Japan and across the United States. In 1994, her first entry to the AQS show, "Delectable Mountain Star," received first place in the Traditional Pieced, Professional category. Several of her quilts have appeared in publications such as: *All Flags Flying, America's Glorious Quilts, Great American Quilts 1995, American Quilter, Quilt Art Engagement Calendar, Quilters Newsletter, Traditional Quiltworks*, and of all places, the cover of a college history book.

Beth Buzbee, LaPorte, Texas

I, Beth Buzbee, was born February 9, 1954 in Marlin, TX. My grandmother, Lilly Kampfhenkel, mother Evangeline Buzbee, and I quilted on a quilt when I was 10 years old. Grandma had the quilt in a frame placed on four chairs in her living room. The quilt frame belonged to my great-grandmother, Caroline Kampfhenkel. As a fourth generation Texas quilter, I enjoy quilting and various other needle arts. Thank God for the talented women in my family who have passed on their knowledge of so many enjoyable talents. I am currently a member of AQS.

Evangeline Buzbee, South Houston, Texas

Evangeline Buzbee was born October 12, 1931 in Marlin, Texas. Now lives in South Houston, Texas. Since 1981 she has made 115 different size quilts. Many are in the homes of her family and friends. She is a third generation of quilters who loves to sew and quilt. Her daughter, Beth, and granddaughter, Mia, are continuing the tradition. She is currently a member of AQS and has received numerous awards for her quilts. Favorite Quilt: Sewing Machines.

Gerrine Buzzell, Romeo, Michigan

Gerrine Anderson Buzzell was born in Cadillac, Michigan, on June 25, 1930. I currently reside in Romeo, Michigan. To keep a four-year-old busy, my grandmother taught me to piece a quilt, which I still have. Sewing has been both a pleasure and necessity; but quilting has always held a special place. I make mostly bed-size quilts for family and friends. I enjoy all patterns, designs, and colors; but especially going to seminars to commune with other quilters. I was co-founder of our local Peaches

& Patches quilt guild. I was chairperson of the quilt calendar project; also co-chair of our local biannual quilt show of 1995. I am also a member of AQS, NQA, AIQA, and a charter member of MQN. My quilts have been displayed in local quilt shows and our calendar. Anytime I can help young people with sewing or quilting is especially rewarding.

Making quilts, I do a little designing, and also help teach some in our quilt guild. Most memorable to me is going to quilting bees with my grandmother.

Susan Vogel, Vivian Brady, Gerrine Buzzell, and Roberta Smelis, a quilt calendar committee, show off the finished calendar. (photo courtesy of Gerrine Buzzell)

Marguerite Decocq, Lillie Eaton, Delma Rae & Louise Bailey. Town and Country Quilters Guild. Demonstration at Joplin Quilt Show. (photo courtesy of Betty Bridges)

Daughters of Dorcas and Sons Chapter 102 NQA, Washington, D.C. (photo courtesy of Mae Bolden)

Quilters learn foundation piecing techniques from Jane Hall, Raleigh, NC, at the 1996 AQS Quilt Show, Paducah, KY.

Debra Wagner, Cosmos, MN, demonstrates her striplate technique at the AQS Quilt Show, All Star Review.

Lorraine Torrence, Seattle, WA, presents a lecture on "Wearable Art for Every Body" at the 1996 AQS Quilt Show, Paducah, KY.

Instructor Katie Pasquini Masopust teaches quilters to draw their patterns at the 1996 AQS Quilt Show, Paducah, KY.

Friends, who moved apart, completed Round Robin quilts via mail. They then got together after a year to baste their quilts. Left to right: Doris Moreloch, Linda Lavendorf, Mari deMoya, Jane Wentlent. (photo courtesy of Mari deMoya)

Courtney Linn Bain, 2 years, 5 months old, helps her Aunt Shorty (Cherita Page Walker), Zeigler, IL. (photo courtesy of Jeanine Linn)

Erma B. Kranstruber, Valley View, OH, talks about quilting to students in her grandaughter's 5th grade class at Cuyahoga Heights Elementary School at Cuyahoga Hts, OH.

Patricia B. Campbell, Dallas, Texas

Photo by Glamour Shots.

Patricia B. Campbell of Dallas, Texas, is a quilt artist, teacher, lecturer, and author known for her unique style of Jacobean appliqué using glorious colors, and for her excellence in appliqué techniques.

Searching for a new hobby, Pat began quiltmaking in 1983. She did not learn from her mother or grandmother. "Neither was a needlewoman," Pat explains, "but my mother did give me her silver thimble when I was 15. I think she knew that someday I'd put it to good use."

Realizing very quickly that appliqué was her passion, and wanting to do something new and different, she adapted 17th century (Jacobean era) crewel embroidery designs to hand appliqué. She explains creating her style, "I knew it had to be floral, it had to be fantasy rather than realism, and it had to be appliqué." She then developed several methods for appliquéing the graceful but tricky shapes typical of crewel patterns.

Pat achieved instant fame when her stunning Jacobean-style quilt "Jacobean Arbor" appeared on the cover of AQS *American Quilter* magazine in 1990. She declares, "I love the fantasy botanicals, the swirls, the curves. Flowers, leaves, trees – I can re-create these lovely things in fabric!" Pat also loves color – choosing fabrics and putting them together. "You're a maverick," exclaimed her favorite quilt shop owner. "It's true," Pat replied, "Magenta is my neutral!" Vibrant, bold, brilliant color brings her quilts to life.

Her quilts have won many national prizes: "Jacobean Arbor" has won eight ribbons, including a blue ribbon at the AQS show in 1990, and a Best of Show in Lancaster, PA; "Elizabethan Woods" is a five-time winner, including another blue ribbon at the AQS show in 1991; and "Vitis Vinifera" has won three ribbons and a Best of Show in Louisville, KY.

Thirteen quilting magazines have featured Pat's quilts, including *American Quilter, Patchwork Quilt Tsushin, Quilting International, Quilting Today, Traditional Quiltworks, McCalls,* and *Threads.* Two books, have featured her quilts: *Award-Winning Quilts and Their Makers, Vol. III* and *A Quilted Christmas,* she has also co-authored four books with Dr. Mimi Ayars: *Jacobean Appliqué: Exotica* and *Romantica, Theorem Applique: Abundant Harvest* and *Summer Splendor.* In addition, she and Michelle Jack design quiltmaking fabric for Benartex, Inc. and co-authored *Red Hot Chili Peppers.* Pat also markets a line of Jacobean appliqué patterns.

Pat has taught at major quilt shows across the U.S., including Paducah, Lancaster, Indianapolis, and Atlanta. She has taught appliqué workshops for quilt guilds all over the U.S. and in England, South Africa, and Australia. To her pride, many of her students have produced prize-winning quilts. Pat encourages her students to be creative and find their own direction. A popular lecturer, Pat a Michigan "transplant" via Florida has a reputation for arriving in Western attire. "I love the Texas look and it's a great place to live, too! Texas is an attitude, not just a place," she says.

Susan Syme Campbell, Hyannis, Massachusetts

Susan Syme Campbell lives in Hyannis, MA, with her husband Peter, two children, and two grandchildren. Currently, she is serving as president of the 400 member Bayberry Quilters of Cape Cod and as producer/director of "The Quilter's Palette" television program. She started quilting in 1987, making over 100 quilts, teaching quilting, and serving as show chairman for her guild. Wanting to record the efforts of quilters in her region, she enrolled in a local access television studio production class three years ago. The results have been spectacular. Twenty-one half hour programs and one hour long special have been produced and cablecast to over 90,000 homes once or twice a week for two years! Sue looks forward to the new television season and the opportunity to continue programs consisting of conversations with quilters; location shoots at quilt shows and studios; and teaching segments with local and national teachers. She is very proud of "The Quilter's Palette," the "first, and we believe the only television program produced for and by quilters in the country."

Christine Carlson, Norcross, Georgia

Author, designer, teacher, lecturer, collector of vintage fabrics. Miniature quiltmaking and designing is Christine Carlson's specialty. She teaches professionally and writes articles on a variety of quick-and-easy techniques especially formatted for her tiny treasures, with paper foundation piecing, bias squares, and strip piecing among her favorites. What started as a fluke almost ten years ago and over 150 miniature quilts later, resulted in her first book: *Bias Square Miniatures*, published in April, 1995, by That Patchwork Place. Her lectures include a large array of her colorful and unusual quilts, some made with vintage fabrics, along with doll beds.

Awards received include: Third place, "Star Struck" wallhanging, Louisville, KY, Fall Festival of Quilts, 1990. Second place, "Lots of Baskets" miniature quilt, Quilt America! Show, 1991. Third place, "Lots of Baskets" miniature quilt, Kentucky Fall Festival of Quilts, Lexington, KY, 1991. Second honorable mention, "Stars, Stars, Stars" miniature quilt, Quilt America! Show, 1992. First place, "Log Cabin Star" miniature quilt, Kentucky Quiltfest, Louisville, KY, 1992. Second place, "Stars, Stars, Stars," miniature quilt, Kentucky Quiltfest, Louisville, KY, 1992. First place, "Stars Galore" miniature quilt, Kentucky Quiltfest, Louisville, KY, 1992.

Linda G. Carlson, Mexico, Missouri

Since the early 70's I have enjoyed enduring "Quilt-a-cus path-o-logcus" according to my pathologist husband. Its symptoms present with a beginner's class and the advanced stages include writing a book and collecting antique quilts. I have been privileged to teach and lecture nationally as a result of this affliction. Author of *Roots, Feathers, and Blooms: 4-Block Quilts, Their History & Patterns* published by AQS in 1994. Collect antique 4-block quilts & patterns, lecture and teach workshops, and design patterns. My most memorable quilting experiences would have to include having AQS publish my first book, and being selected to speak at the 1995 American Quilt Defense Fund/Smithsonian symposium, "What's American About American Quilts?" held at the Smithsonian Museum of American History in Washington, D.C.

Lena Beth Carmichael, Riceville, Tennessee

Lena Beth holds Bachelor's and Master's degrees in agriculture. Along with husband, Rod, and son, Cole, they operate Rabbit Ranch Holsteins, a dairy and poultry farm. She continues to coach 4-H horse judging teams, including state winners, and nationally competitive teams. Lena Beth's quilt career began with collecting antique quilts. She expanded to dealing in old quilts in 1988, selling at antique shows. Marketing has included home-based video and satellite television. Lena Beth has lectured to quilt guilds, elementary school pioneer days, church groups, a community college course, and at Dollywood. She has judged quilts at county fair level. She is a quilt appraiser certified by AQS. Her own quiltmaking goes into group quilts, clothing, and challenge pieces. She continues to collect odd old quilts. Realizing that my own quilt collection had grown larger than my inventory of "for sale" quilts!

Barbara Ann Caron, Cedar Falls, Iowa

Quiltmaker since 1976. Teaches, lectures, designs, and writes about quiltmaking. Assistant Professor of Interior Design at the University of Northern Iowa, Master's and Ph.D degrees in design from the University of Minnesota. Special interest in 19th century design.

Author of *Tessellations and Variations* (AQS, 1995). Quilts have appeared in national judged and juried shows.

Suzanne R. Carroll, Fairbanks, Alaska

Collector, designer, quiltmaker. Suzanne Carroll was born June 5, 1940, in Glenwood, Minnesota, but has lived almost exclusively in Fairbanks, AK, since she was 10 years old. She began sewing as soon as she was tall enough to reach the foot pedal. While raising her children she took tailoring classes and started sewing for people. When she started quilting about five years ago, the wearable art fit right into her realm. She has done many of the traditional quilts but is now more interested in the nontraditional. She is involved in a wearable art group and they have had three shows. She has a wallhanging on tour with the Anchorage Museum of History and Art. McCalls Patterns are photographing two of her vests and she had a garment accepted for the AQS/Hobbs Bonded Fibers show in Paducah, Kentucky. Designing and quilting are Suzanne's favorites of quiltmaking.

Karen A. Hawn Catron, Connersville, Indiana

Collector and quiltmaker with many quilts in home on display and in use. In constructing quilts uses 100% cotton throughout. Karen Ann (Hawn) Catron, born on February 4, 1957, in Rushville, IN. She currently resides in Connersville, IN, with her husband, Rick, 2 sons, 1 daughter, and 1 daughter-in-law. Karen learned to sew in 8th grade and has been sewing ever since. In 1991, a friend introduced her to quilting and a whole new world was opened up to her. She now quilts for the pleasure of it, hand quilting after machine piecing. Several completed projects adorn her home and many projects have been given to friends as gifts. Karen enjoys visiting quilt shows, collecting quilts, and is a member of the Conner Quilters Guild. She considers the art of quilting a gift to be taught and handed down from generation to generation.

Eleanore J. Caulk, Baraboo, Wisconsin

Born August 4, 1933. Lived in Waukegan, IL; Norfolk, VA; Kenosha, WI; and now Lake Delton, WI. I started quilting in 1950's. I started to hand sew and hand quilt. I retired in 1991 and since have become quite active in quilting. Quilts completed: A 6" random square, tied 1950; a 4" random square, tied 1980; Dresden Plate, hand appliqué, 1987; 12 block sampler, 1993; flowered cross stitch, 1994; Broken Star, completely hand sewn and hand quilted, 1995; Snowball Star, machine sewn and hand quilted, 1995; Stormy Sea wallhanging, 1995;. Log Cabin coat and several vests, 1988. Quilts in progress: Tumbling Block Star charm quilt with 1,946 pieces no two alike placement of light medium and darks form the star; a 24" block snowflake design quilted on a muslin background; queen-size candlewicking with a quilted design.

I have taught several crafts and now into quilting. I teach traditional hand sewing and quilting. Will be doing machine quilting also. I am president of the Dells Country Quilters of Wisconsin Dells, WI.

My 12 block sampler took second prize in the Wisconsin Dells Heritage Days Quilt Show, put on by the Dells Country Quilters. We have a challenge project every year for our quilt competition. They are then shown for best of show. We learn new techniques at our regular meetings and show progress on our projects. Currently we are in the process of making our raffle quilt which is the three-dimensional Bow-Tie.

Hazel Jean Centers, Harrodsburg, Kentucky

I was born in Versailles, Kentucky, on March 9, 1938. Married 40 years with 2 sons and 1 grandson. I lived on a farm with my parents and five brothers. I helped my mother with all the sewing and we made quilts for each bed. I've always been fascinated with quilts; how and where they were made. I've made probably 50, since I got married in 1954, giving

most of them for gifts, but the one I appreciate the most is the Log Cabin that I made in 1990 after my dad died and I made it out of all his cotton shirts, pajamas, and robes.

Zimira Charloff, Brooklyn, New York

Born Oct. 2, 1952. B.F.A. in dance from New York University, 1973. Profession: dance teacher. Married, orthodox Jewish mother of nine, ages 8 mos. to 15 years. I have turned down opportunities to teach quilting as I prefer to quilt simply for my own pleasure and for family and friends. I specialize in quilted clothing and objects. I invite input from my children while I am quilting. I especially enjoyed their involvement in the making of my "Sock it to Me" jacket.

A. Jill Christenson-Loll, Seattle, Washington

Born in Seattle, Washington, on Sept. 24, 1955. Quilting since 1991. B.A. in anthropology. Married. Quiltmaker. Administrator for Association of Pacific Northwest Quilters, a five state, two province regional non-profit organization, dedicated to presenting a biennial juried and judged quilt show.

Darlene C. Christopherson, Sioux Falls, South Dakota

Darlene C. Christopherson was born July 29, 1949, in Sioux Falls, South Dakota. Born and raised in quiltmaking in Northern Virginia. Was on the Jinny Beyer Hilton Head Seminar staff for five years prior to returning to Sioux Falls. Teaches hand appliqué, piecing, and quilting as well as many design related classes at retreats and seminars. Many quilts published in books such as *Sensational Scrap Quilts* by Darra Duffy Williamson, and *Soft Edged Piecing* and *Patchwork Portfolio* by Jinny Beyer. A member of the Sioux Falls Quilters Guild, Waterford (Virginia) Guild, Baltimore Appliqué Society, and AQS.

Anne Clayborne, Metairie, Louisiana

Anne Hudson Clayborne, born August 10, 1945, in New Orleans, LA, earned her BS in vocational home economics, a Masters in education and a +30. Anne and her husband, Tom, live in Metairie, LA, where she is a high school teacher.

Anne taught her first quilting class in 1976 and enjoys teaching whenever time permits. She has served as educational director

for Gulf States Quilting Association for 2 years. Anne belongs to AQS, NQA, GSQA, and Bust Fingers, her local quilting guild where she serves as president. Teaching and designing are Anne's favorite parts of quiltmaking. She has received several awards in local and regional quilt shows. At present, miniatures, wallhangings, and designing foundation piecing blocks consume much of her time. Won 1st place ribbon in GSQA quilt show, Miniature Originals.

Barbara Jo Grub Clem, Algonquin, Illinois

Barb began sewing at the age of 10, through the perseverance and dedication of her mother. It wasn't until 1984 that she began to quilt. Her mother-in-law, Ruth, sent her box of fabric and a pattern for a Log Cabin quilt. Ruth had remembered Barb's admiration for this quilt from one of their shopping sprees, and decided she needed a hobby. It wasn't until 1987 that she began to hand quilt upon the insistence of her good friend, Linda. Barb's quilts have won ribbons at the Illinois State Fair, been exhibited in major quilt shows, and published in magazines and calendars. She always tries to make the next quilt better than the last and would someday like to become a quilt judge and an appraiser.

Cindy Cloyd, Austin, Texas

Cindy Cloyd, Austin, Texas, age 43. B.S., M.S., business administration. A native of Southern California, she also lived in France and the UK. She is employed full time as a market analyst and futurist in the computer industry, specializing on information highway trends. Her first quilt was a Sunbonnet Sue, completed in 1973. She has made over thirty quilts and fifty wallhangings and miniature quilts, including one Baltimore Album-style quilt. Her recent quilts emphasize appliqué borders and folk art. She has served on the executive board of the Austin Area Quilt Guild and is active in many quilt organizations.

Maria V. Cobb, Anchorage, Alaska

Designer and quiltmaker. Alaska resident since 1957. Anchorage Log Cabin Quilters Guild since 1986. Background includes University of Alaska – Quilting 1985 – 1986; Conferences – Greatland Quilters, October 1986, May 1988, and May 1990. Workshops with nationally known teachers: Hopkins, Horton, Cory, and Wolfrom. Quilt judge Palmer State Fair, August 1994. Works: "Days of Our Lives," 58" x 60", 8-85 *Quilter's Newsletter*

Magazine 1992. "Ties & Diamonds," 48" x 48", copyrighted original layout, 11-89. *Great American Quilts*, 1993, article Anchorage Daily News, 11-92; *Quilt Craft*, 8-93; "Morning Star," 87" x 87", 1-94, Anchorage Daily News, 5-22-94 & 5-23-94, QNM 5-95; 2nd place ribbon 1994 National Quilting Association Show, memorial quilt dedicated to the oldest "women only" triathlon in the nation, quilt design printed on over 600 shirts. "Caribou," 15" x 19", 7-92. "Born Free," 11" x 13½", 6-89. "Miniature Quilts," summer 1994. Alaska Chapter Coordinator for NQA and 1995 chairman for the first National Quilting Day in Alaska.

Elizabeth Coldwater, Chase, Kansas

I am a self-taught quilter with an interest in many crafts; knitting, crochet, cross-stitch, and sewing. I have been quilting since the middle 70's from an interest in quilts made by great-grandmother, Mamie Caldwell. I have been a member of the Piecemakers Quilt Guild of Rice County, Kansas, since 1989, and the Kansas Quilting Organization since 1990. Currently co-vice president of the guild and have been historian, newsletter person, and on other committees. Enjoy attending classes and workshops and learning new quilting tips and techniques. I prefer to hand piece and hand quilt. I collect books on historical information and quilts and quiltmakers. Single, 37 years old, college graduate, certified dietary manager, and have worked in food service in hospitals and nursing homes. Quilt between work, gardening, and bicycling.

A special memory quilt was made by a cousin, Marsha Vincent, Tulsa, OK, and myself for the Caldwell – Silvas family reunion in Wichita, Kansas, June 24, 1995. Two years ago Marsha and I made album blocks and took them to the last reunion and had family sign them and sent some to family who couldn't make it. Marsha made a beautiful farm scene centerpiece and sewed together the blocks to make a beautiful wallhanging. At the reunion it was raffled off and a cousin, Karen Lutz, won and received it with tears of joy. The quilt contains names of several generations of the family and will be a valuable piece of information for generations in the future.

Bette Grace Rollins Cole, Pioche, Nevada

Born and reared in Utah. Resident of Pioche, Nevada, for 54 years. Grew up enjoying the warmth and comfort of quilts made from used denim or wool pants.

Help make and give dozens of quilts as wedding gifts. For Pioche Heritage Days a unique history portraying quilt is made each year. Have helped design, set together, quilt, and raffle each one for 13 years. Awarded Citizen of the Year for this project as well as many civic activities. President of Pioche Historical Society.

Mable Cole, Greenfield, Illinois

Quilting has been my hobby since I was 13 years old, in 1934 when I made and quilted a Broken Star quilt for home school project, and still have it. Before that I did small fancy pieces which my mother taught me. I have averaged making 15 and quilting 36 a year since 1985 when I retired, making additional crafts to match my quilts, this helps them sell. In 1993 and 1994 I made and sent quilts to 14 states, my unusual year. I have a supply on hand made up and make lots of patterns. I use good materials and work alone. Widow since 1970. I look forward to the Paducah show which I always attend each year.

Derenda Taylor Collins, Flint, Michigan

Derenda Taylor Collins, born November 27, 1936, Colp, IL, learned quilting as a pre-teen from her mother, Derenda Woods Taylor. During her college days, her aunt, Grace Claybrook, and neighbor, Minnie Hinton, encouraged her to get her hope chest quilt finished. Her quilting stopped for 30 years of marriage, motherhood, and careers of school and church musician. Later her grandmother, Maggie Purdue Woods, 94, joined her household and quilting was resumed during the last seven years of her grandmother's life, becoming firmly embedded in the Collins family life style. Her husband, Sylvester; daughter, Sylvia and son, S. Gaffney are quilt enthusiasts, too.

She is a member of AQS and Michigan Quilt Link, travels to quilt shows and classes, and studies color and design. She exhibits at schools, churches, galleries, libraries, and museums in mid-Michigan cities. She liaisons with other guilds to distribute hundreds of charity quilts in Genesee County. She participates in the MSV Folk Art Festival and Crossroads Village Festival. Her favorite quilts are geometric, patchwork, bedsize creations. She is co-founder of the Flint Afro-American Quilter's Guild.

Karen Combs, Columbia, Tennessee

Karen began quilting in 1974 and has been making quilts ever

since! She is known for taking a traditional pattern and giving it her own unique "twist." Karen is intrigued with quilts of illusion and has been designing quilts with illusions for years.

She teaches for many quilt guilds, retreats, and conferences throughout the southeast; including the National Quilting Association quilt show in Charleston, West Virginia. Karen was honored to be nominated for Teacher of the Year by *Professional Quilter Magazine* in 1995. In addition, Karen is co-founder of Maury Quilter's Guild, was their first president, and published their newsletter for several years.

Karen was invited to participate in the 7th Annual Silver Dollar City Wallhanging Challenge in 1993. Being a prolific designer and author; Karen has published articles and patterns in many magazines such as *Traditional Quilter, Quilting International,* and *Quilter's Newsletter Magazine.*

Tia Combs, Coldwater, Michigan

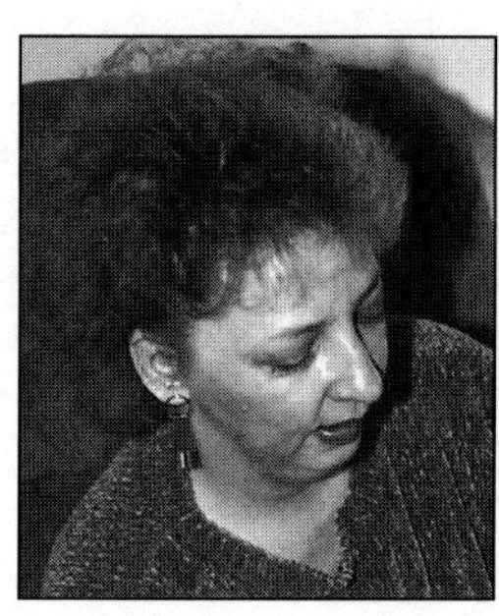

Quiltmaker and designer. My quilting career began in 1980 when I found an unfinished Dresden Plate top which my grandmother had made in 1932. Instantly I became addicted. Through my enthusiasm, my mother became my apprentice and found her niche in cutting out all the pieces for me. Our partnership became our whole lives. I could have produced twice as many quilts by rotary cutting but I found that by tracing all the tiny triangles, etc., it would keep my mother's hands busy cutting out pieces instead of smoking. Gloriously, we sold our "TLC" (my initials) quilts locally and nationally having the most fun of our lives.

Tragically, I lost my beloved mother and best friend in 1993 leaving a hole in my broken heart. The words "Do you have any pieces for me to cut tonight?" are missed so very much.

Finalist in Houston quilt show, two awards of merit in the keepsake quilting "Creating a Challenge."

Jacqulyn Condon, Chandler, Arizona

Born in Pennsylvania, moved to Arizona, then to California where I was a member of the Chula Vista Quilt Guild, began teaching quilting in the Fiji Islands.

Articles published in 1990 *Patchwork Pizzazz,* 1991 in *Country*

Quilt, and 1993 in *Quilt.* Representing the theme of the U.S. Independence Day by a foreign daily newspaper's front page article on my 4th of July quilt; winning awards in international shows; teaching in Fiji, coordinating the first quilt show in the Fiji Islands, watching my students win awards are all memorable.

Taught machine quilting techniques in Japan and knowing one of my Japanese students had a successful one-man exhibit using techniques taught in my classes.

Pepper Cory, Lansing, Michigan

I have been a quiltmaker since 1972 and enjoyed every minute of it. From 1976 – 1983, I owned and operated the first quilt shop in this area. Called Culpepper's Quilts, the shop put me in contact with many different quilters and I became aware of the trends in the craft. When I closed the shop in 1984, I started to write books and haven't stopped since. The titles of the books I have written include *Quilting Designs from the Amish, Quilting Designs from Antique Quilts, Crosspatch-Inspirations in Multi-Block Quilts, Happy Trails-Variations on the Classic Drunkard's Path Pattern*, and *The Signature Quilt,* co-authored with Susan McKelvey. In addition to writing quilt books, I design quilting and painting stencils.

Quilting is both my hobby and my profession. I travel and teach workshops to quilting guilds and at conferences, judge quilt shows, and appraise antique quilts.

Ruth Cattles Cottrell, Irving, Texas

Quiltmaker and designer. BS degree in medical technology, Baylor University, Waco, Texas, 1967. Technical operations manager, Laboratory Corporation of America, Dallas, Texas. I have worked as an operations manager in the medical laboratory field for 25 years. I have sewn since I was 10 years old, doing all sorts of hand and machine work. I became interested in quilting in 1990, joined the Quilter's Guild of Dallas, and have won ribbons on six of seven quilts completed, at Dallas Quilt Celebration, the AIQA show, Houston, and two first places and judge's choice at Quilts UK, 1995. My work was accepted for the AQS show in Paducah, KY, in 1994 and

1995. Won one 2nd place and three 1st place ribbons and best of show for "Crimson and Clover" at Dallas Quilt Celebraion '95.

Brenda Lynn Walker Couture, Chicopee, Massachusetts

Brenda Lynn Walker Couture was born in Detroit, Michigan, Oct. 28, 1946. She was married to Richard Couture, June 1968. Brenda grew up in southern IL, on a farm on the Ohio River, with her mother, grandmother, and three brothers, she now lives in Massachusetts. She learned about quilting from her mother, Cherita Page Walker, and grandmother, Mary Frances Gustin Page, and helped make quilts for their own use. She belongs to AQS, has attended AQS shows with her mother and aunt of southern IL, and aunt of northern MI, and aunt of northern IN. Quilted on the quilt that the Western Baptist Auxiliary had for anyone to quilt on during the AQS show of 1993 and 1994. Brenda is the proud owner of many quilts her mother and grandmother made, and some that she had helped to make.

Richard Gerard Couture, Chicopee, Massachusetts

Richard Gerard Couture, was born in Chicope, MA, June 19, 1945. In 1968 married Brenda Lynn Walker. They currently live in Chicopee, MA. Richard, attended school in Chicopee, he served three tours of duty in the Vietnam War, with the U.S. Marine Corps. Richard became interested in quilting after marrying Brenda who came from a family of quilters. Has attended AQS show and helped his mother-in-law design a quilt pattern. His other interests are ceramics, needlepunch, and embroidery. In 1994 he quilted on the quilt at the Western Baptist Auxillary display. He has no special pattern or favorite quilt. He was a boy scout leader and little league baseball coach. He is very proud of the quilts he and his wife have acquired from his mother-in-law.

Emily Sue Daniel Cox, Paris, Tennessee

Emily Daniel Cox was born March 11, 1939, Henry County, TN, and currently resides in Paris, TN. From her earliest memories she remembers loving quilts. Even before she was born, her mother, Addie Lee Cope Butler Daniel, made baby quilts for her. Emily remembers having matching butterfly quilts for her mother's bed and her great-grandfather's day bed (on which she slept). She asked her mother if there would be enough quilts to last until she died because she never wanted to be without one. Her mother then showed her boxes which contained quilts she, Emily's

grandmother, and great-grandmother had made. They had never been used. What a joy! Three of those quilts are pictured in Bets Ramsey's and Merikay Waldvogel's books.

Almost a decade after her mother died Emily took quilt lessons from Marian Buckley and her first quilt-in-a-day, a Log Cabin ("Chocolate"), won 2nd prize at the local county fair.

Emily's love for quilts continues to grow. She finds it a joy to cherish family quilts (an aunt, Ina V. Butler, gave Emily one in her will) and to make quilts for loved ones.

Patricia Cox, Minneapolis, Minnesota

Quiltmaker, designer, international teacher, lecturer, and writer; living in Minnesota. She has been actively involved in all aspects of quilting since the earliest days of the revival, in the vanguard of the Baltimore Album revival 1980, and is particularly well-known for her fine hand quilting and appliqué skills. Since 1978 she has self-published three books (*Log Cabin Workbook, Every Stitch Counts, Country Children*) which remain in demand, and also produced a video on basic appliqué techniques. A pioneer of the use of plastic for templates and also the use of hand-dyed fabrics for appliqué, Patricia continues to run her own successful international pattern business, One of a Kind Quilting Designs, which she began in 1974. As a NQA certified teacher and judge, Patricia has traveled to Canada, Mexico, United Kingdom, Australia, and New Zealand.

Barbara Lydecker Crane, Lexington, Massachusetts

Barbara Lydecker Crane, a 1970 graduate of Skidmore College (B.S. in fine arts), has been exhibiting her art quilts widely since she began designing in 1981. Juried exhibits include Quilt National '89, and '93, Visions '90, and nine AQS contests (awards in '85 and '91). Her quilts are included in corporate, private, and museum collections.

Her work has been published in many magazines, catalogs, and books, including the *Fiberarts Design Books Three, Four,* and *Five* (forthcoming). Crane has received grants from the Massachusetts Arts Lottery in '86, '87, and '93, and a Fellowship Grant in Crafts from the Massachusetts Cultural Council in '95.

"My goal is to voice my sense of wonderment in the natural world, its beauty and mysteries." She talks about her work in slide lectures and magazine articles, and does some teaching.

Lynn Crawford, Wrightwood, California

Teacher and designer. Lynn Crawford, of Wrightwood, CA, has been quilting for over 12 years. With a fabric collection that is the envy of her friends, she spends time in the morning just playing with fabrics to wake up.

She started teaching about nine years ago and has introduced many quilters to the joys of free-motion machine quilting. Four years ago she started designing some of her own patterns for classes. Designing new quilts and choosing fabrics is her favorite part of quilting, and her long range goal is to have a sewing slave to actually do all the sewing!

Five years ago she and her partner, Pam Overton, formed the Traveling Quilters, a tour service for quilters. They do weekend getaways, trips to local and national shows, and other quilt-related activities. They recently added a third partner, Sue Glass, and are already planning events for 1996 including a Hawaiian trip. Every class I teach is a memorable experience.

Valerie S. Crook, Bel Air, Maryland

Born March 3, 1930 in Baltimore, Maryland. Remarried 1976 to Thomas K. Crook. Daughter Lisa Peterman gave me Georgia Bonesteel's first book plus *Quilters Newsletter Magazine* subscription in 1983, jump starting my quilting. It serves as therapeutic creativity for me. I've three or more quilts in progress at all times. Since 1983, I've made bed quilts, wallhangings, and vests, and have sold many.

I've received ribbons at quilt shows, state and local fairs but quilt only for family and friends now. 1990 QHC Show, Lancaster, PA, exhibited my wallhanging "Amish Footprints in the Nite."

"The Demise of Planet Earth" features a series of four quilts: "Farewell to the Rainforest," "The Lost, Lost Continent," "These Two Shall Pass," "And Then There Were None." The second in the series appeared in *Quilters' Newsletter Magazine* #241, p. 65. These four wallhangings express my concerns for our environment.

Mary Bywater Cross, Portland, Oregon

Quilt historian, author, curator, artist, consultant, also Columbia-Willamette quilt study group leader, judge, and teacher. My interest in quilting was nurtured by sharing family heirlooms

and history with my Iowa grandmother. Then, studying the broad field of quilt history and quiltmaking, I focused my work on making woolen quilts and researching quilt history for public presentations.

My quilts are in collections across the country. My award-winning books on quilts of migration have been products of in-depth research into the lives of westering women.

One of my greatest joys in the world of quilts as visual records of women's experience is helping family members discover their past through the clues stitched away in their textile treasures.

Idabel Crowell, Montaque, California

Born November 15, 1934, Schulter, OK. My original design bias tape appliqué "Balloons" wallhanging was viewer's choice, Siskiyou Piecemakers Challenge Etna, CA, 1993. Displayed Hall of Banners AQS show 1994. Photo American Quilter magazine fall 1994. "Magic Spiral" wallhanging viewer's choice, Siskiyou Country Quilter's Guild show Yreka, CA, 1995. First place Siskiyou Country Quilter's Challenge "My Favorite Place," August 1995. Began quilting in 1987. Presently editor of Siskiyou Country Quilter's Guild newsletter. Cathedral Window quilt in progress for daughter using fabrics from her childhood dresses.

Melody Crust, Kent, Washington

Melody is a first-generation quilter whose love of fabric and quiltmaking have led her to design, teach, lecture, and publish. She is fascinated and inspired by nature and has learned to really "see" and to appreciate color, value, and brilliance from her photographer husband.

Melody is a quilt teacher and lecturer active in a variety of quilt-related projects. Although established in the Northwest, she teaches and lectures worldwide. Books and magazines have featured her work. Her art quilts are in private collections, and galleries, and have been exhibited internationally.

In addition to designing and making quilts she also designs and self-publishes a line of quilt label patterns to encourage quilters to permanently identify their quilts.

Melody co-founded and is vice president of the Association of Pacific Northwest Quilters. In 1994, APNQ produced the first judged and juried quilt exhibition in the Northwest.

Linda L. Culbreth, Jackson, Missouri

Designer, quiltmaker, teacher, and pattern printer. Born in Houston, TX, on March 3, 1951. Made first quilt top at age 9 or 10. Designed "Rainy Day Ducks," "Calico Cows," "Deb's Tea Party," "Jo's Carousel."

While pregnant with last child (now 17) started a baby quilt: "Rainy Day Ducks." Almost finished hand quilting it. He came early – so finished it by machine. Made quilts for friends & family.

Beth Garrison Culp, Atlanta, Georgia

Born in Gastonia, NC; 1968 graduate with honors from Ashley High School, recipient of the Betty Crocker Award for outstanding home economics student; received BS in home economics from Meredith College, Raleigh, NC, in 1972. Married for 23 years with three daughters.

Quiltmaker for 12 years. So far have made 10 full-size, 15 lap-size, 20 wall-size, and several vests.

Participated in the Georgia Quilt project by making and donating a quilt to be presented to a participant in the 1996 Olympics, to be held in Atlanta. In 1990, I designed, coordinated, and made, along with five novices, a quilt for Pace Academy. The project took 18 months, and over 300 man hours to complete. It was purchased at an auction for $1,500 and donated to the school, where it hangs today.

JoAnne Cuoghi, Arrington, Virginia

Born in New York City, JoAnne spent most of her adult life in New Jersey. Recently moved to Arrington, VA, where she conducts quilt workshops at Harmony Hill Bed & Breakfast, which she operates with her husband, Robert. Quilting since 1978, her work is equally divided between bed quilts based on traditional designs and innovative, contemporary wallhangings. Currently focusing on machine embroidery. Chairperson, Tercentenary quilt committee, old Tennent Presbyterian Church, Tennent, NJ, 1992. Has taught for South Brunswick Twp. adult education, and Molly Pitcher Stitchers Guild, Tennent, NJ. Member AQS, Molly Pitcher Stitchers.

Diane Current, San Rafael, CA

Award-winning designer, quiltmaker, and lecturer whose work is included in national and international collections. B.A., clothing, textiles and art, University of Washington; Seattle, WA. Married to Jerry Hall Current, 3 children.

Wall quilts and wearable art have been seen in numerous juried, one-person, and invitational shows including Stitchery International, Pittsburgh, PA, 1981 and 1985; and "Two Textile Artists," North Hills Art Center, Pittsburgh, PA., 1981. Awards include Best of Class, Marin Needlework and Quilt Show, San Rafael, CA, 1988; and Juror's Award and Mellon Bank Purchase Award, Fiberarts Guild of Pittsburgh Bienniel Show, Pittsburgh, PA, 1980. Other activities: instructor, quilted clothing, quilting, and design, North Hills Art Center and City Quilt Shop, Pittsburgh, PA, 1977 to 1982; featured speaker, 1st "Fiber Gathering," Cedar Lakes Craft Center, Ripley, WV, 1983; president, Fiberarts Guild of Pittsburgh, 1981 – 82. Presently designing and making quilt-related children's clothing under the label, "Current Image."

Barbara Cutts, Portland, Oregon

Born in London, England. Lived and worked in Los Angeles in the film and television industry doing wardrobe/costume. Have always been interested in fabrics and design. Made my first quilt in 1984 for the first grandchild. Moved to Oregon in 1992. I now have more time to quilt and sew, mostly for pleasure. I like to do patchwork, appliqué, embroidery, bead work, painting, walking, and gardening. I'm just about to try some miniature quilts to use up some of the myriad ideas that are piling up.

Elinor Grabske Czarnecki, St. Francis, Wisconsin

Elinor researched shadow needlework techniques back to the 15th century and the display of her work in 1981 triggered industry interest in these techniques. (The resurgence of interest in these techniques are once again apparent.) Elinor's interest in others motivated her, in 1983, to embark on a 16 month endeavor to bring the art of quilts to the Ronald McDonald house of southeastern Wisconsin. This house was the first in the nation to have a quilt on every bed. The 75 quilts are said to be the largest collection of quilts brought together, in the shortest period of time to be given away as a gift. (The quilts were gifts from 75 cities and 14 states.) Elinor is an accomplished designer and has had over 100 patterns/designs/articles accepted for publication, for magazines, books as well as manufacturers. Elinor is an innovative and enthusiastic teacher, sharing her needlework knowledge since 1974, conducting workshops in virtually all aspects of quilting and hand needlework across the country. Most recently created the "Chartline" tools, and the method of "No Math – Template Free Angles on Rectangle Patchwork." As well as writing two books using this technique, *Angled Strip Patchwork Made Easy, The Protea and Other Flowers*, 1988, now in its second printing, and *Angled Strip Patchwork Christmas 'Round Town* 1989. In 1994 Elinor was named Craft Designer of the Year Finalist by *Craft and Needlework Age* magazine and Loctite Corporation. Elinor currently presents a three minute craft spot for the Fox Network television station in Milwaukee, WI, and is an active board member with the Wisconsin Quilt History Project, and is once again soliciting and making replacement quilts for the southeastern Wisconsin Ronald McDonald House. Elinor's versatility has been reflected in her occupational experience. Her fiber art work has been accepted in private and public collections.

Ann I. Czompo, Williamsburg, Virginia

Quiltmaker and teacher. Ann Reed Czompo was born June 15, 1939, in Youngstown, Ohio. She earned a B.A. degree in sociology and music from Kent State University, an M.A. in dance from Texas Woman's University, and did graduate work in dance ethnology and ethnomusicology. She taught dance at University of Cincinnati, Northern Illinois University, and SUNY, College at Cortland, retiring in 1991 after 30 years of teaching. Ann and her husband, Andor, moved to Williamsburg, VA, in August 1995. Ann has been quilting since 1975, doing patchwork and appliqué, traditional and innovative designs, quilts, wallhangings, and clothing. Themes include dancers, dogs, breast cancer, logos, and advertising graphics. She has taught quilt workshops for schools and guilds, and has won numerous awards locally, regionally, and nationally. She is a member of AQS, NQA, Thumbstall Quilt Guild (Marcellus, NY), Cortland County Quilters, and frequently attends quilt workshops, shows, and festivals.

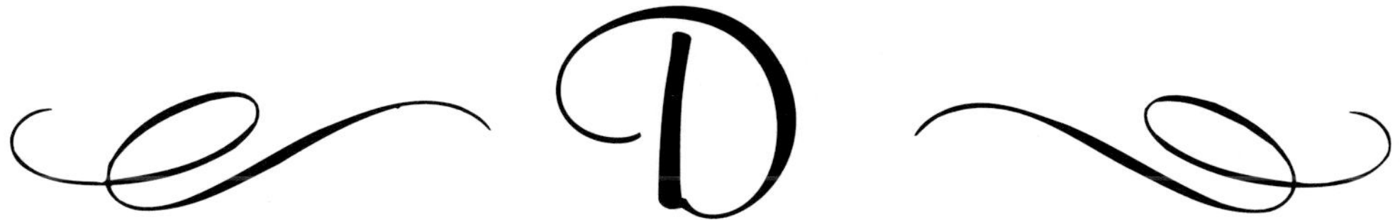

Wanda Stolarun Dabrowski, New Britain, Connecticut

Quiltmaker, collector of antique quilts and antique fabrics. Born and raised in New Britain, CT. Received a BS degree in education from Central Connecticut State College. After retiring from Central Connecticut State College in 1986 where I worked as an administrative assistant, I attended an adult education class which was my introduction to quilting. In January 1990 a new quilt chapter in Berlin, CT, Sisters in Quilting was organized and I became a charter member. We are a chapter of Greater Hartford Quilt Guild. I organized and ran our bus trips and wrote chapter news items for the GHQG newsletter. I am also the liaison for my guild to the CQSP. I am a member of a Textile Study Group and the Connecticut Quilt Search Project. We are documenting pre-1950 quilts and it is still an on-going project. As part of this project, we anticipate publishing a book on the history of Connecticut quilts and quiltmakers. I love all types of quilts and have not narrowed a preference to making only one type of quilt. Most of my quilts were for family members and also for AIDS infected babies.

Received several first place awards at regional country fairs, and also from the Association of Connecticut Fairs.

Kathleen M. Daniels, Miami, Florida

Collector, designer, quiltmaker. I've been sewing since age 12. I have over 30 quilts which I've collected and sewn. My collection contains several quilts over 100 years old. My first quilt was a yo-yo quilt, which I made from old clothes in 1971.

Also, I do embroidery, needlepoint, cross-stitch, and I have a sewing business on the side with my sister which we call – "Two Crafty Sisters."

Current projects include a family history quilt which includes appliqués and embroidery, a 4th of July holiday quilt, and a Presidential embroidered quilt.

M. Susan DeLongchamp Danielson, Golden, Colorado

M. Susan DeLongchamp Danielson was born December 1, 1950, in Ishpeming, Michigan, graduated from Ishpeming High School

in 1968, and Northern Michigan University in 1981 with biology and chemistry degrees. Susan is a molecular biologist working in the Molecular Diagnostic Laboratory at the Children's Hospital of Denver, CO.

Susan began quilting in 1987 and since then has completed 16 wallhangings, 14 crib quilts, and 12 full-size quilts. She has had quilts published in *Quilter's Newsletter Magazine*, issues #246 and #251; *Dance of the Logs* by June Ryker; *Great American Quilts*, 1994; *Star Bright Quilts – Quilts Made Easy* by Oxmoor House, 1995; 1992 contestant in the AQS show and her quilt, Feathered Friends II received a 3rd place award at the 1996 AQS show. Susan is a member of the Colorado Quilting Council, Columbine Quilt Guild, Rocky Mountain Quilt Museum, American Quilter's Society, and the American International Quilt Association.

Marjorie Wood Dannis, Portsmouth, New Hampshire

Marjorie Wood Dannis, born March 4, 1916, in Winchester, MA, graduated from Simmons College, Boston, MA, with a BS in library science. I took my first class in quilting in the late 70's with Mildred Soffellard. I have been happily at it ever since. I joined the New England Quilt Guild in 1978, and have served as state representative, chair of the museum search committee, and parliamentarian off and on since '78. I am presently librarian for the New England Quilt Museum which has over 1,300 books, extensive pattern collections, both in pamphlets and in single sheets: vendors catalogs; quilt show catalogs; teachers brochures; newsletters from New England and national quilt organizations. We are open most days of the week; we also enjoy doing reference questions for quilters.

Cathy M. Dargel, Tucson, Arizona

Professional quilter. Cathy Marie Lechota Dargel was born July 25, 1955, in Flint, Michigan. She was graduated from the University of Michigan and the University of Arizona and resides in Tucson, Arizona.

Beginning quilting in 1983, she is currently a professional quilter. Specializing in machine quilting, but also doing hand quilting and complete commissions, she has more than five years and

hundreds of quilts to her credit. Cathy has taught quilting at local shops, but now devotes her quilting time to her business, appropriately named, Imma Quilter. Winner of numerous ribbons for her work, Cathy is a member of many quilting groups. Her first quilt, which was made in 1976, recently won Abominable Mention in the Worst Quilt in the World contest.

Lyn Daugherty, Sandy, Oregon

Quiltmaker, designer. Until 1988 I was a quilt lover, and especially loved the quilts my mother made. For mom's 70th birthday I made a quilted coat in tribute to her. We then celebrated the joy of quilting by entering our coat in the Sewn Wearables Contest offered in our favorite magazine, *Creative Ideas Needle & Crafts*. We didn't win the Bernina, but the coat was chosen as runner-up. I was asked to write directions for making the coat as part of the "Quilt" Classics feature article, October 1989 issue. Then as the coat returned from New York, I received a letter from mom suggesting we enter the coat in another contest – the 2nd International Art Competition offered by the Museum of Church History and Art, Church of Jesus Christ of Latter Day Saints. The coat was chosen to be displayed in the Museum Art Show. In time, the coat returned to mom (Myrtle Smith) in Victoria, B.C., Canada, where she enjoys it today.

Since my first attempt at patchwork and quilting, I have developed my own passion and have quilted many memories with mom, sisters, children, and friends. My latest quilting companions are my Girl Scout troop. Quilting with my daughters, granddaughters, and their friends is wonderful. They love to make baby quilts for special needs babies.

Melody David-Baker, Tucson, Arizona

Melody has loved quilts forever. She is a member of the Arizona Quilting Guild, Log Cabin Quilter's Chapter. She hosts a work day with Susan Standley and Terri Johnson once a month where the three work on scheduled projects they have all agreed on. Her house is a busy place with seven children!

Melody is a very energetic quilter and can not put them down until they are ¾ done! Melody started quilting when she took time off from work seven years ago with her first baby. She has always been attracted to quilting, but now it is a passion.

Melody, born June 16, 1956, in Tampa, Florida, now lives in Tucson, AZ, with her husband, Michael Baker, and their children, David, Melissa, and Moriah.

My favorite project is one that Sharon and I did together, we picked all the fabrics together.

Annie Ruth Davis, Kennesaw, Georgia

Co-author of *Georgia Quilting on my Mind*, Georgia quilt patterns and history collector, and lecturer. Born and reared in Cartersville, GA. Now lives in Acworth, GA. Quilter for 15 years, have 3 daughters, 1 son, and 9 grandchildren. She has made a quilt for each one including sons and daughters-in-law. Annie learned the art of quilting at her mother's knee. Fabric has always been a fascination to her. Sewing since she was old enough to hold a needle, making her children's clothing, and teaching classes in the shop, "Annie's Workshop." The shop brought her in contact with other people whose interest was also in textiles and the art of quilting.

After the death of her mother, she was given all her mother's sewing paraphernalia in boxes and brown bags, in which she found a quilt top pieced 20 years earlier by her mother. Annie quilted the top; gave it signed and dated to her first granddaughter, Brooke. From that moment, she has been hooked on quilting. She and her partner, Pat Prewett, added quilting to their fabric shop and began quilting classes. They later incorporated and Annie's Workshop became Allatoona Quilt Shop, Inc. Unfortunatley, Allatoona Quilt Shop burned while Pat was attending Emory University in clinical pastoral education.

Annie is a charter member of Allatoona Quilters' Guild and a past officer. She was also the president of North Georgia Quilt Council. Designed "Genelogy Quilt" over 600 names and dates. Won several blue ribbons at quilt shows. Quilt shop owner for 5 years. Served as president of Georgia Quilt Council, 1990.

Trudy Davis, Advance, North Carolina

My name is Trudy Davis, I was born in Rockford, IL. I received my first quilt, a satin quilt to be exact. My grandmother, Guffy, made the quilt when I was born in 1948. I remember this quilt so well because of the beautiful bright colors and the feel of the material. I remember laying on it as a child during the summer because it felt so cool and then in the winter under it to keep me warm.

My parents moved to southern California when I was very young and my quilt went with me. I didn't think to much about quilts till I moved to San Diego and went to the local swap meet. There I found a quilt top that was being used as a table cloth. I asked the young lady if it was for sale and she said yes, that it was her grandmother's who just passed away and she didn't know what to do with it. I asked her about her grandmother: name, age, birthplace, and anything else she wanted others to know about her. With this information in hand, along with the top, I embarked on a new second job. My husband calls me the "Quilt Rescuer." It doesn't matter where I go, yard sales, auctions, swap meets, you name it and I always seem to locate unfinished quilt tops, squares, and even pieces that were cut that need a little attention.

I have put together four so far, each with their own quilt history plate on the back with the story of the person who started it. I know that's not too many but working and family, I am unable to do this full time like I would love to do. Hopefully when I retire, I will be able to finish them all and rescue more from the scrap pile or trash bins.

Daisy S. DeHaven, Lansing, Michigan

Have been quilting since 1979. Active in Capitol City Quilt Guild, Lansing, since 1985; have served as secretary, vice president, and currently (1995 – 96) as president of the 200+ member CCQG; in 1990, established a President's Block to honor outgoing CCQG presidents. Member of AQS, AIQA, NQA, charter member and benefactor of MAQS, charter member of Michigan Quilt Network, serving as Region IV Showcase treasurer in 1993. Started small quilt group in my church called Presbyterian Piecemakers in 1987. Designed and am coordinating the making of a signature quilt for the Lansing First Presbyterian Church's Sesquicentennial Celebration in 1997, teaching basic quiltmaking to volunteers working with me.

Have collected antique quilts for 20 years, make both traditional and contemporary quilts, mostly bed size. Chair 18-member charm quilt group which meets each month, and which becomes a round robin group each September to December for a change of pace. Have presented guild programs on round robin quilts. Worked with CCQG volunteers (Sunbonnet Sues in Canoes) to produce three quilts to commemorate the 33 month, 21,000 mile, two continent canoe expedition from the Artic Ocean to Cape Horn undertaken by Explorers Valerie and Verlen Kruger, 1989 – 91; write-up and photographs in #85 (December, 1992) issue of *Lady's Circle Patchwork Quilts*; quilts were exhibited at Houston International Quilt Show in 1992 and Sunbonnet Sues traveled to Houston for the exhibition. Won 3rd place for CCQG's annual challenge in 1992 and 1994.

My masterpiece to date is "Love Ring – A Wedding Quilt" made for the wedding of my daughter and her husband on July 30, 1994. Quilt won 4th place Viewer's Choice at the 1995 Going to Pieces Quilt Show (over 300 entries).

Lenna DeMarco, Chandler, Arizona

Lenna DeMarco born in 1947, in Chandler, AZ. I am a self-taught quilter and amateur quilt historian. I have only been quilting for the last ten years and focus primarily on traditional and historic patterns. I keep in my cupboard my first quilt, a wallhanging, as an example of how not to make a quilt! In addition to my own quilts, I collect, restore, and repair antique quilts and quilt old tops. My oldest quilt is a red and green Missouri Rose appliqué that Barbara Brackman dated to the 1850's (purchased at at thrift store for $45!). Although I teach college full-time, much of my off hours are spent in quilt study and working on my seemingly endless supply of old quilt tops. As I work on each top, I feel as though I am reaching across the centuries and helping to complete the work of one woman's life. It truly is a labor of love. Member: AQS and AQSG.

Mari Yamashita deMoya, Middleton, Wisconsin

Mari belongs to Mad City Quilters, WI Quilters, Inc., and the Madison area chapter of the EGA. At seven Mari stitched pajamas on her mother's Kenmore and has been saving fabric scraps ever since. A graduate degree in Asian and Pacific art history has provided inspiration for incorporating Asian motifs in her quilting and a slide lecture. Her favorite projects include friendship challenges and exchanges that remind her of the Army community and life before her husband's retirement from the military.

Rita Denenberg, Wellington, Florida

Retired artist, self-taught quilter. Quilting since 1983. Started exhibiting in 1988, turning professional in 1989. I utilize both hand and machine techniques. Designer, quiltmaker, instructor, lecturer. Represented Florida in Great American Quilt Festival, 1989. Received 2nd place in professional appliqué at AQS show

1990. Numerous other awards. Exhibited throughout U.S. and Japan. Featured in numerous books and magazines for patterns and feature articles.

Violette H. Denney, Carrollton, Georgia

Quiltmaker! I was born July 5, 1933, in Carroll County, Georgia, a farmer's daughter. Became a bride at age 17 and moved to Atlanta, GA. We have two wonderful sons, and in the early 60's we bought part of my "grandmother's flower garden" (farm) and when the boys were in their early teens, we built a cabin in the country. I worked 20 years. In 1975 my mother gave me two quilts that she had started about 1960 and said "I believe that of my 7 daughters you are most likely to finish these." Our boys married, my husband retired, and we moved to Carrollton. That's when I wanted quilts for my country home, and I learned to quilt from a book. My first quilt was a "Cathedral Window," next I put my counted cross-stitch flowers together in a quilt. Yes, I did finish my mothers quilts (Six Point Star & Grandmother's Flower Garden). My mother died in 1982. In about 10 years I have made 50 – 60 bed and wall quilts. These remain in my family! In addition to being a wife, mother, grandmother, and quilter, I am an active church member and teach Sunday school. I am an active DAR member; currently keeping our chapter scrapbook and serving as treasurer.

I am a member of AQS, NQA, Georgia Quilting Council, East Cobb Quilt Guild, and W. Georgia Quilter's Guild (past president of WGQG). I am currently serving my 2nd year as treasurer of Georgia Quilt Council. This is the 5th year to co-chair our local quilt show at the regional library. We have prepared exhibits in the 6 large display cases along with our quilt show and usually 1 or 2 other months each year. One of the favorite displays is "Bears and Decorative Tins" with mini quilts. Our guild has participated in the County Fall Festival for several years with an exhibit and a quilt in progress to demonstrate quilting. I have, with other guild members, presented several programs at schools in our area. I try to share my quilts in local shows. I have entered quilts for the past 7 years in the Great American Cover-Up, at Bulloch Hall in Roswell, GA. My quilting experience has been useful at church also. I made a signature quilt during Vacation Bible School for a child with leukemia. We mailed it to him in Seattle, WA, while he was there for bone marrow transplant. I have made 7 banners to be used in choir programs.

I have several awards, but the most exciting is being a member of the Georgia Quilt Project and making an Olympic Quilt to be given away during the 1996 games. I have been involved from the beginning in the Georgia Quilt Project to document Georgia's quilts.

Sarah A. Dickson, San Antonio, Texas

After a short time of making traditional quilts in 1979 – 80, I began collaborating with Maureen H. McGee and making quilts from traditional patterns but with a definite contemporary look. We were strongly influenced at first by Roberta Horton's "Amish Adventure." The play of color, both bold and subtle, against black was very appealing to both of us.

We have been fortunate to have been awarded a blue ribbon at the AIQA show for our quilt "Cygnus X-1" and have shown at the AQS show as well as numerous quilts shows, particularly in Texas and Kansas. Our work has been featured in *Quilter's Newsletter Magazine, Patchwork Tsuchin,* and two books by Joen Wolfrom, the Lang Calendar, along with exhibits here in the United States, Europe, and Japan. We were also chosen to make the raffle quilt for the AIQA show in 1990. We continue to collaborate and to grow as individuals in this artistic endeavor.

Barbara Dieges, So. Pasadena, California

I taught kindergarten for nine years. While raising three children, I designed stitchery kits and won Best in Cross Stitch at Good Samaritan in 1981.

I took to quilting in 1983 and am a member of two guilds. I designed two opportunity quilts. "Lotus Blossom," won Honorable Mention at AQS 1994. I have had three other quilts at AQS.

"Christmas Celebration!" and "Turquoise Night" won blue ribbons at Glendale Quilt Guild show. "Shaded Nine-Patch" won Honorable Mention at NQA 1995.

"Christmas Celebration!" was on the cover of *Quilting Today* #22. I was featured teacher in *Traditional Quiltworks* #33. I am a local and national teacher.

Mary Evangeline Dillon, Tucson, Arizona

Mary Evangeline Dillon was born July 1, 1955, in Tucson, AZ, and currently resides there. She graduated from Blue Ridge High

School in Lakeside, AZ, and earned a Bachelor of Science degree from the University of AZ. A 6th generation quiltmaker, she began to learn the skill at the age of three. During college Mary became more involved in quiltmaking and designing and is now a full-time quilt designer, author, historian, and teacher. Her specialties are stained glass appliqué, southwestern design, and a technique she developed to create "pictorial star quilts." Her books are: *Windows of Peace Quilt, Contemporary Southwestern Quilts,* and is currently at work on the star quilt book. One of Mary's strongest interests is the history of the art and she is a charter member of the American Quilt Study Group which works to find and document this history. Other affiliations include AQG, AQS, and NQA. She has won numerous awards and her work has been shown in local, state, national, and international shows, winning awards at all levels. Her quilts are found in many private collections.

Carol Doak, Windham, New Hampshire

Author, designer, teacher, and prize-winning quiltmaker. Carol Doak is an author, designer, teacher, and prize-winning quiltmaker. Her blue-ribbon quilts have appeared on the covers of national magazine publications such as: *Quilter's Newsletter Magazine, Quilt World, McCall's Quilting, and Quilting Today, Ladies Circle Patchwork Quilts.* Carol has authored the following books: *Quiltmaker's Guide: Basics and Beyond, Country Medallion Sampler; Easy Machine Paper Piecing; Easy Reversible Vests;* and *Easy Paper-Pieced Keepsake Quilts.* She writes the "Tricks of the Trade" column for *Quick and Easy Quilting.* Carol travels internationally to teach workshops and present lectures. Her lighthearted approach and ability to teach have earned her high marks and positive comments from workshop participants. My 1993 teaching tour to Australia is a very special memory not only because it provided me with the opportunity to meet and work with so many delightful Australian quiltmakers, but because my mother joined me on this trip. We spent three weeks traveling in Victoria and the Sydney area where I presented workshops and lectures. From the farm areas to the cities, I found warm hospitality and instant connections through our mutual love of quiltmaking, emphasizing that the sharing and giving for which quilters are known can be found the world over.

Dorothy Barrick Dodds, Tempe, Arizona

Dorothy Barrick Dodds was born March 28, 1933, in Enid, OK. She currently resides in Tempe, AZ. Dorothy is co-owner of Quilters' Ranch and co-author of the book, *Triangles on a Roll.* She has taught both hand and machine quiltmaking methods for the past 13 years. Dorothy states that quiltmaking is very

engrossing and a wonderful way to shut out life's little irritations and concentrate on a creative process. That creativity has resulted in her award-winning quilts entered in the Arizona Quilters Guild show.

Sandra Donabed, Wellesley Hills, Massachusetts

Artist, fibers of all sorts. Collector of antique and just plain old fabrics, pack rat of buttons, beads, and flea market junk! Sewer of threads. Made Ginny doll clothes, made my own clothes, made my own curtains and bedspreads. Painted, wove, macraméd, and embroidered. Now I make quilts and don't sew buttons. The time my machine needle went through my index finger and broke off inside is very memorable! The nurse in the E.R. was another quilter!

Beth Donaldson, Lansing, Michigan

Beth Kolodziej Donaldson was born May 1, 1957, in Wayne County, Michigan. She is married to Tom Donaldson and the mother of Katy and Colleen. She currently resides in Lansing, Michigan. She started sewing in her early teens and took up quilting after the birth of her first daughter. In 1984 she became a charter member of the Capitol City Quilt Guild (and its president). She has volunteered and worked on many local quilt shows and exhibits. She is a member of AQS, AQSG, and MQN (Michigan Quilt Network). Her first book, *Block by Block* was published by That Patchwork Place in 1995. Since 1990, Beth has organized The Northern Michigan Quilters Getaway, a biennial retreat that features nationally known teachers in an intimate setting. One and two day classes are offered at the Terrace Inn, a small hotel in historic Bay View, Michigan. Beth loves and makes all styles of quilts. Her teaching specialties are rotary cutting, machine piecing, and machine quilt-as-you-go techniques.

Sandra Larkin Douglas, McKinney, Texas

Plying a needle since the age of 9, I began with embroidery and went on to crochet, knitting, sewing, and cross-stitch through the years. Not until retiring from 20 years of public school teaching did I come to quilting. It has become an addictive obsession that continues to challenge and inspire me to ever advancing

degrees of creativity. I have added silk ribbon work and tatting to my skills to embellish my quilts. Professionally I teach quilting classes for adults and children, present programs and workshops for quilt guilds, and enter challenges, competitions, and shows. The ribbons I have received are incentives to continue learning and growing. I enjoy attending guild meetings, friendship groups, and retreats, and making quilts and other handcrafts as gifts for my family and friends.

Kathy DuFrane, Henrietta, New York

Quiltmaker. About 13 years ago my sister had a poem published in a quilt magazine; as I flipped through the pages, I fell in love with the beauty of the designs and color. After three more years of looking at magazines, I finally convinced myself to cut into that beautiful fabric. My first quilt was a fleet of sailboats for my son. After that success and a few classes to bolster my confidence, hardly a day goes by that I'm not working on some quilt project. When I'm not busy with my own, I have a continuous stream of customers for my custom hand-quilting business. I love traditional quilts, have designed several wall quilts, and enter local shows. The highlight of course was winning that first blue ribbon. My non-quilting time revolves around my husband, Dan; children, Jeremy (14), Amanda (9), Jessica (2), and a home-based business.

Linda Dumanowski, San Jose, California

Dreamer, designer, quiltmaker, infector of others with the quilting bug. Born August 20, 1946 in Warroad, Minnesota, I was first introduced to family quilts that had been made by my grandmother. I made my first not-so-successful quilt top at the age of 9 or 10. Since then I have been caught up by the creative aspects of quilting, have exhibited quilts at shows and the county fair, and am a member of the Santa Clara Valley Quilters Association. I am married, have two children, and two grandchildren, and work as a registered nurse.

I most enjoy involving children by incorporating their interests and/or photographs into quilts, which they then become a part of. It is an honor to be considered a mentor to others who are entering the land of quilting. One of my favorite quilts commemorates the occasion of my future son-in-law's immigration to America.

Beverly Dunivent, Green Valley Lake, California

Author, collector, historian, teacher, lecturer, certified quilt appraiser. Beverly Dunivent has been a quiltmaker and has studied the history of quilts for the past seventeen years. She has taught quiltmaking for the past fifteen years and has lectured about quilts and their history for ten years. Her first article, "The 1930's Revisited" appeared in issue 23 of *Quilting Today* magazine, and she has since had an article published on making reproduction quilts in *Traditional Quiltworks*. She and Anne Copeland have had articles published on quilt kit history in the Winter 1994 issue of *American Quilter*, and on the care of quilts in May 1994 *Lady's Circle Patchwork Quilts*. Their paper "Kit Quilts in Perspective" is published in *Uncoverings 1994*. They expect their book on the subject to be published soon. Beverly speaks and teaches at guild workshops, quilt shops, quilt conferences, shows, and retreats, specializing in 1930's quilts, kit quilts, string piecing, as well as scrap and reproduction quilts. She taught at the American Quilter's Society Quilt Show in Paducah, Kentucky, in 1994 & 1995. Beverly is also an AQS Certified Quilt Appraiser.

Being part of the group that furnished the Ronald McDonald House in Orange, CA, with quilts for each bed was a wonderful quilting experience.

Alice L. Dunsdon, Glenwood, Iowa

Designer and quiltmaker. Alice Dunsdon was born and raised in the Midwest, where she presently resides with her husband. Their two children and four grandchildren live nearby.

Alice has spent a lifetime designing and making her own clothes so it was a natural for her to slip over into quilting. She has made approximately 60 quilts, many of them being original designs and most being appliquéd. Her quilts have won numerous awards in national shows, some having been featured in national magazines as well as *The New York Times* newspaper. Her quilts are in private as well as corporate collections.

Her most recent experience was being asked to design an historical quilt to celebrate Iowa's sesquicentennial. In conjunction with this project, she was also asked to design a flag for her county which will be flown on special occasions at the state capitol along with 98 other Iowa county flags.

Annie Ruth Davis, 3rd from left, was presented with the President Quilt 1993, by members of Allatoona Quilt Guild, Kennesaw, GA.
Left to right: Margie Zamporti, Teresa Ross, Annie Ruth Davis, Dianne Worley, Shirley Poe, Sarah Davis, Sheliah Robertson, Carolyn James, Jeannine Hartman, and Ruth Stormark.

Alexandra Capadalis Dupré, Long Beach, New York

Alex designs quilts & wearable art. She authored *Men's Wear: A Guide to Designing Wearable Art for Men.* Twice she has designed garments for the Fairfield Fashion show. Her quilts & garments vary in theme from folk art to architecture. Her classes focus on design & technique. Following a B.S. in art education & 20 years in the graphic arts, Alex turned to quilting to channel her creativity. She is a 3-time winner at AQS & 5-time winner at NQA. She designed the NY State Quilt: Poets, Authors & Playwrights. Her motto is: Do what you love, do your best, and it shows.

Mamie Clemens Durbin, Bardstown, Kentucky

Mamie Clemens Durbin was born April 28, 1921, and now resides in Bardstown, Kentucky. She remembers learning to quilt about 25 years ago and leaving the knots on the back of the quilt! She has made Cathedral Window, patchwork, and handkerchief quilts. She also likes to embroider and makes quilts for her children, grandchildren and great-grandchildren.

Mini Quilt Exchange – 1990, Ft. Leavenworth, KS.
Ft. Leavenworth Ladies Wednesday Afternoon Quilting Society.

Anne Waddell Dutton, Chandler, Arizona

Anne Waddell Dutton was born January 3, 1941, in Charlotte, NC. She currently resides in Chandler, AZ. Anne is co owner of Quilters' Ranch and co-author of the book, *Triangles on a Roll.* She also was the designer of the Frame Mate, a lap held holder for hoops and frames for quilting and needlework. Her love of quilting has enabled her to develop a quick piecing method of making scrap quilts known as, Scrap'N'Patchwork. It is a technique she enjoys teaching at seminars. As a shop owner Anne really enjoys the art of the quilting business. She loves the creativity it takes to keep a business afloat and interesting.

Working on the Peterborough's 250th Anniversary Commemorative Quilt, Peterborough, NH.
Left to right: Connie Bastille, Shelly Osborne, Sue Butler.

Fairy D. Hillman Earnest, Orange, California

Fairy D. Hillman Earnest was born December 31, 1925, in Rock City, IL. She currently resides in Orange, CA. Her mother always made quilts for their beds, so they were always a part of her life. When she was starting a family, the first thing that entered her mind was to make a baby quilt. That was the start of a long wonderful, rewarding hobby. She makes mostly bed-sized appliqué, hand-quilted quilts. She has won many ribbons at county & state fairs and also quilt shows. An active member of two local guilds, member of AQS & NQA. She can count close to fifty quilts that she has made. Many keep her children and grandchildren warm and cuddly.

Ellen Anne Eddy, Chicago, Illinois

Quiltmaker, teacher, and author.

Ellen Anne Eddy was born May 5, 1953, in Streator, Illinois. She studied education and fine arts at both Knox College and Boston State University. She currently lives in Chicago, IL. She's a member of AQS and F.A.C.E.T.

She began quilting in 1976. She has shown in numerous solo artist shows across the country and won prizes including first place small wallhanging at Quiltfest, 1994, in Louisville. She's been featured in articles in *American Quilter, Quilting International, Threads Magazine, Quilting Today, Art Quilt Magazine, Surface Design Journal, Quilter's Newsletter,* and *Fiber Arts.*

She has developed a series of classes and lectures for quilters on Thread Magic, a technique focusing on usage of delicate and difficult embroidery threads in the sewing machine. She is currently teaching classes nationally at guilds and conventions, including the New York Quilt Festival in New York and at the Honeybee Quilt Retreat in Jacksonville, FL.

Janie Hendrick Edwards, Murray, Kentucky

Janie Hendrick Edwards was born in Calloway Co., KY, on Dec. 14, 1914. She currently lives in Murray, KY. Janie began quilting at the age of 16 by helping her mother make bed quilts for home use. An active quilter for 65 years, she has made numerous quilts for her children, grandchildren, and great-grandchildren.

Janie also makes quilts to sell. Her favorite pattern to quilt is World Without End. Her overall favorite is Double Wedding Ring.

Sylvia Einstein, Belmont, Massachusetts

Artist, quiltmaker, teacher, lecturer, and author. Born and educated in Switzerland, I came to the United States in 1965. In 1975 I made my first quilt, a bicentennial appliqué quilt, which was exhibited in "Quilts '76" in the Boston Center for the Arts. I am primarily making contemporary crazy quilts in vivid colors. I use mostly commercial fabrics. I have exhibited in the USA, Europe, Japan, and South America. I teach and lecture regularly in Europe and the USA. I have been a longtime and active member of the Arlington Quilter's Connection and I have worked for the New England Quilt Museum on the Exhibit committee. My quilts are biographical and express my reactions to the world around me. Quilting has become the focus of my life.

To have my work on the cover of the *Danish Patchwork* (kludemagasinet) and the *Patchwork Gilde Heft, was a wonderful honor.*

Carol H. Elmore, Manhattan, Kansas

I grew up in Morton, IL, and graduated from Greenville College, Greenville, IL, in 1969 with a BA degree in English. This was followed in 1975 by a Master's degree in library science and in 1983 by a Juris Doctorate degree both from the University of Missouri, Columbia, Missouri. I have been around quilts all my life with both my mother and grandmother being quilters. I made doll quilts as a child and worked on quilts with my mother from the 1960's – 1980's. In 1990 I moved to Manhattan, Kansas, and started restoring antique quilts and appraising both contemporary and antique quilts. I work primarily as an appraiser of quilted textiles and lecture on quilt history. My most memorable quilting experience was when I successfully passed the American Quilter's Society appraisal certification exam on April 28, 1995. I am also a member of the American Society of Appraisers – Quilted Textiles, the American Quilter's Society, Kansas Quilter's Organization, Konza Prairie Quilt Guild (Manhattan, Kansas), and Kaw Valley Quilt Guild (Lawrence, Kansas).

Judy Elsley, Ogden, Utah

Judy Elsley holds a Ph.D in English Literature from the University of Arizona, and is presently an associate professor at Weber State University in Ogden, Utah. She has published a number of articles on the relationship between quilting and literature, and quilting and culture, including work on the AIDS quilt, *Aunt Jane of Kentucky*, and *The Color Purple*. Her paper on the Smithsonian Controversy was published in AQSG's *Uncoverings* in 1993, and her discussion of the different kinds of scholars within the quilting community was part of the 1995 edition of *Uncoverings*. Her anthology of academic essays on quilting, *Quilt Culture: Tracing the Pattern*, co-edited with Cheryl Torsney, was published by Missouri University Press in 1994.

Janet B. Elwin, Damariscotta, Maine

Janet B. Elwin was born in Malden, MA, and currently resides in Damariscotta, Maine. Nationally and internationally known quiltmaker, Janet has been exploring quiltmaking as a teacher, lecturer, and workshop leader since 1973 when her husband Bud's grandmother, Eva Hoyt Maze, introduced her to the pleasure of patchwork. In 1976 she was one of the founders of the New England Quilters Guild. During her term as president (1980 – 1982) she initiated the long range goal of the guild – the establishment of a quilt museum in New England. To help this goal, she chaired New England Images, the first fund-raiser which raised over $21,000. The museum opened in Lowell, ME, June 1987. Janet's quilts (well over 250) have won many awards and have been exhibited across the United States and abroad. Starting with traditional designs and theories, she has used the hexagon and triangle shape to interpret her ideas into colorful, intriguing quilts and wallhangings. While quiltmaking and teaching are her primary goals, she also designs and markets quilts and sophisticated patchwork skirt patterns. She is the creator of the famous necktie skirt. A dynamic speaker and enthusiastic teacher, Janet has two books to her credit, *Hexagon Magic*, by EPM, VA; and *Creative Triangles*, Chilton, PA. She is the author of a new AQS book: *Ties – Ties – Ties*. Janet is also the hostess in a Video Guide to Quiltmaking, a 2-hour instructional guide to quiltmaking distributed by Quilts, Etc., Janet's business in Damariscotta, Maine.

Marie Hollerbach Engelbach, Pevely, Missouri

Marie Hollerbach Engelbach was born April 1, 1919, in St. Louis, MO. She now lives in Pevely, MO. Marie was taught as a young girl the art of quiltmaking mostly out of necessity. The first quilt she made for herself was the Pickle Dish. She made a quilt a year after she married while also working on their dairy farm. Her quilting slowed down when she went to work outside the home, but started up again full swing in 1976. Now she does the hand quilting herself on at least two a year. She also quilts once a week with the quilting ladies at the St. Joseph Catholic Church. She has given each of her 2 children and 4 grandchildren a quilt when they married and one every five years after. Her 6 great-grandchildren have also received quilts. She's passed the art of quiltmaking down to her daughter Cecilia Engelbach Portlock and granddaughter, Barb Engelbach Hudson and great-granddaughter, Jennifer Hudson who has made her first quilt at 9. In 1989 her appliqué Christmas quilt was displayed at the AQS Quilt Show.

Kaye England, Indianapolis, Indiana

Born in Glasgow, KY. Owner of two quilt shops, author, and fabric designer. Travels around the country teaching and lecturing. An avid collector of antique quilts and vintage fabrics.

Helen M. Ericson, Emporia, Kansas

I began making quilts in the 1960's to use scraps from clothing construction. Began studying history and doing talks and workshops, then purchased the Mrs. Danner's Pattern business in 1970. Since the death of Betty J. Hagerman in 1986, I market her Sunbonnet Pattern book and mine. I have made over 200 quilts, and do all my quilting in a hoop. I collect 1930's patterns and fabric, especially unfinished quilts from a bygone time. I have quilts from five generations of my ancestors and enjoy corresponding with quilters with similar interests. I am not so interested in the new innovations in quiltmaking as in preserving its traditional past, and the appreciation of those who worked with what they had to make the beautiful quilts we now cherish.

Laura Estes, Odessa, Washington

I am married to Patrick Estes. We have two cats. We enjoy living in this rural semi-arid desert country of eastern Washington.

I have enjoyed quiltmaking since the late '70's and am currently preparing to market my own line of quilt patterns, under the name: Laura's Sage Country Quilts.

I was pleasantly surprised to tie for third place in the Keepsake Quilting Spring '95 challenge, this was the first time I had entered.

Jean M. Evans, Medina, Ohio

Quiltmaker and designer. Jean M. Evans was born August 6, 1939, in Benton Harbor, Michigan. Her twin sister is quilter Joyce M. Murrin, New York. After graduating from Holland High School and Central Michigan University, she began a 30+ year career in art education. She resides and teaches in Medina, Ohio. In 1975, Jean added quilting to her other interests in art and sewing. She enjoys designing, creating, and constructing quilts from original designs using lots of color, patterns, and textures. Her quilts and those collaborated with sister Joyce, have won numerous awards in regional and national shows as well as inclusion in the Museum of the American Quilter's Society permanent collection, and various publications.

Joanna E. Evans, Bloomington, Indiana

Joanna E. Evans was born July 29, 1959, in New York, NY. Today she is a quilter and freelance writer and editor from Bloomington, Indiana, where she lives with her husband and twin sons (born in 1993). She is the vice president of the Bloomington Quilters Guild and a member of the Indiana State Quilters Guild, NQA, AQSG, and AQS. She holds a Bachelor's degree in biology and education and a Master's degree in education, both from Smith College in Northampton, Massachusetts.

Joanna's quilt "Nectar" appears in *America's Best Quilting Projects: Scrap Quilts* by Rodale Press (1994). Joanna has written quilt patterns for *Traditional Quiltworks* and *Quilting Today*. She has designed quilts and written patterns for two books published by Publications International, Limited.

Afro-American Quilters of Los Angeles, CA. (photo courtesy of S. Brandon)

Susan Jean Gilleland Faber, Dyer, Indiana

Susan Jean Gilleland Faber was born in Wauseon, Ohio, January 10, 1947. She graduated from Adrian (Michigan) High School. She and her husband now live in Dyer, Indiana.

Sue began sewing at age 9 and dressmaking in her teens. She has had her own sewing business, Cloud Nine, since 1979. She began quilting in 1988 and is currently an AQS member.

Her unique designs in art quilts and wearable art reflect her flair for color, design, glitz, and all types of machine work. Her work is almost totally done on the sewing mahcine and has won local and national awards. She does commission work and sometimes teaches sewing or quilting and gives quilt-related talks.

Ann Fahl, Racine, Wisconsin

Ann Fahl is a quilt artist, lecturer, teacher, and writer. She is challenged by quilt competitions. Her very first quilt won an honorable mention, and today has collected a number of awards and prizes. To her students, her message is: "Believe in yourself, try to be more creative with each quilt that you make! You can do it." Her biggest thrill comes from seeing one of her quilts published in a magazine or book. Selling a quilt is also exciting. It means that someone loves her work enough to buy it! She's rarely sad about selling a quilt, "There are always more quilts in my mind, I can always make another one! I love making quilts, not owning them." Ann was born in Honolulu, Hawaii. She received her B.S. from the University of Wisconsin. She lives in Wisconsin with her husband and two sons.

Caryl Bryer Fallert, Oswego, Illinois

Caryl is well known for her unusual and striking works of fabric art. Her award-winning art quilts have been shown in numerous national and international juried exhibits, across the United States, as well as Japan, Australia, Europe, and Russia. Caryl's work is also included in a number of private, corporate, public, and museum collections. Many of Caryl's quilts have been

commissioned by private and corporate clients. The dimension and character of these pieces are determined by the client, and the environment for which they are intended. In addition to her commission work, Caryl reserves time to create a body of very personal, experimental quilts. Caryl travels extensively, and has lectured and conducted workshops for quilt and textile arts groups throughout the U.S. as well as in Japan, New Zealand, Australia, Ireland, and the People's Republic of China. In 1969, Caryl received her BA from Wheaton College. She also studied art at Illinois State University, University of Wisconsin, and College of DuPage. Her studio is in her 115 year old farm house in northern Illinois.

Tracy Faltersack, Fargo, North Dakota

I decided to join the Quilter's Guild of North Dakota after my mother and sister began making quilts and I saw how fascinating they were. I joined our local quilt block club and became familiar with techniques and ideas about quilting. My husband and I have triplet boys and the guild made them each a quilt when they were born. It is a custom that the guild does this for new babies. I enjoy sew-on-the-line quilting, hand appliqué, and machine and hand quilting. I am going to school to become a nurse.

I have worked on the Indian Summer Quilt Show and Conference for two years. I have won ribbons at our local quilts show. My great aunt, Bethyl Lueck; my mother, Connie Rodman; my sister, Lisa Satermo; and I visited Paducah, KY, for AQS Quilt Show in April 1995.

Victoria A. Faoro, Paducah, Kentucky

Quiltmaker, Writer/Editor, Educator, Museum Director.

Growing up on dairy farm in rural Grand Gorge, New York, I learned to embroider when 5 or 6 years old, and was using the sewing machine by the time I was 10 – primarily to make Barbie doll clothes for younger sisters. My first quilts were made in the early 1970's, using dressmaking scraps saved over the years. I was by then teaching high school English in Walton, NY, and made these quilts to commemorate marriages and births among my friends and family.

In the late 1970's – early 1980's I became involved in publishing in White Plains, NY, and soon after began making part of my living as a professional quiltmaker, selling work through national craft shows, where I also secured commissions. In addition I was soon teaching quiltmaking through colleges, in shops, and in my home.

In the mid 1980's I began writing occasional articles for quilting publications, including *American Quilter* magazine, and became more involved with teaching and arts administration and less involved with making quilts myself. By the late 1980's I was director of a regional community art council, had become very involved in developing an extensive artists-in-the-school program, and was teaching writing at a local college.

In January 1990 I moved from Oneonta, NY, to Paducah, KY, to become Executive Editor for the American Quilter's Society and to help with the planning of the Museum of the American Quilter's Society. During the next exciting years I had the pleasure of editing *American Quilter* magazine, working with AQS staff and authors to develop many quilting books published by AQS, and helping with plans for the museum.

When the Museum of the American Quilter's Society (MAQS) opened in April 1991, I served as its director, to help it become established nationally, while continuing editorial work at AQS. During subsequent years I have worked with both AQS and MAQS, at this point serving as full-time director of the Museum of the American Quilter's Society.

For the past six and a half years I have not made many quilts myself, but I have had the great pleasure of enjoying many thousands of wonderful quilts made by AQS members and other quilters of the past and present – and have also had the pleasure of helping AQS and MAQS share these quilting accomplishments with others. My activity with AQS, MAQS, and all of their friends and members continues to be a most exciting adventure!

Louise Feldt, Dodge City, Kansas

Quiltmaker. Louise Feldt was born Aug. 26, 1932, at Park, KS. I have lived in Dodge City, KS, since 1973. Mom started me with embroidery at age 5. I used a sewing machine in high school. Made clothes for our family, then there were fabric scraps. Quilts were a way to use them. Scrap quilts are my favorite, but memory quilts are special. I helped nieces make one for their parents in 1976, and have been involved in 3 dozen since then. I use garments from our closets to make "fun" memory quilts: the

jeans with a hole; a dress that has a spot; and those T-shirts!

I belong to Miss Kitty's Quilters & AQS, but mostly I make quilts for family and gifts – All using my "Elna."

Linda Filby-Fisher, Overland Park, Kansas

Linda Filby-Fisher born July 26, 1948, in KS. Graduated with a BS in nursing from KU in 1970, and with an MS in social work from UTA in 1975. Linda and her family live Overland Park, KS, where she divides her time between her private psychotherapy practice and her quilt studio. With some advice from her grandmothers, Linda began quilting in 1970, became a professional quiltmaker in 1987, and a quilt artist in 1989. Presently she divides her studio time between full commissions for residential/commercial clients, studio originals (noncommissioned pieces), quilt completion, restoration, and appraisal. She is a member of AQS, AQSG, SAQA, QRS, Quilters Guild of Greater Kansas City, and East Bay Heritage Quilters. Linda works to create high quality quilts with personal meaning, visual impact, and detailed design. Her quilts can be found in collections across the country.

Kerry Finn, West Fargo, North Dakota

I began quilting 10 years ago and joined the Jamestown Quilter's Guild. I have sewn clothes and crafts for many years, working in a fabric store at one time. I enjoy hand quilting, hand piecing, and hand appliqué. I favor folk art quilts. I work for Job Service of North Dakota, am married, and have three sons, 15, 16, and 18. I finished college after my children went to school.

I have taught classes in Fargo and Jamestown, ND. I have won many ribbons at our Indian Summer Quilt Show and Conference in Fargo, ND.

I had been very active in the Jamestown Quilters Guild before moving to West Fargo in 1991. I joined the Quilters Guild of North Dakota in Fargo and served as vice president of the guild in 1993.

Patricia Anne Bolden Flannery, Phoenix, Arizona

Quiltmaker. Patricia Anne Bolden Flannery was born May 19,

1938, in Johnstown, PA. Relocated to Phoenix, AZ, in 1953. She began quilting in the late 50's; self taught. Her favorite quilts to make are pieced and bed sized. The most ambitious quilt she has made contains the autographs of 22 Indian artists located in the Southwest. The quilt design is based on a Navajo rug design from the late nineteenth century, named "eye-dazzler." The quilt contains over 3,350 pieces and took three years to complete. Pat is a member of AQS and the Arizona Quilter's Guild. Her quilts have won many awards at the Arizona State Fair, including best of show.

Theresa Bowden Fleming, Aurora, Colorado

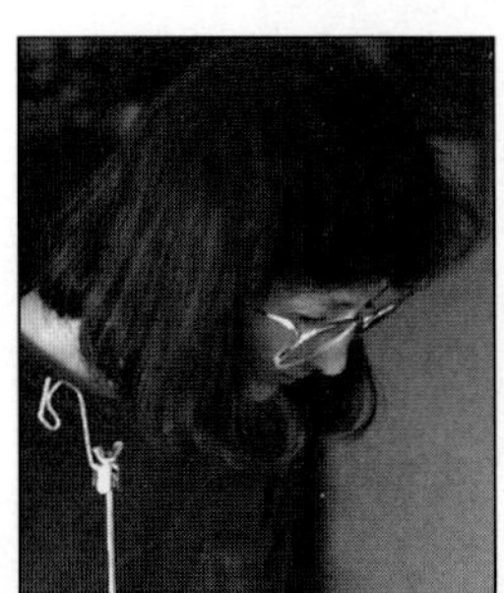

Author/photographer, quiltmaker, designer, and businesswoman. Theresa Bowden Fleming is a Colorado native, being born in Ft. Collins, Colorado, and currently living in Aurora. She has a photography degree from Colorado Mountain College in Glenwood Springs.

Her interest in quilting began in 1988. In 1991, her paternal grandmother, Velma Smallwood-Bowden, bought her a commercial quilting machine to start a home-based quilting business.

She loves to do miniature quilts, design and mix block patterns, design original quilting patterns for the commercial machine, and use photographs in an artistic way in quilts. She is also a published writer/photographer.

Having her first photo/writing submission published, plus having her first original block design published was a memorable quilting experience. Also, doing the machine quilting for charitable organizations, like a quilt for Habitat for Humanities and crib quilts for a special pregnancy center for girls who decide to keep their babies.

Glenna Broderick Fletcher, Cannonville, Utah

Glenna was born March 16, 1943, in Salt Lake City, UT, raised in southern Utah, and now resides in Cannonville, Utah. I started making quilts by tying five graduation quilts for children, then helping my daughters tie two more. With some scraps I made two All-Around-The-World quilts each taking over a year to match, cut out, piece, and sew together. I learned to quilt in Relief Society, an organization for women to learn homemaking skills. What I liked most was to embroider beautiful quilt squares and then put them together in a quilt. I plan again to

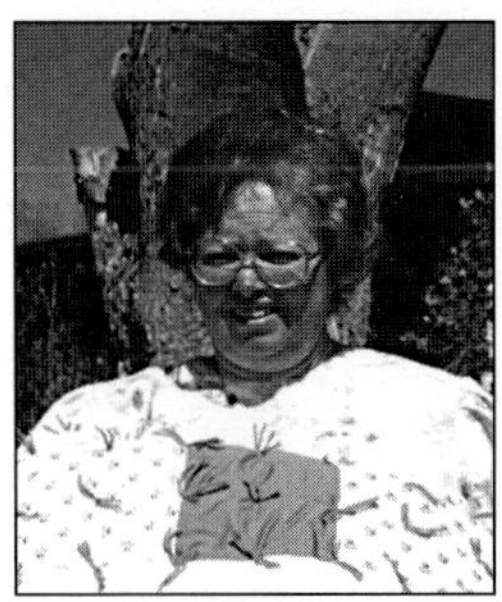

embroider and appliqué material into a work of art. My goal now is to quilt five wedding quilts for a "hope chest." I have quilted 55 quilts in the last 12 years, 36 of which were baby quilts. I enjoy matching colors and getting a quilt finished so I can start another. They remind me of beautiful thoughts and God's beautiful world. Creations and accomplishments are wonderful! I quilt once a week with women on a quilting project for our church.

Judy Florence, Eau Claire, Wisconsin

Quiltmaker, designer, lecturer, workshop instructor, judge, and author. Born April 30, 1945, in Waupaca, Wisconsin, Judy Florence is married and the mother of two sons. She holds a B.A., B.S., and M.S. from the University of Wisconsin. She has been making, writing, and teaching about quilts since 1974. She began quilting with scraps from sewing projects and pieces "handed-down" from her grandmother. Her quilts have been exhibited at local and international shows. One of her most cherished awards is the "Best Quilt with American Indian Influence" at the International Quilt Exhibit in California.

Teaching and writing have occupied most of her time since 1978. She is the author of numerous articles and six quiltmaking books with the seventh to be released in 1996. She has taught throughout the United States, Australia, Scotland, Canada, and Japan. In 1994 she was selected to represent Wisconsin in a "sister-state" cultural exchange delegation to Chiba, Japan.

Lois H. Flowers, Flint, Michigan

Quiltmaker, designer, and instructor. I was born December 12, 1924, in a small town in Tennessee (Newbern). In 1946 I received a Bachelor's degree in home economics, with a specialty in sewing.

When I was nine years old, I would watch my grandmother teaching my two older sisters to make quilts and how to quilt them. They would say I was too young to learn. I would notice them quilting and those memories stayed with me.

After retiring I decided to stop making clothes and go into making quilts. For the past four years I have been teaching an eight week course of quiltmaking at my church, and once a year I teach a six week class in my home as a community project. I am a member of the Afro-American Quilter's Guild, Michigan Quilt Network Inc., and AQS. Received 2nd place ribbon in a contest of approximately 150 quilts.

Catherine Jean Funderburk, Lincolnton, North Carolina

Jean Hamilton Funderburk was born March 3, 1956, in Gastonia, NC. She currently resides in Lincolnton, NC, with her husband, Buddy, and daughter, Sara. She taught herself the basics of quiltmaking in 1986 because she felt women have little of themselves to pass on to their children. Large or small, her quilts are for the most part of traditional construction. People recognize her work because of her use of jewel-tone fabrics, which are her favorites. Lincoln Quilters was formed in 1990. Jean was quick to join and has served as an officer in some capacity ever since. She teaches an annual quiltmaking for beginners workshop in the hopes of passing on the skills and happiness shared by those who quilt. When the opportunity arises she also teaches a sampler class to help others learn more varied skills. She is a member of NC Quilters and AQS.

Susan Fuquay, Arlington, Texas

Susan was born in Chicago, IL. She received a degree in design from Purdue University in West Lafayette, IN, in 1975. After living in Atlanta, GA, for a few years she now lives with her husband and two children in Arlington. While owning an antique shop in 1980, Susan discovered her love of quilting while trying to duplicate the antique quilts which were fast becoming collectibles. She moved on to designing a line of Seminole patchwork clothing patterns while teaching and working at a local quilt shop. Her style continues to follow a traditional path, often combining pieced patterns and appliqué. Currently Susan is the publisher of *American Quilt Retailer*, a bimonthly trade newsletter for quilt store owners.

Susan's Tree of Life quilt was the Texas state winner in 1994, Good Housekeeping/Lands' End All American Quilt Contest.

Myra M. Furse, Baraboo, Wisconsin

I began quilting in 1972. Quilting has been my rudder through many personal ups and downs. I have taken lessons from many people, but my most inspiring teacher was Betty Peterson, who taught at Shorewood High School in Shorewood, WI. I retired from Milwaukee Public Library in 1986, and moved to Baraboo, WI. I founded Baraboo Quilters through the recreation

department in 1987 and have been president ever since. I have taught quilting at Baraboo High through Madison Area Technical College for about 8 years. I also belong to Dells Country Quilters. I have made many quilts, some for my five children's families, some for charity, some for sale. Quilting is still my rudder; my interest in and enthusiasm for it have never flagged but continues to grow.

Carrie Morrison, Fort Worth, TX, still quilting at 89 years of age.
(photo courtesy of Peggy Morrison)

Victoria Renee McElroy (Future Quilters of America).
(photo courtesy of her grandmother, Roxanne McElroy)

Janet Moody Gaglione, Ellicott City, Maryland

Designer and quiltmaker. Janet's background in theatrical costume design and stage lighting has made her crossover into quilt design quite natural. Her design philosophy for quilts is based on a theatrical lighting approach; blending and adding colors until the stage, quilt, and the palate comes alive with depth and luminosity.

Like most quilters, she is an avid fabric buyer. While on tour with various dance companies and Broadway shows, she has compiled an eclectic collection of fabrics for her unique geometric designs.

Janet's quilts have traveled North America extensively and have been seen worldwide. While most of her work centers on her hand-quilted original designs, she also welcomes commissioned projects and special orders.

Georgia Ward Gaiser, Cincinnati, Ohio

Photo by Olan Mills.

Born June 5, 1925, in Whitley County, KY, now residing in Cincinnati, OH. I have been quilting as long as I can remember. My mother Judy Ward, taught me as a child. I loved it and have continued. I use old patterns and today's, and often create my own. I sketch them. My husband, Tony, drafts them and we choose colors together. It's rewarding to see our very own efforts become reality and beautiful works of art. I have been sewing by machine since I was 6. Have studied sewing eight years and love all aspects of the needle, having won prizes during my years of study, earliest age 9. I'm a long-time member of AQS. Thanks mom and thanks AQS for the opportunity to be mentioned in this wonderful book.

Kristen LaDuke Gallup, Indianapolis, Indiana

Born April 12, 1963, in Michigan City, IN, to Norman and Janice Gangwer LaDuke. I had quilts from my great-grandmother McKee, as a child, but I didn't learn to piece and quilt until 1984. After learning, I took a six year hiatus, then started again in 1990 when neighborhood ladies all got together to make a quilt for "Baby" Maria Sejnoha, born premature and with cerebral palsy to one of our neighbors. A 1991 block-of-the-month class in Barrington, IL, culminated in not only a completed quilt

top but also my first completed bed quilt (in 1994). Currently, I am historian for the Quilters Guild of Indianapolis, Inc., a 400-member guild. I also serve on committees for our biennial guild quilt show. No awards won to date.

Donna Marie Gordon Gamble, Toppenish, Washington

Photo by Olan Mills.

Donna Marie Gordon Gamble, born May 21, 1930, in Multnomah County, Portland, Oregon. Residing in Toppenish, Washington, married 43 years, four children, 10 grandchildren. Began quilting in 1952 after marriage and coming to Washington State. Was taught basics of quilting by members of Sunshine Circle Ladies, a group of farm women, formed in the mid 1930's. Our life is a farm and cattle ranch. Have attended many quilt shows and workshops in this area, also AQS in 1986, and NQA at Lincoln, NE, 1991. I am a strong traditional quilter, piece by hand and machine and appliqué by hand. All my quilting is done by hand. Machine sewing done on Singer Featherweight. I have made 38 full-sized quilts and 15 baby quilts. Have 56 quilt tops to be quilted, fabric for at least 30 more. Always have a quilt in my floor frame. Have quilt book collection of 430. Eldest granddaughter, Hannah, 6, has started hand piecing. Past member 5 years, and past president 2 years of Yakima Valley Quilters Guild. Presently belong to AQS, NQA, Horizon Quilters Unlimited of Grandview, Washington. Quilt most Thursdays with others at Lou's Thursday Quilters, Yakima, Washington. Jan. 1995 was guest quilter with one week display at Toppenish Historical Museum.

Vyvyan M. Gardner, Canyon City, Oregon

Born August 27, 1925, in Ashland, OR. Retired 1986 from social work, 1989 started quilting, 1990 moved to rural area. Books and TV lessons are my teachers. Due to osteoarthritis I quilt on my lap without a hoop. I just finished a two-sided quilt; crazy quilt front, Fan quilt back. I am designing my first original pieced

quilt with a 40 inch 32-point hobstar as the center medallion. I have received ribbons at small county fairs and at the large show in Portland, Oregon.

Minnie Gartner, Glendive, Montana

Have been a member of the Sacred Heart quilter's group since 1984. Have done much other quilting in my lifetime.

Charlotte Gasker, Tucson, Arizona

Born in Indiana in the late 40's. Introduced to quilting by mother and grandmothers at an early age. Started my first quilt when I was 14, and finished it several years later.

In 1983 joined the San Fernando Valley Quilt Association (SFVQA) in Woodland Hills, CA. Over the next ten years I exhibited in their annual quilt show, participated in challenge quilt competitions and served on committees. In 1989 I joined the Simi Valley Quilt Guild, of Simi Valley, California. Became a member of the Blockheads mini group and served on the board for SVQG. The Blockheads met once a month to talk quilts, work on our latest project, and seek advice from each other.

Having moved to Tucson, Arizona, in need of a quilt guild. I found the Arizona Quilters Guild (AQG). This guild is made up of individual chapters located around the state. The Log Cabin Quilters group was in the process of chartering with the AQG when I joined in October 1994. In December 1994, I became chairman for the Log Cabin Quilters chapter.

Over the years I have made numerous quilts. Most of them have been machine appliquéd and machine quilted. Several of my quilts were awarded blue ribbons at the Ventura County Fair in California, between 1983 and 1992.

Jeanne E. Glenfield, Pepperell, Massachusetts

Jeanne Gibson Glenfield was born in Lancaster, Pennsylvania, graduated from Germantown High School in Philadelphia, and moved to Massachusetts where she met her husband, John. A mother of four and a grandmother of three she began quilting in 1970, thanks to a second grade program held at a local historic site – the Old Chelmsford Garrison House. The program allows the pupil to live a day in the life of a Colonial child and teaches them to churn butter, dip candles, make soap, and QUILT! Since she had always sewn, she chose quilting and has been bitten by the bug ever since. In 1988 Jeanne and her partner, Marie J. Geary, founded the Eastcoast Quilters Alliance. They produce "A Quilter's Gathering" each November and "A Quilting Sampler" each June in Wextford, Massachusetts. Both events feature nationally known teachers, classes, exhibits, and vendors. Jeanne has exhibited at New England Images, the New England Quilt Museum, the Bank of Boston, Vermont Quilt Festival, and local shows. Her major focus is to produce a new quilt to hang in the Westford Regency Inn lobby each November. She is very proud of her two quilt covers – *Traditional Quilter*, Sept. '94 and a special Christmas issue of *Traditional Quiltworks*, Fall '91. My favorite part of my passion is sharing. Wherever you travel in the quilting world you can always find friends. I don't know of any other field where you are surrounded by people so giving and caring.

Flavin Glover, Auburn, Alabama

Teacher, designer, and quiltmaker. Flavin Glover is a designer and quiltmaker who has a degree in clothing, textiles, and related arts from Auburn University. She specializes in original patchwork quilts inspired from landscapes and architecture and wearable quilted fashions. Her patchwork quilts and quilted garments have been exhibited and published extensively since 1979.

Flavin travels thoughout the U.S. as a teacher and lecturer. A chapter featuring her quilts and her Log Cabin Possibilities Workshop was recently published in *Quilt with the Best*, published by Oxmoor House. Her work has been selected for Quilt National and the Tactile Architecture Show in Washington, D.C. A one-person show of her work was reviewed by *Art Papers*.

Margaret Ann Godwin, Santa Barbara, California

Quilt artist, teacher (quilting & computer designed quilts), and lecturer. Born in Santa Monica, CA, October 26, 1951, to Shirley Margaret Sebring and Robert Dedrick Godwin. Lived in San Diego, La Habra, San Luis Obispo, Lompoc, and Tarzana. Graduated from Bringham Young University, 1973. Started quilting in 1983 in quilting class by Mary Russell.

Garment, "Yes, Virginia…" featuring a dozen 3-D Santa Clauses was juried into the AQS Show in Paducah 1990. "Starry, Starry Geese" in *A Log Cabin Notebook* (Mary Ellen Hopkins) and juried into Natural Impressions (1991). "From Cabrillo through

Cousteau" juried into Natural Impressions II show (1995). Lone Star (24" sq.) with over 1,100 pieces, "Let There Be Light," toured with Hoffman Fabric Challenge ("A" Group 1993 – 94). "To Be a Friend" invited to be exhibited at Womenspeak at UCSB Women's Center (1994). "More Perfect Union" won American Pie contest, West Coast Quilters Conference 1992. Assistant to Mary Ellen Hopkins at Quilt Camp, Las Vegas, Nevada, 1992. Developed quick methods for Mariner's Compasses, and Lone Stars. Latest works have multiple, partial, skewed Mariner's Compasses, or use multiple blocks combining into secondary patterns.

Candy Goff, Lolo, Montana

I started quilting in 1986 and, after receiving Best of Show in the local county fair, decided to enter juried and judged shows. Since then, I have won first place ribbons in shows including American Quilters Society, Assoc. of Pacific Northwest Quilters, and Washington State Quilters. I also received Best of Show in 1995 at Quilter's Heritage Celebration in Lancaster, PA, and was the Montana winner in the 1994 Land's End/*Good Housekeeping* competition.

My quilts reflect a desire to carry on the tradition of the fine heirloom quilters of the past. I most enjoy creating my quilts entirely by hand in our Montana log home. Tillie, the peekapoo, my new helper, is just learning proper quilting etiquette.

Marilyn Goldman, Selma, Indiana

Marilyn Goldman was co-author of *Quilts of Indiana: Crossroads of Memories*, 1991. She served as a charter member of the Indiana Quilt Registry Board as secretary and newsletter editor. She is also a charter member of the American Quilter's Society and the Indiana State Quilt Guild and a current member of the American Quilt Study Group. She lectures on Log Cabin quilts and Marie Webster designs. She is president of the Muncie Quilters Guild and past newsletter editor. In addition to commission work, she has quilted for the National Organization of Women (NOW), Ball Memorial Hospital Auxiliary, Muncie Civic Theater, and the "Yes Mam" project.

Maria R. Goodwin, Washington, DC

Historian, U.S. Mint; co-author of *The Guide to Black Washington*; Maria lectures and writes on black genealogy; also volunteers at the Smithsonian Castle Docent.

Quiltmaker and co-designer with my mother. Combining family research with designing "heritage quilts" to document family history. Always looking for photo transfer methods and slave quilts.

Sarajane C. Goodwin, Washington, DC

Retired federal government employee; born in St. Louis, MO; printing specialist; 20-year volunteer for the Smithsonian Institution; co-editor, *COHRON Connection Family Newsletter*.

Quilter and instructor for the Washington Senior Wellness Center's SEW-ciables; member of the Daughters of Dorcas; designs quilts. Memorable quilting experiences are working with the SEW-ciables; designing "heritage quilts" with my daughter; and having my work exhibited at G Street Fabrics.

Patricia Gould, Santa Fe, New Mexico

Designer and quiltmaker. Patricia Gould was born October 9, 1954, on Long Island, New York, one of 5 children. Her parents encouraged in all the children a deep love for all the performing and visual arts in addition to an insatiable desire to explore the world through traveling. At age 8, her mother and grandmother taught her to sew by hand and machine on an old Singer Featherweight. She made doll clothes and as she matured, sewing enabled her to create unique outfits for herself which were personal statements.

Patricia studied creative writing and photography in high school and attended S.U.N.Y. at New Paltz, New York, where she obtained a BA in art history with a concentration on ancient and non-western arts. She minored in studio arts including painting, printmaking, ceramics, and silversmithing. An adult-education class in stained glass led her to spend several years in the late 1970's creating window hangings in both abstract and landscape designs.

When space limitations made stained glass making more difficult in the mid 1980's, Patricia taught herself hand quillting, learning from books and magazines. She began her quilting by making traditional bed quilts and soon began designing her own abstract designs for wallhangings. She is currently concentrating on hand-pieced machine-quilted landscapes, based on ideas inspired by her travels to exotic places such as China, East Africa, and Russia. A trip to Antarctica is planned for 1996, which is sure to inspire plenty of quilt ideas.

Patricia is a member of AQS and AIQA and has exhibited in their quilt shows and in the Mid-Atlantic Quilt Festival, the New York Quilt Festival, and Quiltfest USA in Louisville, KY. She was the New Mexico state winner in the All-American Quilt Contest sponsored by Good Housekeeping and Land's End in 1994. She met her husband while working as a letter carrier in Santa Barbara, CA, and they now reside in Santa Fe, NM, where they are building a house that Patricia designed with plenty of studio space for her creative endeavors. New Mexico state winner for "Tanzania Reverie" (appliquéd wall quilt) in All-American Quilt Contest 1994 was a memorable honor.

Cathy Grafton, Pontiac, Illinois

Quilter, designer, teacher, and author. I have been making quilts for 24 years. I have been a teacher and lecturer since 1976, and regularly participate in quilt shows and historical festivals where I demonstrate quiltmaking. I design my own "Prairie Quilts," an ongoing series based on farmland and prairie remnants in central Illinois. My work has been featured in over 13 books and magazines. I have authored articles on quiltmaking, and am currently working on a book about silk ribbon embellishment on quilts. After first teaching classes on miniature quilts I now teach free-form dimensional appliqué, silk ribbon embellishments, hand quilting, and non-threatening quilt design.

In 1984 I made a quilt in collaboration with Edward Larson. Making "Washington Island" stretched my abilities and set me firmly in the direction of appliqué and picture quilts. It was after making this quilt that I began to develop my own folk art style.

Helen Granmoe, Glendive, Montana

An advanced seamstress; have been a member of the Sacred Heart Quilter's Group since 1984.

Tina M. Gravatt, Philadelphia, Pennsylvania

Tina M. Gravatt, born Jan. 22, 1947, Trenton, NJ, currently resides in Philadelphia, PA. Self-taught, she became interested in quiltmaking in the 70's. In 1985 she challenged herself to create miniature quilts representing 200 years of American quilting history. Her quilts relate to specific time periods and are displayed on her collection of doll beds. Tina has made a name for herself not only as a quiltmaker but

also as a teacher, lecturer, and author. Her books, *Heirloom Miniatures* and *Old Favorites in Miniature*, published by AQS, and her column in *Ladies Circle Patchwork Quilts* have enhanced her reputation in the quilt field. She has exhibited her miniature quilts throughout the US and Europe including: MAQS, Paducah, KY; VT Quilt Festival; McMinn Co. Heritage Museum, TN; American Folk Art Museum, NYC; Paisley Museum, Scotland. Tina holds memberships in AQS, AQSG, AIQA, NQA, British Guild, and Heartstrings Quilting Guild.

Laura Elizabeth Green, St. Petersburg, Florida

Laura attended Florida Presbyterian College, receiving B.A. degrees in fine art and psychology. Laura makes art and portrait quilts, and hand-painted silk, she was selected to teach at the International Quilt Festival in Houston in '93 and '94. Laura was featured in *American Quilter* Vol. VI, No. 1; *National Surface Design Journal*, fall 1994; and *Fiberarts Design Book III*, 1987.

Peggy Ann Meadows Greene, Indianapolis, Indiana

Peggy Ann Meadows Greene was born July 26, 1940, in DeRidder, Louisiana. She graduated from Merryville High School in 1958, McNeese State University in Lake Charles, LA, in 1962, and Louisiana State University in Baton Rouge, LA, in 1964. Since 1967 she and her husband, Jim, have lived in Indianapolis, Indiana, where she taught kindergarten for many years. They are the parents of two sons and the grandparents of three.

As a child, Peggy learned to piece scraps from her grandmother. In the early 1980's she began quilting with the Hill Valley Quilting and Travel Society, a dozen friends who meet weekly to make quilts for each other. She is a member of the Quilter's Guild of Indianapolis, Inc., and has served on its board as vice-president, president, show chairman, and on other committees for the past ten years. Other memberships include AQS, NQA, ISQG, Charm Club, and Quilt Connection Guild. She assists in coordinating guild volunteers to hostess at Quilt America! each year. Appliqué and quilting are the areas of quiltmaking that Peggy enjoys most. She also collects books on quiltmaking and its history and older quilt patterns. Most of her quilts have been wall quilts. Some have received awards at local, regional, and national quilt shows and have been pictured in the AQS *Quilt Art Engagement Calendar* and in *Quilter's Newsletter Magazine*.

Ruth K. Greene, Ashville, New York

Ruth Green was born October 8, 1940, in Fairbanks, AK. Currently resides in Ashville, NY. BA, Buffalo State College, June

1973. Self-taught fabric artist working in the areas of dimensional and monochromatic portrait quilting by machine. Also creates wearable art using old linens. Lectures and teaches throughout western NY. Received grant from the Embroiderers Guild of America to begin book on dimensional portrait quilting; grant from Arts Council of Chautauqua County to attend Surface Symposium '95; 3rd place 1993 NQA Quilts in a Series, "American Indians That Live in My Sewing Machine"; Scholarship to QBL, 1993; solo exhibits at Adams Art Gallery, Dunkirk, NY, April 1994; and Chautauqua Institute, December, 1994. Many portraits in private collections. Member AQS, Westfield Quilt Guild, EGA, Chautauqua Art Association.

Verena Grieder, Newnan, Georgia

I made a quilt for my younger son and designed each square after a special event in his life. I'm a flight attendant and have enjoyed quilting for the past 9 years.

Marie Thowe Grieshaber, St. Marys, Kansas

She was born in Kansas shortly after the beginning of the 20th century, taught in a one room school, and was married during the Great Depression. They farmed, raised a son and daughter, and she continued quilting with her sister, sisters-in-law, cousins, and friends. In her mid 80's, she occasionally quilts with a church group, hand quilts a top each winter on her own, and waits for spring so she can continue gardening.

Michele Grimmett, Westminister, Colorado

I am an amateur quilter who has been quilting for about seven years. I enjoy making traditional quilts as well as designing my own patterns. Quilting has become more than a hobby; it has added a significant creative dimension to my life by giving me the opportunity to create something beautiful and original that can be passed down for others to enjoy. Quilting is not a solitary sport; the fellowship among quilters is an added attraction.

Mary Alyce Grow, Sutherland, Nebraska

A traditionally educated teacher, Mary Alyce Grow took her first traditional quilting class in 1984. Her hand-pieced and hand-quilted queen-size sampler won a blue ribbon and visitor's choice in the first quilt show entered. Shortly thereafter she discovered rotary cutting and took every class available. During ten years Mary Alyce made over 80 quilts and recently held a one-woman quilt show. One of her original wallhangings is on display at the University of Missouri. A companion piece was presented to the University of New South Wales, Sydney, Australia. Mary Alyce and her husband, Charles, are retired teachers and the parents of three children, David Grow, PhD., Carol Befort, and Paul Grow, M.D. They have eight grandchildren. Mary Alyce has had three surgeries on her hands the past seven years, including a bone replacement and no longer does hand quilting. She shares her expertise in lecturing and teaching quilting classes.

Marjorie Gunden, Blairsville, Georgia

Marjorie Gunden was born at Hopedale, Illinois. She taught thirty years in the public schools in Indiana and Florida. She quilted for family as a hobby. Her hobby grew during retirement and she opened The Quilt Patch, near her summer home in Blairsville, GA. The shop is open May through October where she specializes in custom quilting, sells old and new quilts, and has classes. In the winter she quilts in her Naples, FL, home, her work has circled the globe: Africa, Australia, Saudi Arabia, England, France, Germany, Georgia (Russia), the Marshall Islands, and most of the U.S. including Alaska and Hawaii. Having customers return to her shop each year with their friends is most rewarding. Marjorie is a member of AQS and Misty Mountain Quilters (North Georgia).

Lisabeth Robbins Polouski Gutierrez, Balbuena, Mexico

Quiltmaker, student of quilt history. A native of RI, born June 17, 1965, a graduate of Rutgers University, I live in Mexico City with my husband and two daughters. Since late 1993 I have been teaching myself quilting with the help of great books and magazines. At first my projects were machine pieced and quilted, but now I am in love with hand appliqué. My goal is to design a line of appliqué patterns. Another goal is to participate in contests so I can refine my skills. I hope my future includes creative growth and opportunities to learn from more experienced quilters. I am also learning from the next generation of quilters. My 3 & 5 year old daughters, Lauren & Eva, are already designing blocks for me to appliqué.

Ladies quilting on a raffle quilt for Heritage Days, Pioche, Nevada.
Left to right: Martha Bleak, Bette Grace Cole, Kathleen Riding.
(photo courtesy of Bette Cole)

Needle Benders Bee quilting at Dottie Settergrin's house in San Antonio, TX.
Left to right: Dottie Settergrin, Kay Chambers, Doris Sanders, Kolodzie Harper, Doris Bunge.
(photo courtesy of Kolodzie Harper)

*Working on a quilt depicting the contributions and history of the women in Mecklenburg County, North Carolina.
Left to right: Roberta Seeman, Sarah Woodring, Nancy McGinnis, Sue McCarter, Vickie Paradise.*

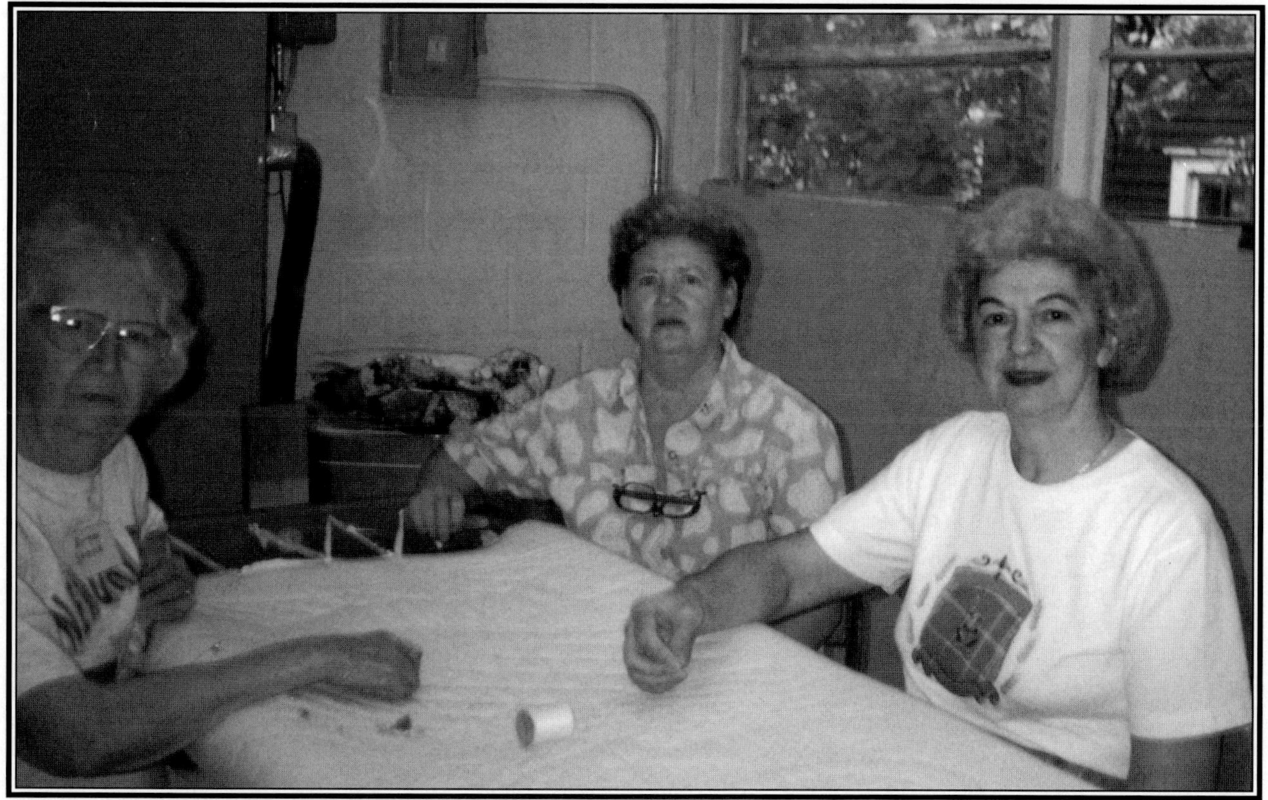

*Members of West Georgia Quilter's Guild working on a Queen Anne's Star quilt to benefit Carrollton Community Activities Center.
Left to right: Erma Stone, Ollie Wright, Violette Denney.*

Karen Schoepflin Hagen, Genesee, Idaho

Karen Schoepflin Hagen was born September 25, 1943, in Moscow, ID. She resides in Genesee, ID, where she works in the school system as a one-on-one aide with a disabled child and accompanist in the music program. After school hours she teaches piano and flute students.

Each summer Karen tours with her quilt exhibit. She began quilting in 1975 and sees fabric art as her calling. She belongs to AQS, Palouse Patchers, and the Genesee Quilt Guild.

Putting in many night hours in quilt creation, Karen prefers hand appliqué and hand quilting, and loves to experiment and discover unusual techniques. Quiltmaker, lecturer/presenter, and arranger of summer tours to exhibit quilt works.

Enjoyed Viola, ID, quilt group where I learned quilting. Refuse to list many awards – as do not believe in judging competitions, etc. I feel that they are a great detriment to quiltmakers.

Linda J. Hahn, Manalapan, New Jersey

Quiltmaker. After I divorced and moved back to NJ with my then 2 year old, I tried different crafts to keep occupied. My boss's wife encouraged my first efforts at quilting and still encourages and critiques. My husband, Allan, makes custom quilt racks and my 4 year old cuts my threads, so the whole family gets involved with a quilt.

Member – Molly Pitcher Stitchers. Located and made fireman quilt for new husband.

Jane Carroll Hall, Raleigh, North Carolina

Jane Carroll Hall was born May 31, 1932, in Rochester, NY. She graduated from Cornell University in 1953. Jane and her husband, Robert, have lived in Raleigh, NC, since he retired from the army. They have six children and five grandchildren.

An award-winning quiltmaker, Jane has taught quiltmaking at quilt conferences and guilds across the country for the past twenty-five years. She is an NQA Certified Teacher, an NQA Certified Judge, and an AQS Certified Appraiser. Her quilts are

in public and private collections in this country and abroad.

With Dixie Haywood, Jane has co-authored *Perfect Pineapples* (C&T Publishing, 1989), *Precision Pieced Quilts Using the Foundation Method* (Chilton Book Company, 1992), and *Firm Foundations* (American Quilters' Society, 1996).

She enjoys all facets of quiltmaking, from designing to collecting, and works most often with traditional patterns, using innovative sets and coloration. Pineapples are a favorite, as are designs using foundations.

Cindy Vermillion Hamilton, Pagosa Springs, Colorado

Born in Long Beach, CA, in 1949, Cindy Vermillion Hamilton (formerly Davis) is a self-taught quilter who began her first quilt 25 years ago at the age of 19. As a new Colorado bride, she wanted a quilt to put on a brass bed, so she went to the library, checked out the two books on quilting that were available and got to work.

Quilting for love rather than money, Cindy has never sold a quilt, but she enjoys giving her work to family members. She's currently reproducing a family heirloom red and green appliqué quilt as a marriage quilt for her oldest daughter.

Her favorite quilt styles include circular sunbursts, originally designed medallions, and large four-block red and green appliqué quilts inspired by the Pennsylvania Germans.

Cindy's work has appeared in magazines such as *Quilter's Newsletter* (cover no. 257), and *Stitch 'N Sew Quilts*, American Quilter's Society calendars, and books by Oxmoor House, Leman Publications, and AQS. Her quilts have been awarded blue ribbons at the Colorado State Fair and at Paducah, Kentucky (Olde English Medallion, 1st place, Traditional Pieced Professional, 1992). She has taught quilting in Pagosa Springs and Durango, Colorado, and frequently provides programs for her home town group, the Pagosa Piecemakers.

Currently, she is teaching at the middle school in Pagosa Springs, Colorado, where she resides with her two younger children and her new husband. Quilts are a part of the curriculum in her remedial reading and math classes; she uses them to incorporate measuring, geometry, history, art, and literature.

Gloria Hansen, Hightstown, New Jersey

Coming from an extensive background in arts and needlework, I began quilting in 1982. From there, my love of quilting and my affinity for color, line, and pattern grew.

I strive for original design and color use in my quilts. Line drawings are first created and explored using my Macintosh computer. Color and fabric palettes are then formed away from the computer guided by my emotions and intuitions. Often a theme emerges in the midst of this process. I include fabric in my quilts that I created either by dyeing, airbrushing, or painting, and I find my painted fabric to be the most expressive. It is the interplay between the structured line base and the emotions of the color and fabric usage that I find most satisfying in my work. My quilts are both true to my feelings and expressions while showing deference to traditions in quiltmaking.

It has been my pleasure to have my quilts exhibited across the country, and I have been honored to win many awards. My quilts and fabrics have been published in several magazines and books. I have published two successful patterns, have taught quilt classes and given lectures/workshops on fabric painting, and have appeared on a local TV talk show to discuss my quilts. My computer modem connects me to an electronic mail quilt study group. I am also an active member of the GEnie online quilt guild and am electronically connected to other quilt groups. During the week, I am employed as a paralegal/office manager at a law firm in Princeton, NJ.

Klaudeen Grenlie Hansen, Sun Prairie, Wisconsin

Quiltmaker, instructor, judge, editor, lecturer, organizer. Born January 12, 1940, Scandinavia, WI; educated at UW Stevens Point & Madison; married, husband Mervin, 3 children. Competition chair for the AQS International Quilt Competition, Paducah, KY, 1985 to present. Co-editor, *Quilt Art*, 1985 to present. Articles, puzzles, and quilts published in *American Quilter*, *Quilt World*, and *Quilter's Newsletter*. Began teaching machine piecing and quilting in 1971. Travel to teach

and judge at quilt events nationwide. Solo artist exhibit at American Embassy, Oslo, Norway, 1994 – 1995. Originator and chair, Prairie Heritage Quilt Show, 1974 – present. Adult education administrator. Community education task force. Presented with Award of Excellence, Downtown Association, 1990. Certified and accredited judge of over 12,640 quilts at shows and fairs nationwide. Current chair of Master Quilter program for NQA.

Rose Hansen, Glendive, Montana

Am a member of the Sacred Heart quilter's group since 1984.

Sue Hanson, Chagrin Falls, Ohio

Quiltmaker, collector, fabric designer, and consultant. I have been quilting personal family items for 20 years. Now I customize quilts professionally. Currently I manufacture neckties using quilt shop fabrics, design turn of the century baseball motifs, and teach tie making classes at a local fabric shop. Currently I belong to an informal unstructured quilt group. We have no dues, officers, or agenda. Our goal is to promote and encourage each member in their own personal endeavor and function as a barnstorming team. It has been successfully functioning for over 10 years. My background is in rug hooking and braiding, having exhibited a five strand braided rug in The May Show at the Cleveland Art Museum in 1969. My training is a BA degree from the University of Missouri at Columbia in 1955.

Donna Faye Jacques Harden, Englewood, Kansas

Quiltmaker and collector. As a child I sat across the quilt frame and visited with my grandmother. It was from her that I learned to love quilts. For years I made a quilt each winter until 1987 when I went to a quilt camp. From then on I was hooked. I belong to two quilting groups and consider each person that belongs as dear friends. I have taken lessons from many teachers and have learned much from each of them. Quilting camp and a trip to Paducah, KY, in a van with nine friends are memorable quilting experiences.

Priscilla Harding, Chatham, Massachusetts

Designer, quiltmaker. I have done everything from appliqué to painting a quilt. Fortunate to have won eight National Cranberry Quilt Contests and three National Fairfield Contests. *Early*

American Magazine gave me their Merit Award for my Fairbanks Family Genealogy Quilt. It has 32 squares around the coat of arms. The first square begins with Jonathon's birth date in West Yorkshire, 1595, and down through my family to 1924. "The Greatest Detective That Never Lived" (Sherlock Holmes) Quilt was featured in the *Sherlock Holmes Gazette*, London. A most memorable result was an autographed picture from Jeremy Brett to me and a "Bravo" written on it.

Hilda Nell Kolodzie Harper, Converse, Texas

Quiltmaker. Hilda Nell (Kolodize) Harper, born in Karnes City, TX, Oct. 21, 1927. Wife of Wood T., mother of three, and grandmother of four.

Exposed to quilting at age 9 at my mother's quilting bee, when given a flashlight and a pair of pliers to go under a quilt to find a stuck needle and pull it through and then stick the needle back through to the top. I imagine some of you don't remember or know how tight a needle can become stuck in a layer of cotton batting. At the time, I thought my chore was very important.

With a B.S. & M.Ed. I taught mostly elementary grades. The 32nd (last yr.), I worked with a group of 5th graders to make a wall quilt. The next year the students quilted it.

As an adult I have made many quilts, wall quilts, pillows, and baby comforters. I am a member of the Greater San Antonio Quilt Guild; Needle Benders Bee; quilter at the Institute of Texan Cultures; entrant winner in the San Antonio Rodeo and Stock Show's Country Fair; taught small quilt groups (children to seniors), also my young granddaughter.

Gloria Harries, Grandview, Washington

Quilt teacher. In lectures and classes I try to teach color! Make quilts with a sense of humor: Dog with bowtie bones; cats breaking Dresden Plates; etc.

Past 14 years I have been a quiltmaker, quilt artist, and the only active quilt teacher currently in the Yakima Valley.

Won first as co-designer with Joyce Peaden chapter row NQA 21 show; Judge's choice St. Nick Challenge; also have had quilts and article in five national quilt magazines.

Pauline Harrison, Corpus Christi, Texas

Quiltmaker and designer. I started quilting at age 70, and am now 77. I've made 50 full-size quilts plus many wallhangings and baby quilts, mostly originals and have won 18 ribbons. As a member of the Coastal Bend Quilt and Needlework Guild, I have worked on many community projects including A.B.C. quilts for Aids babies and children.

Linda Harshbarger, Opelika, Alabama

Linda Harshbarger, born in Detroit, Michigan, has lived with her husband and two sons in Alabama since 1974.

After many years of home sewing, a friend introduced her to quiltmaking in 1981, and the rest is history. Linda enjoys the competition of quilt contests, and has several ribbons from over the years. A favorite wall quilt is shown in *America's Best Quilting Projects*, Rodale Press. Most recently, one of her quilts was chosen to represent Alabama in the 1994 All-American Quilt Contest sponsored by Land's End and *Good Housekeeping*.

She is a charter member of the Cotton Boll Quilters, having served a year as president, and chairperson for their first two quilt shows. She has also taught a 7-week beginners class on the art of quiltmaking through the Outreach Program at Auburn University. Linda feels that although traditional quilt patterns will always serve as our roots, original innovative designs are her favorites.

Bernice Hartley, Jefferson City, Missouri

Bernice Hartley, born Jan. 17, 1918, lives in Jefferson City, MO. Learned to quilt from my mother, Emma Hager, when I was a child. Had pieced 13 quilts before I was 21 years old. I repair old quilts, and finish old quilts that have been started. I do all hand piecing and hand quilting. I like to make tiny blocks and see them grow into a large quilt. My favorite was the Cathedral Window. Piecing quilts is a past time for me and a help to others.

Karen Cochran Hasler, Franklin, Indiana

In 1961, after Indiana State College in Terre Haute awarded me a BS degree in home economics, I married Victor Hasler and moved to Indianapolis where he is employed by Eli Lilly. Our children have moved on after college graduation, H. Vic to

Tennessee, Lane to Chicago, and Treva to California where they have found jobs and now have spouses. Our three wonderful grandchildren living in far eastern Tennessee speak "southern."

In 1981, quilting became my passion and I became active in the Quilt Guild of Indianapolis. I joined the Indiana Quilt Registry Project which was a stretch for any quilter. In 1985, I started a guild on the Indianapolis south side so that working women and young mothers would not be forced to drive an hour to learn about our craft. My interest continues in the history of quilting; textiles, judging, and constructing them. Occasionally I teach a class but really only do so to be with other quilters. When asked to speak, my talks tend to be of historical nature focusing on dating, styles of the eras, etc. Currently I am president of the Indiana State Quilt Guild and a member of three small bees. Each year the History Museum of Johnson County conducts a show, which I coordinate.

The Indiana Quilt Registry Project was my education on quilting and quilters. As a novice quilter I joined the Board of Directors and spent the next five years traveling throughout Indiana learning about our quilting history. Statewide documentary days introduced me to new quilt-loving friends as well as developed my knowledge of colors, fabrics, patterns of the different eras. What a rare opportunity; a college course in itself. Co-authorship of the book *Quilts of Indiana* summarizing our findings was a challenge to me with a sense of pride in our accomplishments as the final outcome.

Betty Luse Hatfield, Union Hall, Virginia

Quiltmaker and pictorial quilt designer. Began quilting in 1975 when 17 friends in New York state met weekly to appliqué the history of Putnam County. This quilt was featured on *Quilter's Newsletter* magazine cover Feb. 1977. Member of Northern Star Quilters 1979 – 84. Retired to Virginia, presently in Roanoke Star Quilters and Lake Quilters Guild which I co-founded.

Balloon entry accepted for exhibition 1990 AQS, wall quilt "New York Skyline" juried into 1994 AQS. Wall quilt "Winter Sunset" won viewer's choice and judges award for color and design in Northern Star Show, Somers, NY, 1987. Also viewer's choice in Inland Empire Guild Show, Riverside, CA, 1988.

Rose Wiebe Haury, Topeka, Kansas

Designer, quiltmaker, and fabric buyer. Rosemary Wiebe Haury was born March 2, 1949, in Freeman, SD. She and her family now live in Topeka, KS. Rose began quilting in 1974 and never intends to quit! Most of her quilts are fairly traditional. She likes to use simple patterns (Nine-Patch is her favorite) and add interest with color and fabric design. Rose is currently a member of AQS, Kaw Valley Quilt Guild of Lawrence, KS, and the Kansas Capital Quilters Guild of Topeka where she has served for several years on the board. Two of her wallhangings were part of the exhibit Beyond Tradition: Mennonite Art Quilts in North Newton, KS.

One of Rose's greatest joys is sharing the common interest of fabric collecting, show attending, and quiltmaking with junior high daughter, Emily.

In 1986 two of us pieced a 15' x 15' quilt for the play "The Quilters." We used a small photo from *QNM*, no rotary cutter, and lots of cardboard and time. It was quilted in five sections and then "pieced" again. It turned out beautifully and has hung in a place of prominence for many years.

I just completed a Round Robin/Friendship Quilt with five quilting friends. We had a great time and the results are amazing – the same, but different. Now we are all making and trading 4" blocks. It's wonderful to be a part of a group that likes to quilt and eat together!

Bettina Havig, Columbia, Missouri

She has been quilting since 1970, teaching since 1974, and owned a quilt shop from 1977 to 1985. Bettina Havig is a quiltmaker, teacher, lecturer, judge, quilt historian, and consultant. She has been on the programs of Quilters' Heritage Celebration, Quilt America, Quilters' Unlimited Showcase, AQS Annual Show, The National Quilt Festival, and has taught throughout the US and in Germany, England, and Scotland. She has served as consultant to EZ International on the development of a new product for quilters. She directed the Missouri Heritage Quilt Project and was a consultant to the California Project. As consultant to the National Quilt Festival for Silver Dollar City she developed the concept of the quilt challenge, coordinates that challenge each year.

Her work has been featured in *Quilters' Newsletter* magazine, *Quilt*, and *Quilting Today*. She has authored four books: *Missouri Heritage Quilts*, published by AQS; *Amish Quiltmaker*, Sterling Publishers; *Quilts of the Booneslick Trail Quilters' Guild*, ASN, and *Amish Kinder Komforts*, AQS.

Lisa Jo Hawn, Indianapolis, Indiana

Lisa Jo Dougherty Hawn was born August 21, 1961, in Benton, Illinois, graduated in 1979 from Marion High School in Marion, IL, and attended one year at Olivet Nazarene University in Kankakee, IL. She currently resides in Indianapolis, IN.

Lisa began quilting in 1987 by doing a crib-sized Nine Patch completely by hand. Since that time, she has hand quilted ten quilts in various sizes. Most of her quilts are made as gifts. Hand quilting is Lisa's favorite style of quilting. She is currently a member of Quilt Connection Guild of Greenwood, IN.

DaNelle Haynes, Phoenix, Arizona

Quiltmaker, guild member, guild leader, student, and teacher. I am a 40 year old quiltmaker, wife, and accountant. Besides quilting, I enjoy our weekend home at Apache Lake, camping, my family, and my dog, Bailey. In 1991 I was treasurer for Cactus Patchers of Tempe. I was then chairwoman for Cactus Patchers from 1992 – 1994. I was also chairwoman for the Arizona Quilters Guild 1994 Fall Meeting convention. I have been making quilts for only 5 years, but have been involved in handwork such as embroidery, needlepoint, and crochet since I was 5 years old. I have taught workshops in crazy quilting and binding technique in recent years. I am an active member of NQA, AQS, AQG (Arizona Quilters Guild), Cactus Patchers, S.C.A.D. (Small, Creative, and Done), and The Swarm.

Had a miniature featured in *Miniature Quilt Magazine* in 1995; served as hostess for the 1994 Arizona Quilters Guild Fall Meeting convention (over 300 in attendance, 16 vendor mall, Hoffman fashion show, and Betty Boyink teaching classes); recieved 2nd & 3rd place ribbons in the 1993 Arizona State Fair.

Dixie Hamer Haywood, Pensacola, Florida

Born May 6, 1933, in Seattle, Washington. Married Robert C. Haywood, June 14, 1952. Children: Brent Hamer, Todd Robert, Dana Claire (Howard).

First quilt made in 1955; second in late 1960's; continuous quiltmaking since. Award-winning quiltmaker. NQA certified teacher and judge. Author of the *Contemporary Crazy Quilt Project Book*, (Crown, 1977); *Crazy Quilting With a Difference*, (Scissortail, 1981), both reprinted by Dover; and with Jane Hall, *Perfect Pineapples* (C&T, 1989), *Precision Pieced Quilts Using the Foundation Method*, (Chilton, 1992); and *Firm Foundations*, (AQS, 1996), and numerous articles. Helped found quilt guilds in California, Oklahoma, and Florida. Served as consultant on Florida Quilt Heritage project.

Evelyn Healy, Glendive, Montana

Have been a member of the weekly Sacred Heart quilter's group since 1984.

Mildred Alyeene Malm Hensley, Woodward, Oklahoma

Mildred Alyeen Malm Hensley was born July 13, 1928, in Tulsa, TX. She now lives in Woodward, OK, with her husband of 49 years. Alyeene is from a large family whose mother Lola Pearl Bartlley Malm made quilts because of necessity for bed covers. Alyeene became interested in quilts quite early and helped her mother piece and quilt. Her first effort by herself was a doll quilt made from yo yo's which is still hanging prominently on her quilt rack today. The first large full bed quilt was pieced and hand quilted in 1949. It was a Double Wedding Ring made from pieces of her school dresses and feed sacks. It is also on her quilt rack. Alyeene has not kept track of the number of quilts she has made but today she averages 8 – 10 quilts per year. "I like scrap quilts best. I get most of my patterns from pictures then draw them to the scale I need for each project."

I am registered with the Oklahoma quilt guild. I do hand quilting for other women and make quilts to order. I set up at craft shows each year where I sell some of my quilts.

Alma May Henson, Kingman, Indiana

Quiltmaker. Born in early 30's, in Oxford, Indiana. As a child I enjoyed Grandma Robbins' homemade quilts and the quilting bees held in her home. I threaded needles. My other grandma, Pearl Fife, pieced quilts by hand and appliquéd. She used satin scraps. My mother made a quilt every winter. Started helping mother at age 10; and at age 14, I completed a quilt for my hope chest.

After marriage in 1948, I started quilting for my family needs. In the 1970's, I started quilting for fun. One of my daughters, active in California quilt guilds, inspired me to join Sugar Creek Quilters in 1994. Some activities include monthly meetings, workshops, and in-home quilting

Joined the Indiana State Guild in 1995. Old Jail Museum Challenge Quilt and quilt show in Library, Crawfordsville, IN.

Becky Herdle, Rochester, New York

Becky Arnold Herdle was born August 18, 1922, in Atlanta, GA, and now lives in Rochester, NY, with her husband Lloyd.

Quilting entered Becky's life for the first time in 1977, after her family of six children were mostly grown. At that time she took a course from Suzzy Payne on "Patchwork on the Sewing Machine" and since then quilting has become her full-time avocation. She is a certified quilt judge, lecturer, workshop instructor, and author. In addition to magazine articles, she has published a book: *Time Span Quilts: New Quilts From Old Tops,* AQS.

She is a member of AQS, NQA, and the Genesee Valley Quilt Club (thought to be the country's oldest) and has displayed her quilts locally and nationally, winning a number of ribbons and awards. In addition, the "Time Span Quilts" which she has made amount to a sizable collection.

Connie Hester, Bryan, Texas

Connie Hester is an award-winning quilt artist, author, instructor, and designer of patterns for quilts and quilted clothing. Her quilts have appeared and won awards in Paducah's American Quilter's Society Show; Houston's International Quilt Festivals; Texas' Sesquicentennial Quilt Associations "Great Texas Quilt Round-Up" tour; Midland's Museum of the Southwest's "Contemporary Texas Quilts"; San Diego's International Quilt Exhibit; Pacific International Quilt Festival; Jacksonville, Florida's Quiltfest 1993; Indianapolis' Quilt America!; Germany's Quilt Expo IV; *American Quilter* magazine; *Quilter's Newsletter Magazine; Lone Stars; Quilt* magazine; *Country Quilts* magazine; and others.

She created Speed Grids® for speed piecing triangle blocks in 1989 and wrote *Winning Ways to Make Quilts* in 1992. Currently Connie is finishing two more quilting books and pursuing a more improvisational style in her art. With her husband, George, and her two children (Morgan, 11, and Matthew, 9), she lives in the historic district of Bryan, TX.

Wanda Hickman, Atlanta, Georgia

Designer, quiltmaker, and teacher. I became involved in quilting as a child, accompanying my grandmothers to quilting bees. In high school my grandmothers and their friends gave me piles of quilt squares to assemble into quilt tops. I still have two of those quilts, tied. At sixteen who has the time or patience to hand quilt? For the next 25 years as a mother, teacher, and counselor, I dabbled in quilting. My creative interests expanded to crafts, painting, and graphic design. When we were transferred to England in 1991, I became involved with one British and two American quilting groups. I immersed myself in quilting and discovered a hidden passion I had been seeking all my life.

Upon returning to the United States and with the encouragement of my husband, Bill, I decided to combine my teaching experience with my graphic design skills and my love of color and fabrics to become a professional quilt designer and teacher. It's the best career decision I have ever made!

My most memorable quilting experiences revolve around the many challenge projects I do. They push me to use fabrics and techniques I might not otherwise choose. They force me to generate ideas that, once flowing, have over-filled files. They help me provide opportunities for students who think they are not creative or original. You should see their surprise and satisfaction at the outcome. Recently, I taught a class based on the 1995 Hoffman challenge. Five of the eight students submitted their final projects. We celebrated!

Sharla R. Hicks, Anaheim, California

Sharla Hicks is a self-taught artisan and teacher. In 1981, she turned to quilts and began teaching the craft a year later. In 1988, Sharla began a formal education in art which she incorporated into her quilting and teaching. She currently gives lectures and workshops for quilt guilds and shops in northern and southern California. Her goal as a teacher is to help quilters find their own individual expression. As a quilt artist, Sharla sees herself as a colorist who makes innovative and orginal quilts that reflect her personal journey.

She has been an active member of Antelope Valley Quilt Association, Glendale Quilt Guild, and Flying Geese Quilters in southern California serving on several boards as program chair, publicity, secretary, and philanthropy chair.

In 1993, Sharla coordinated with Jane St. Pierre and Patty McCormick the completion of 85 quilts for House of Hope, a center for the homeless women and children. In 1994 – 95, she organized the first juried and judged southern California regional quilt show, "Crossroads." She also developed the Computer Quilting Exhibit for Laguna Art Museum held in conjunction with the Amish Quilt Exhibition, "Lit from Within, Amish Quilts of Lancaster County." Sharla wrote an informational computer slide show that highlighted the style differences between Midwest and Lancaster Amish quilts and American quilts of the same period and set up three additional computers with quilting software and instruction manuals.

Sharla has been invited to exhibit her work at American Quilt Museum, San Jose, CA, 1984; West Coast Quilter's Conference, Sacramento, CA, 1992; Brandstater Gallery, La Sierra University, Riverside, CA (5 woman show), 1993; Muckenthaler Center,

Fullerton, CA; and Quilt Show of Glendale Quilter's Guild, Burbank, CA, 1994. Her work has also been accepted into many juried shows like American Quilter's Society, American International Quilt Festival, and Natural Impressions II. Sharla has won several awards: 1990, "Ruel's Kaleidoscope," 3rd, Schweinfurth Art Museum, Auburn, NY; 1991, "Ruel's Kaleidoscope," 3rd, International Quilt Festival, Houston, TX; 1991 "The Power of Freedom," 1st, Freedom of the Nations Contest, Piecemakers, Costa Mesa, CA; Also published in *Quilting Today*, June 1992; 1994, "I Love Chartreuse," 2nd, Orange County Fair, Costa Mesa, CA; 1994, "Adam's Outer Realm," Judges Choice, "From Our Hearts and by Our Hands," Flying Geese Quilt Show, Costa Mesa, CA; 1995, "Chinese Red," Honorable Mention, National Quilting Association, Riverside, CA.

Jackie Miller Hill, Aiken, South Carolina

Having been born in New Mexico, raised near NYC, attended Trinity College & Georgetown Law in D.C., moved to Baltimore, Texas, Illinois, and South Carolina, because of my husband's Army, academic, and surgical careers. I have come to love the diversity and unity of America, our quilting heritage. While keeping horses alive in the winters of IL, rotating water buckets to thaw in the kitchen, I was struck with how hard life must have been for the pioneers. I also saw quilts for the first time. The fact that busy women take the time to make beautiful functional art for their families, with recycled fabrics, is an inspiring example of seeking balance and putting meaning into life.

I make quilts of my own designs, often with an embroidered quote, to bring the written word into the visual art. I collect quilts, quilt tops, blocks, and books. I have made quilts with my grade and middle school art students. I introduce women to quilts by organizing simple group projects and lecturing. Six blue ribbons at the SC State Fair for the children's quilts, one red ribbon at the state fair for my own.

Jacqué J. Holmes, Big Bear Lake, California

Jacqué J. Holmes, was born November 14, 1930, in Omaha, NE, she was raised in Des Moines, IA, and moved to California in 1951. I crafted, painted, and designed needlework kits for Bucilla for my business, Jac-Line. I was a buyer for Port O' Call Pasadena, a chain of specialty stores until my husband suffered a stroke. We moved to our mountain dream home in Big Bear Lake in 1984.

I opened the Bears Paw Quilt Shop in 1985 and set out to learn everything about quilting. To say that quilting took over my life would be an understatement. Since closing the quilt store I've concentrated on designing, teaching, and publishing patterns of my original designs. I also create the designs for the Eagle Crest Quilt Retreats in Big Bear Lake. My daughter and 15-year-old granddaughter also quilt.

Have shown and received numerous awards in local and national quilt shows. I belong to AQS, NQA, and Busy Bear and Wandering Foot Quilt Guilds. Have two children, five grandchildren, and one great-granddaughter. In March 1994 I lost my husband of 42 years and I've found quilting to be a great source of solace for me.

Linda R. Honsberger, Racine, Wisconsin

I'm mostly a self-taught quilter. My husband's grandmother got me interested around the time of the Bicentennial. Two years later, before my second son was born, I took a four week quilting class. I was piecing a Log Cabin quilt at the end of it. Three years later I was teaching, lecturing, doing commission work, and repairing old quilts.

I have received awards and am currently quilting for internationally known quilt artists and quilt shops. My work for them has been featured in magazines, books, and PBS.

Two projects I truly enjoyed out of the hundred or so quilts I've done were my son's third grade class quilt and making my parents' 40th wedding anniversary quilt.

Lyn Honzel, Mendocino, California

Collector, designer, and quiltmaker. "I get to live in the most beautiful place in the world, and make quilts," says Lyn Honzel. Eight years ago she moved to Mendocino, an artist colony on the northern California coast, where she lives in a cottage overlooking the Pacific. Her quilts start from there: surrounded by 2½ acres of redwoods, she takes her inspiration from the trees she sees from every window and from the ever-changing ocean.

Lyn has been sewing all her life and discovered quilting by playing with scraps of fabric. She became fascinated with the geometry and the three-dimensional quality of quilts, and with the dedication that goes into making them. For her, quilts are more of a process than a product, a way of giving something in her head a physical form. Always working in seclusion, she is happiest when quilting with her two dogs curled up at her feet, losing complete track of time. "Quilts are the most tangible way of saying I love you," she says. "They express what I can't.".

The owner of Cross Blends, our local quilt store, asked ten local women to make a quilt of an historic building for Mendocino's 150th anniversary celebration. Some of the women had never quilted before, but all the pieces went together into a larger quilt. Since I always quilt by myself, this was the only time I have been a part of a communal project.

Janice H. Anderson Horn, Clarion, Pennsylvania

Born July 16, 1935, in Claire, WI. I am a librarian who graduated from Luther College, Decorah, IA, and the University of Michigan. I began making quilts by sewing the tops for quilts to be raffled for fund raising for the local service to victims of domestic violence. I am about to begin my 6th one for that effort. In between I have made wallhangings and quilts, entering them in shows and selling them.

I particularly like working with colors. I assist at an annual local show and organize an annual exhibit. Through those activities I've become acquainted with quilters and quilt owners which will help with the work for a regional quilt documentation project. I am a member of AQS and NQA.

Marie Sturges Houston, East Aurora, New York

Marie Sturges Hoston was born March 10, 1940. She grew up outside New York City and now lives with her husband Fred in East Aurora, NY, 20 miles southeast of Buffalo.

Marie's first quilt was a queen-size Log Cabin quilt made for her daughter, Virginia, when she graduated from high school. Her first original quilt (inspired by a wall in Bologna, Italy) was made for her son, Tom, when he graduated from architectural school.

As a member of the Southtowns Piecemakers Quilting Guild, Marie worked on the World University Games Quilt in 1993 when the games were held in Buffalo. With other members of SPQG she makes quilts for Haven House, a shelter for battered women and children. In 1995 she received a fourth place for her entry in Buffalo's Architectural Quilt Challenge.

Now that she is a grandmother, many of Marie's quilts are crib size. It's the perfect size for trying out new ideas, and they actually get finished!

Nancy Menard Howard, Rolla, Missouri

I was born in Buffalo, New York, and graduated from Buffalo State College in 1977, with a degree in art education. I became interested in quilting in 1970 and made a few quilts as gifts for friends. My husband and I moved to Missouri in 1984 and I joined the Piece and Plenty Quilt Guild in 1987.

The quilts I make are usually machine pieced, hand appliquéd, or a combination. I enjoy hand quilting. I have held several offices in our guild and have led workshops on various quilting techniques.

3rd place, Guild Challenge Project, May 1991 "Wild Rose at Christmas" (this quilt was exhibited in the first State Quilt Show at the Capitol in May, 1995). 1st place, Guild Challenge Project, May 1992 "Ode to Mrs. Columbus." Viewer's Choice Award, "There's a New Critter on the Farm" wallhanging, October 1992. "Ode to Mrs. Columbus" wallhanging accepted at Silver Dollar City exhibit, September 1993. Viewer's Choice Award, "Stardust Jacket," October 1994. 1st place experienced category, "Tiffany's View from my Kitchen," May 1995.

My son, Benjamin is locally famous for his early prowess with scissors. While I was in the next room cutting out a dress pattern, he was in my bedroom cutting my handmade quilt in half (while it was still on the bed). He was 4 years old at the time. There was nothing left to do but sew it back together with a black strip (my mood at the time), appliqué a pair scissors, his name, and the date on it. I guess he did me a favor – his wedding present is done!

Shirley Hoy, Paducah, Kentucky

Shirley Hoy, Executive Director of the Rotary Club of Paducah, KY, and the Rotary Antique Quilt Show & Sale, which is held each April. Shirley has coordinated all aspects of this show, arranging for the antique quilt exhibit and contracting with vendors of unique goods and services.

"The thing of which I am most proud is that our Rotary Antique Quilt Show proceeds fund the Rotary Education Assistance Program (REAP). To August 1995, we have invested $223,000 in over 130 Paducah/McCracken County students, who otherwise would have been unable to attend college."

In the past, Hoy has majored in collecting and exhibiting antique quilts, but now has designed a new quilt which she hopes to complete in the near future for a special person. Shirley is synonymous with Rotary and with quilts in Paducah.

Jenny Frank Hubbard, Ft. Collins, Colorado

Jenny Frank Hubbard was born June 24, 1961, in Winfield, KS. She currently lives in Fort Collins, CO, with her husband and their four children. Jenny began quilting in 1982 and to date has made 200 quilts. She is a home sewer for *Quiltmaker Magazine* and a quilt teacher at a local shop. In 1993 she was awarded a New Forms grant with funding from the NEA and the Rockefeller Foundation administered by Helena Presents & the Colorado Dance Festival. She has had quilts displayed in Paducah, Lancaster, Peoria, and Denver as well as Rome, Italy, and Kyóto, Japan.

She is a member of AQS, AIQA, CQC, FRCQ, and local quilt groups. Her sisters, Amy Lindberg and Tina Woodall, also quilt.

Carol Hudson, Richmond, Illinois

My name is Carol Hudson. I have always liked sewing and doing craft projects with family and friends. In 1984 I took a beginning sampler quilt class at a local quilt shop; the focus of my leisure time changed to quilting. I love all facets of quilting; especially the new friends I've made in the classes and in Country Quilter's Guild of McHenry, Illinois. During the school year I quilt most evenings and weekends because I teach third grade at Prairie Grove School in Crystal Lake, Illinois. In the summer I visit quilt shops and machine piece; I hand quilt on our cabin cruiser which my husband and I keep at Menominee, MI, on Green Bay. Each July I take a class on Washington Island, Wisconsin, and we live on the boat. Since I take several classes throughout the year, I happily have "homework" quilts in progress.

Shirley Hudson, Newark, Ohio

Born into a family of quilters on March 1, 1931, she was inspired by aunts Una Brown and Dillie Holdsworth of Coshocton. After raising 7 children, wanted to learn new and faster ways of the art. Joined Heart of Ohio Quilters.

Charlene Hughes, Pukalani, Maui, Hawaii

Designer and quiltmaker. Charlene Hughes has resided on the island of Maui for 20 years. She blends the European and  Midwestern influences of her youth with contemporary quilting methods and designs, as well as traditional Hawaiian quilting techniques. Ms. Hughes brings an artist's sensibility to quiltmaking, preferring to create tactile wall pictures, rather than quilts that are exclusively utilitarian. She embellishes many of her quilted wallhangings with antique lace, buttons, hand-painted silk, dolls, and other found objects.

Member of NaPo'e Humukuiki O' Hawaii, Hawaii Quilt Research Project, Hui Noeau, AIQA, AQS, and NQA.

Sue Ann Huitt, Yarnell, Arizona

Sue has been quilting since 1985. She majored in weaving in college. Nancy Crow was her most influential quilting instructor. In 1995 she opened a home studio.

Her semi-abstract improvisational landscape quilts are inspired by rural Arizona, the English countryside, and Samoa, where she lived for two years. She uses cotton hand-dyed fabrics, seed beads, and couching.

She has shown quilts in Quilters' Unlimited Kansas City show in '94 and '95, won Best of Show in the '95 Yarnell Art Show.

Mildred M. Hundley, Tempe, Arizona

Born in Kentucky and lived in Illinois most of my life and retired in Arizona in 1988.

Amateur quiltmaker, presently serving as librarian and historian for Cactus Patchers of Tempe, AZ.

My real love for quilts developed after I attended the AQS Quilt Show in Paducah, KY, in 1985. Prior to that I was only familiar with the traditional patterns. The show opened up a new world of interest.

Since then I have attended as many classes and quilt-related shows as possible and I've learned much from the quilters in my group about design, fabrics, color, and quick construction methods. I am fortunate to be living in an area where there is so much interest in quilting.

Lois K. Ide, Bucyrus, Ohio

Teacher, designer, author, collector, and quiltmaker. Lois K. Ide was born in 1920; is a registered nurse; married Dr. Carl J. Ide in 1943 and they live in Bucyrus, Ohio.

A world traveler, GCO Flower Show judge, a decoupeur with journeyman status in the National Guild of Decoupeurs, quilter, teacher, and writer. Taught to sew by her mother.

Her quilt, "World Peace" was one of 41 finalists in the Quilts – Visions of the World contest in '88; discovered by UNICEF & printed in '93 as a greeting card for its European collection and selected by Fairfield Batting Co. for its early 1995 advertising.

Received an Ohio Arts Council Grant in '89, via the NEA, to teach dimensional appliqué techniques to apprentices Holly Ross from Stow & Anita Shackelford of Bucyrus, Ohio.

Lois's quilts and writings have appeared in many calendars, books, and magazines. Her "Galaxy of Quilters" quilt is in the permanent collection of MAQS. Her quilts have won Best of Show, Technical Excellence, and many other special ribbons. However, Lois feels her greatest achievement is teaching young people how to reach their highest quilting potential.

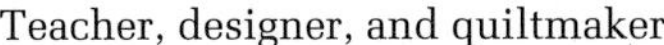

Cathy Isdale, Houston, Texas

Teacher, designer, and quiltmaker.

Quilting teacher at Houston Community College from 1970 to 1992. Completed 40 quilts. Fabric purchased for 56 quilts in various stages from planning to near completion. My quilt projects range from pieced, appliqué, embroidery, creative personal history to spiritual interpretation. I design and make custom quilts from other people's ideas and color choices.

Merl and Fay Pritts, Mt. Pleasant, PA.
Merl machine quilting & Fay hand quilting.

Gwen Marston having fun during her folk art appliqué class at Asilomar, California.

Vyvyan Gardner and her mother enjoy the PSU Quilt Show, Canyon City, OR.

Karen Elaine Jamell, Greenwood, Indiana

Karen Elaine Hadley Adrian Jamell was born September 5, 1949, in Beech Grove, IN, and attended Indiana University-Purdue University at Indianapolis.

She resides in Greenwood, IN, with her husband, Bob, and daughter, Alyson. Although, she made her first quilt in 1970 for her daughter, Nicole, she didn't make another until she began quilting seriously in 1987.

Her love of quilts began as a child when her grandmother, Mildred Wright Patterson, took her to see a collection of quilts made by her great-grandmother, Beda Quinton Wright, of Barren County, KY.

Karen has entered only one quilt competition and won the First Place-Viewer's Choice Award. She finds hand piecing and hand quilting the most enjoyable aspects of the quiltmaking process. She is a member of AQS, Indiana State Quilt Guild, Quilt Connection Guild, and Quilters Guild of Indianapolis. As a member of Quilt Connection Guild, she holds the office of secretary and has served on many other committees, including chairperson for donation quilts, co-chairman for sew day and a quilt show, nominating committee, and arranging quilt displays at local libraries.

Marlene H. Jensen, Benson, Arizona

Quiltmaker. Born and raised at Pender, Nebraska. Moved to Arizona about 40 years ago. Self-taught quilter. My quilts are given to the family.

Mary Beth Noonan Jensen, Lena, Wisconsin

Mary Beth Noonan Jensen was born February 2, 1944, at Oconto, WI, was raised mostly in Marinette, WI. She earned a Bachelor's

of Fine Arts at the University of Wisconsin – Milwaukee where she became a K-12 teacher of art. While teaching she earned a Master's degree in curriculum & supervision then served as an elementary school principal. Mary Beth was in teaching 9 years and administration 15 years in Hartford, WI, before retiring with her husband, Glen, in 1993. They now live at a beautiful site on a bluff over looking the Machickanee Flowage on the Oconto River near Oconto Falls, WI. The wildlife sanctuary type atmosphere is as much an inspiration to quilting as are the many shops in the area that display area quilters' creations.

With only several experiences in quilting, Mary Beth now enjoys canvassing the magazines and shops studying quilting and becoming familiar with contemporary quilting and quilt art. Collecting ½ yards and fat quarters of a variety of cottons and blends has become as much of a delight as creating small pillow tops, lap quilts, mini wallhangings, and future projects.

Mary Beth's "Mother's Day" lap quilt won first place at the Oconto County Fair in Aug. '94 and it's matching pillow won second place, building a feeling of success. The lap quilt was made from her mother's old "silky" clothes and decorated with her grandmother's antique buttons and lace. Her mother now treasures the lap quilt in the nursing home. Taking a quilting class in fall '94 helped greatly in updating & learning special techniques.

Mary Beth is a member of the American Quilter's Society, collects quilt books, instructions, and subscribes to quilt magazines for ideas, tips, and information.

Denise Jeppson, Corinth, Texas

I have been quiltmaking for the past 13 years, and collecting antique quilt tops and blocks for almost as long. I have taught various quiltmaking classes for the past two years, hand quilting being my favorite. I have also given free lectures on quilt-related topics to quilt guilds and school classes, to promote the art of quiltmaking. I especially enjoy the history of quilting and derive great pleasure from finishing and repairing old tops and blocks. I am a quiltmaker, teacher, collector of antique tops, and an amateur appraiser.

I have won several blue ribbons for my quilts at the Texas State Fair, the North Texas Fair, and my quilt guild challenges. My goal, someday, is to be an AQS certified quilt appraiser.

Christina E. Johnson, Philadelphia, Pennsylvania

Christina Elizabeth Richardson Johnson was born May 31, 1942, in Davenport, IA, but was raised in California where she lived until 1990. In addition to quilting she has experimented with needlepoint, weaving, crocheting, and knitting.

Having moved to Philadelphia, PA, and desiring to meet people with kindred spirits, she initiated the founding of Quilters of the Round Table in 1993. She is its first president. Although she considers herself a new quilter, she has led the guild to demonstrating quilting at the Museum of the University of Pennsylvania and at the Philadelphia Museum of Art.

In April 1995, the guild hung a very well received month-long show at the Afro-American Historical and Cultural Museum in Philadelphia. Two of Christina's quilts were chosen to be in the exhibit. One was a design incorporating blocks signed by 37 members of her husband's extended family as a family history. She is currently working on grants to document quilts in southeastern Pennsylvania.

Lee Johnson, Kingsville, Texas

I am a traditional quilter partial to red, white, and blue. I like to hand quilt best, but time pushes me to use the machine more and more. I like to teach beginners.

For nine years I have taken squares entered in our county livestock show, designed a top from them and quilted it for a drawing the following year. All monies earned go toward the four year college and two vocational scholarships awarded each year to the kids.

I collect a lot of different quilt and craft books and magazines. They inspire me to try new and old ideas. I like attending my bees and guild. For two years I enjoyed being program chairman. I was president of Coastal Bend Quilt and Needlework Guild in 1995. It was a great privilege and learning experience.

Marjorie E. Johnson, Wheaton, Illinois

Designer, lecturer, and teacher. Marjorie E. Johnson tells stories

with fiber art. Her work has been featured in galleries from Baltimore to San Francisco and she has been published in Japanese magazines. Her stories are inspired by her intensive travels, personal triumphs, the love of those close to her, and her Christian faith.

Marjorie's previous work in a variety of other mediums (oil, acrylics, clay, basket weaving) is reflected in her fiber art. Her fabric is layered, pieced, quilted, appliquéd, and embellished. Her finished works are full of surprises – the more you look, the more you will find.

Have participated in: AQS/Hobbs Bonded Fibers Fashion Show; Textile Art Center, Chicago; Paper-Fiber, Iowa City; Tapestry Gallery, Madrid, New Mexico.

Terry Johnson, Tucson, Arizona

Terry Johnson is currently a member of American Quilter's Society and the Arizona Quilters Guild, Log Cabin Quilters Chapter. She is also involved with friends Melody David-Baker and Susan Standley in a group they call "Never a Dull Needle." They meet once a month at Melody's house with their young children, all seven of them! The children range in age from seven years to seven days. We recently helped the children make blocks to exchange with each other so that each child will have a friendship quilt.

Terry has loved quilts since childhood when she lay on her grandmother's quilts tracing the patchwork patterns with her finger. She was intrigued with the beautiful and intricate designs made of simple squares, triangles, and rectangles. That's why she has a special fondness for patchwork, although she admires all quilting techniques.

Terry has been quilting for little more than a year. She does it because she has a passion for it. The foundation for this passion was laid unknowingly by her grandmother, Loki Stratton, who quilted out of necessity. She was taught, encouraged, and supported by Melody David-Baker. How do you thank someone who has taken you by the hand and helped you fulfill a life-long desire? Melody has always been there with humor, generosity, and friendship.

Terry, born August 17, 1958, in Pikeville, Kentucky, now lives in Tucson, AZ, with her husband, David Johnson and their sons, Casey and Spencer.

Vicki L. Johnson, Soquel, California

Designer and author. Since 1970, artist Vicki L. Johnson has been creating quilted and painted art works. She has worked with clothes, dolls, and quilts. Currently, her emphasis is on quilts which use the California coast as inspiration, and integrate painted and pieced fabric surfaces.

Vicki is a graduate of the University of Michigan with a degree in graphic design. She worked in that field for ten years before devoting her time to quilts. She has taught classes in traditional and contemporary quilting, fabric painting, dyeing, and soft sculpture for quilt stores, guilds, and the College of the Redwoods. Currently, she is a freelance teacher lecturing and teaching for guilds and national quilt conferences. The American Quilter's Society published her book, *Paint and Patches* in September of 1995.

The quilted paintings of Vicki L. Johnson have been seen in international exhibitions and collections, private and corporate. She has won many awards and recently won a 1st place at the American Quilter's Society Show 1995 in pictorial wall quilts. Her quilts are owned by the Oregon Coast Aquarium, the Museum of the American Quilter's Society, Valley Oak Dental Group, Fairfield Processing Corp., Mountain Bell, and private collectors in America, Canada, England, Sweden, and Switzerland.

Quilting awards received: 1995, 1st place AQS; 1994, PIQF, Best Interpretation of Theme; AQS, 2nd place; 1993, AIQA, 1st small art quilt.

Virginia Johnson, Ferryville, Wisconsin

Teach quilting and promote quilting to anyone within ear shot. All aspects of quilting parallels my interests; drawing, painting, sculpturing, watercolors, and using fabric. Quilting has become a vocation since 1979. I have a small quilt shop where I design and make quilts on order and for myself.

Written several articles for the local senior citizen's paper. Designed several equilateral design quilts and hand-painted fabric for my quilts. Owner of the Olde Tyme Quilt Shoppe, Ferryville, WI. Quilting with others is one of Virginia's favorite quilting experiences.

Anita Peeples Jones, Ardmore, Pennsylvania

My mother taught me to sew and appreciate the pleasures of

needlework when I was young. I made my first quilt 27 years ago. As I quilt I remember my mother's lessons and take comfort in carrying on the skills she taught me. I feel my creations leave a tangible example of my existence for future generations — in them they will see a bit of what my mother instilled in me.

I prefer traditional patterns with a twist, and use colors that surprise the observer. I teach classes in the creation of wearable art, and I am a guild president.

I am most proud that a wallhanging of mine is on permanent display in the school that my two sons attended and I had three pieces in a recent exhibit at the Afro-American Museum in Philadelphia. I am also delighted that my daughter-in-law has begun to quilt.

Carolyn Jones, Houston, Texas

Born December 21, 1929, widow of Dee Jones, mother of Jayne, 46, and Jill, 44. Retired from So-Fro Fabrics, craft department.

I made a few quilts years ago but I really started quilting in the last five years. I am now trying to make up for lost time. I love to quilt tops more than I like to appliqué or piece. Like most quilters, I love fabric and would have a room full if I could.

My daughter and I visit quilt stores whenever we can and we really enjoy the huge quilt show each November in Houston. I have several quilt tops ahead of me to do so I know I'll be an active quilters until I'm older and grayer!

Claire T. Jones, Nashville, Indiana

Wife, mother, homemaker. Husband is now retired. Have been a nursery school teacher, pianist for their music program after I stopped teaching. Legal secretary before marrying.

Have done some local teaching in a small way. Chairman for four years of Brown County Pioneer Women.

Being chairperson on the Historical Society's Annual Quilt show has been a rewarding experience. Getting everything to come together at the right time is the challenge. The fun part is getting to know the quilters, and hearing their stories, in person, before anyone else. I have submitted the application to become a certified appraiser in the AQS program. Will be working hard, studying, this next year.

Olga Spanhoff Jones, Telluride, Colorado

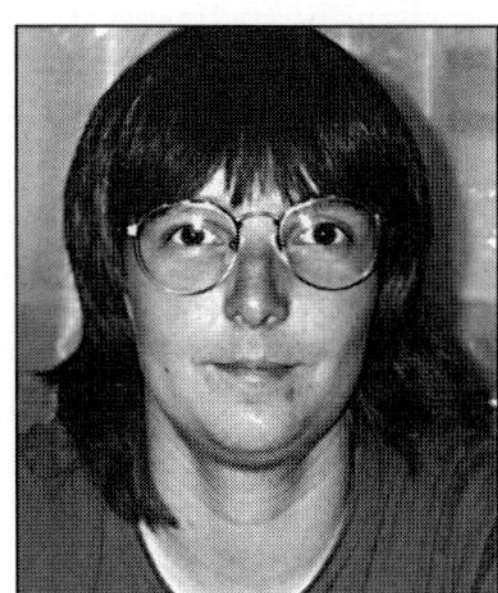

I am a novice quilter who has learned from books. My mother-in-law encourages me to continue to perfect my stitches. I prefer to work with large pieces, muted colors, and traditional patterns.

My first full-size quilt was a gift for my parents which included photographs of my husband, myself, and our horses.

Theresa M. Jones, Glendive, Montana

I have been an avid admirer of the art of quilting for many years, but did not become an active quilter until after my retirement.

I am a member of the San Francisco Quilters Guild; Sacred Heart Church Quilters, Glendive, Montana; Quilters Guild of Fargo, North Dakota; Badland Quilters Guild; and charter member of Patches On the Prairie Quilters Guild, Glendive. Also serve as secretary and newsletter editor.

Wendy Mathiesen Jordan, Indianapolis, Indiana

Wendy Mathiesen Jordan was born in Glendale, CA, August 2, 1963. She graduated Georgia-Cumberland Academy in 1982, and the University of Indianapolis in 1986. Almost immediately she left her degree in biology behind in search of work she could truly love. Finally in 1990, she stumbled into quilting and never plans to leave. She is self-taught and has a studio in Franklin, IN, where she designs and creates her quilts as well as jewelry. She is a member of Quilt Connection Guild in Indianapolis and the Indianapolis Art Center.

She is a designer/quiltmaker whose favorite part of the process is handling the fabric and watching the new piece come together.

In 1995 she had a quilt juried into an art show at the Indianapolis Art Center and won an award.

Tuscon, AZ, children working on friendship quilt for each other, using fabric markers and tracing hands.
Left to right: Casey Johnson, 6; David Baker, 8; Spencer Johnson, 2; Melissa Baker, 5.

Schoolhouse Quilters, Morro Bay, CA, show off their sweatshirts.
Back, left to right: Kathi Settle, Carol Orona; front left to right: Carole Fairbanks, Kim Zerbe, Jill Sabol.

Martha Bell Kappers, Venice, Florida

Designer, quiltmaker. Attended Kent State University, asst. children's library, married, mother of 6 boys and 2 girls. Volunteer work: school librarian. Member of Greater Hamilton, Ohio, Arts Exhibit Committee, member of Hamilton – Fairfield Arts Council board as secretary. Maintained HFAC Gallery at Fairfield, Ohio, City Building. Chaired the Fairfield City silver anniversary arts & crafts show. Have won ribbons for my paintings, wallhangings, and quilts. I have had a quilt pattern published in a *Quilt World* magazine, August 1983. Won ribbons at the Ohio State Fair for my original designs. Was juried into 1986 AQS show, and was awarded the "Lil Brinkman" Brush and Easel club award, 1987, for dedication to the art community. I designed a quilt for St. Philip's Church in Franklin, TN, and taught the Arts Environment Ministry the quilting process. Aided in creating decorations for changing seasons and holy days. I also created banners for St. Michael's Church in Sterling Heights, MI. At present I am finishing a quilt beginning a fabric screen and painting and enjoying retirement.

Lita Karlstrand, San Francisco, California

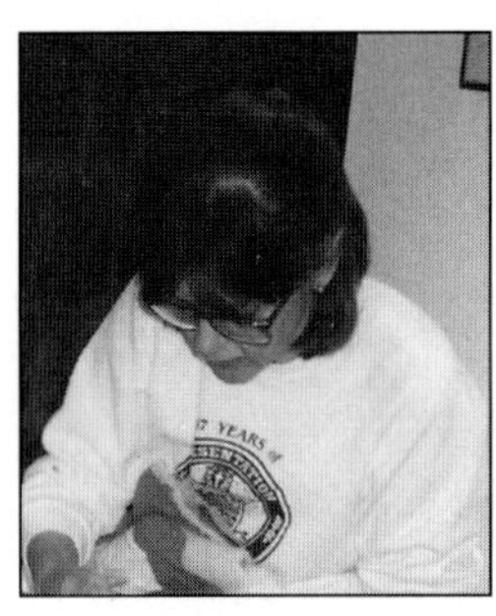

Quiltmaker, collector of antique American and foreign quilts. My grandmother, Elsie Michels Sandelin, had quilted her way around the world as an army wife. I had always admired her work and I made my first quilt in Texas in 1988, just to prove to myself I could do it. I caught the bug and haven't stopped since. I'm following in my grandmother's footsteps, quilting my way around the world as an air force wife.

My biggest thrill in quilting was winning the blue ribbon at the Wichita County Fair (TX) with my first quilt. Since then all of my quilts have won awards, but nothing will ever top that.

Helen Kelley, Minneapolis, Minnesota

Helen Longfield Kelley was born April 28, 1927, in Englewood, NJ. Helen has lived in Minneapolis, MN, for 33 years. She is an author, lecturer, historian, designer, quiltmaker, and travels

extensively to teach and research. She was the organizing president of Minnesota Quilters, a 1,500 member organization, and serves on the board of the Minnesota Quilt History Project. Helen has written four books and is well-known for her monthly "Loose Threads" column in *Quilter's Newsletter Magazine*. She has taught throughout the U.S., Canada, Great Britain, Holland, and New Zealand. She has a particular interest in Native American star quilts and ribbonwork design. Helen speaks frequently to humanities classes and art organizations in her area in appreciation for what her community has done for her. Her quilts have won prizes in the AQS, NQA, and AIQA shows. She received The Award of Distinction as Minnesota Fiber Artist of 1995 from the Minnesota Fiber/Metal Council.

Margo W. Kelly, Boise, ID

Quiltmaker, designer, teacher, author, and owner of Cotton Comforts (a monthly newsletter and fabric club for quilters).

Born in 1969, Margo was first introduced to quilting by her mother-in-law, Nancy F. Kelly in 1988, but did not take a quilt class until 1991. The quilting bug bit Margo hard at that class, and she has been quilting ever since.

Margo Kelly is the owner of Cotton Comforts, a monthly newsletter and fabric club for quilters. She originally started the company (in 1993) when she was pregnant with her first child and wanted to find a way to work out of her home once her child was born. She loved quilting, writing, and business, and concluded if she could carefully put the three together, she may have a successful venture. Unexpectedly, Margo had two children within eleven months, and as a result she quickly learned that 24 hours in a day were not enough to run her business, clean the house, make meals, and care for two small baby boys. However, she had an inner drive to be successful, so by carefully planning daily chores and manipulating her business schedule to fit the babies' sleep patterns, Margo has been able to accomplish the goals she has set.

Early in 1995, Margo began teaching quilt classes at the Quilter's Frame in Prescott Valley, Arizona. Then, when she and her family (along with her business, Cotton Comforts) relocated to Boise, Idaho, in June 1995, she began teaching quilt classes at the Quilt Crossing in Boise, Idaho. Occasionally, Margo adds to her busy schedule by designing and making custom quilts for interested people; and freelance writing for magazines.

Angela Justine DeWilde Kennedy, Andover, Kansas

A lifelong interest in needlework and apparel design is reflected in Angela's artistic fashions. During her childhood in Kansas City, MO, she studied voice which led to a degree in music. As a result of these paralleled interests she continues to sing in solo and group performances and she designs and creates wearable art. Her work has been in both solo and group exhibits and invitational shows. Several of her fashions have been juried into the AQS/Hobbs Bonded Fibers Fashion Shows and have received awards. She also designs vestments and other fabric pieces for liturgical use. Quilting, embroidery, fabric manipulation, and bead embellishment are artistically blended in Angela's work. She enthusiastically shares ideas and techniques with students and friends she has met in various guilds over the last 15 years.

Carol Kennemuth, Mayport, Pennsylvania

Carol Laraine Kennemuth resides with her husband, Bob, in Clarion County, PA, where she was born in August of 1941.

Having always been a seamstress, many fond memories lingered of days watching her grandmother, Sarah Wyant, piecing quilts. This interest rekindled, and she began quilting in 1989 and within 4 years had organized the Nimble Thimble Quilt Guild in Shannondale, PA, of which she is president. In recent years, Carol has made 10 quilts and won several awards at local quilt shows.

Eager to explore all facets of quilting, she soon discovered she enjoys piecing, appliqué, and hand quilting equally well. Several of her best efforts are now cherished possessions in the homes of loved ones. For Carol, her favorite part of quilting is the camaraderie and personal friendships gained in the past several years. Her quilts have been on display at many area quilt shows.

Linda Fry Kenzle, Fox River Grove, Illinois

Editor of *Stylepages*, an art-to-wear sewing journal, pattern designer, married to Don Carlo, mother of one child, Joshua.

Known for new techniques — fusible appliqué, confetti cloth, etc. Author: *Embellishments,* a book on art-to-wear (Chilton, 1993), *Dazzle* (1995).

Won 1st place in first show entered with "Fantasia" quilt. My work is shown in galleries & shows. Memorable quilts made as contributions to Aids babies and residents of our local old folks home; and work in AQS Fashion Show '94.

Marjorie M. Kersch, Herscher, Illinois

I'm another of those Depression era ladies when every little scrap was as precious as jewels, they still are to me.

I've been teaching for the last ten and more years around a banquet table in my family room.

I like to teach the basic course and see the lights come on and the excitement when a student finishes her first project. My goal is to teach as many as I can at a reasonable price. I give scholarships and gifts of teaching at charitable drawings and needlework shows, etc.

I have three ladies' groups making utility children's quilts for the Luke Society Mission in the Mississippi Delta. I never get tired of quilt books, magazines, fabric stores, other people's collections, and other quilters and would-be quilters.

I belong to AQS, NQA, Illinois Regional Quilters Network, subscribe to lots of magazines, and the *Professional Quilter*. My house is, of course, full of quilt fabric, books, and quilts!

Sara Newberg King, Pine Island, Minnesota

Born in California, graduated from University of Washington in occupational therapy. Lived throughout U.S., in Canada, and Italy.

Currently designs quilts, clothing, and patterns. Has her own King's Kreations quilting patterns and silk ribbon embroidery kits. Teaches, lectures, and leads quilting tours. Juried into shows at Museum of AQS; Rochester, MN, Art Alliance Center; QNM; Wisconsin History Project; Pine Castle Center for the Arts Orlando, FL; and East Coast Quilters. Received Forecast 1995 Public Arts grant. Published in *Double Wedding Ring*

Quilts from AQS and *Great American Quilts*, 1996, from Oxmoor House. Exhibits work at S.E. Minnesota Visual Arts Gallery in Rochester, MN.

Sharon Elizabeth King, Miami, Florida

Quiltmaker. I discovered the art of quilting during a trip to Europe with my mother. Rich in tradition, I instantly knew I had to make one. I had to create this object of beauty with pieces of fabric, hours of labor, and emotion, only the quilter could understand. It's amazing how cutting colors of material into tiny pieces, rearranging them into a puzzle and quilting a design can bring such satisfaction to oneself. The end-less hours of labor is really pure joy... for once you see the fin-ished product, you know you have created a personal masterpiece. You can see love, pride, and history all at once. I have made many a quilt since my first calling and cannot wait to discover my next creation! Hopefully, they will be treasured and appreciated by many generations to come. There are many addictions in life and I am glad mine is quilting!

Upon attending a quilt show in Key Largo, Florida, I never expected to be the proud owner of the famous "Celebrity Auto-graph Quilt" made by Tonya Sledd. With persistence of my boyfriend, I purchased five raffle tickets. Was I ever shocked when my name was chosen! There are fifty famous signatures that include President Clinton, movie stars, musicians, athletes, and comedians. It is an honor to own such a valuable quilt knowing that one day it will be donated to a museum for so many people to admire. Because I am a dental hygienist, I designed a "Tooth Quilt" to hang in my office. I love hearing my patients' comments on my originality! My dog, Sarita, is so jeal-ous when I am working on a quilt, that she does everything to try to disrupt me to give her attention. So I finally decided to make her very own quilt. Now everytime she see's me making a quilt, she goes and snuggles on hers!

Virginia L. King, Kissimmee, Florida

Quilter, quilt shop owner, teacher, charter member of Patchers of Time quilt guild. Homemaker for 29 years, realtors license, quilting for 11 years, three children, married to an electri-cal engineer, who also owns a restau-rant. We own Queen Ann's Lace.

Second quilt was a commemorative quilt, bearing 350 signatures of church families for pastor's anniversary.

Karen Stanek Kirchhofer, Mountain Home, Idaho

Born in New York. Nurse and mother of Kathleen, Courtnay, and Evan.

Designs some quilts. Enjoys hand quilting whole cloth quilts. Has won 1st prize. Member of El-Y-Hee Quil-ter's, Boise Basin Quilters, Utah Quilt Guild, Association of Pacific Northwest Quilters, and Boise Peace Quilters.

Malvia Kiser, Jeffersonville, Kentucky

Quiltmaker. Malvia Adams Kiser was born Nov. 25, 1929, in Knott County, KY. I currently reside in Jefferson-ville, KY. For reasons of necessity my mother taught me to quilt at about the age of 10. My favorite pat-terns are the Double Wedding Ring, Lone Star, and the old traditional patchwork quilts. I also do lots of appliquéd quilts. Most of my quilts cover our beds, and the beds of our family. I have sold some quilts in consignment craft shops and word of mouth advertis-ing. I quilt alone but have made into the hundreds of quilts.

Beatrice Klein, Glendive, Montana

Have been a member of the Sacred Heart quilter's group since its formation in 1984.

M. A. Klein, Portola Valley, California

Designer/artist, maker. Trained as an artist, I have been a quiltmaker since 1980 creating contemporary, narra-tive, one-of-a-kind, mixed-media col-lages using only hand-dyed fabrics, hand and machine stitchery, over-painting, and hand quilting. Most notable of my commissions are "A Most Unusual Watering Hole," 42" x 108", for the Library of Congress, Washington, DC, and six permanent banners, each 78" x 42", for St. Timothy's Episcopal Church, Danville, CA. Other pieces can be found in nine corporate and 38 private collections. My work has appeared in numerous juried and invitational exhibits throughout the country and pieces are included in *Fiberarts Design Books II & III*, and in the *Guild Designer's Books of Artists 8, 9,* and *10,* published by Kraus Sikes, Inc., Madison, WI. I am also listed in *Marquis Who's Who in the West,* 1994 &

1995. I lecture and teach workshops in my unusual technique for fiber groups around the country.

Chosen for large commission for the Library of Congress, Washington, DC.

Esther Knowlen, Eugene, Oregon

Quiltmaker and quilt artist. Esther Knowlen was born in 1923 on a North Dakota farm and started to sew on a treadle machine at age four. Quilting, however, did not become a hobby and a passion until after retirement at age 63. In nine years of quilting, Esther has made 90 quilts of all sizes, and garments, for her own use and gifts. Most of these are original designs. She has also made 37 small quilts for children for donation individually and through guild charities. She prefers machine piecing and does both hand and machine quilting. Designing and carrying out complex pieced designs holds the greatest interest for her. She enjoys design challenges, taking an active role in guild activities, and entering her work in local and national shows; but works primarily for personal creative satisfaction. She has won an award at Houston Quilt Festival, and numerous awards in local shows and fairs.

Greatest thrill was winning a blue ribbon at AIQA show in Houston in 1991 in the "First Quilt" category, and then having that quilt chosen for inclusion in a calendar to be published by Lane.

Evelyn Jane Baumer Kocher, Greenwood, Indiana

I was born September 7, 1933, in Indianapolis, IN. My husband of 43 years, Jim, and I now live in Greenwood, IN, after living all of our lives in Indianapolis. We have two daughters, one son, and one son-in-law. I taught nursery school for 19 years.

I started quilting in the mid-seventies and was going to use all my scraps in a Cathedral Window. I soon found out that wasn't going to happen so went on to patchwork and appliqué.

I have had quilts shown at local shows and at AQS and NQA. I had a block in a JCPenney quilt at the Great American Quilt Festival. A wallhanging was included in *Quilt Art '95*.

I am a member of the Hill Valley Quilt and Travel Society, Quilters Guild of Indianapolis, Quilt Connection Guild, Indiana State Quilt Guild, AQS, and NQA.

Marlene A. Koons, Auburn, California

Marlene Ann Kennedy Koons was born November 16, 1942 in Philadelphia, PA, graduate of Syracuse University. She and her husband, Howard, reside in Auburn, CA.

Wearable art designer and teacher. Quiltmaker, branching out to art quilts using her fabric manipulation ideas.

Exhibitions of Marlene's creative pieces have occurred at local shows and shops, and she has received awards at state fairs. Invited artist 1993 P&B Textile Exhibition on a national tour.

Carin Leigh Cornish Krafft, Bayville, New Jersey

My name is Carin Leigh Cornish Krafft. I was born on March 29, 1957, in East Orange, NJ. I currently reside in Bayville, NJ.

I have been sewing since age 12 and am a self-taught quilter. My first effort was a pastel pinwheel crib quilt. It was machine pieced and quilted. Mainly my quilts are larger wallhangings, but I do make baby quilts and smaller wall quilts. Many of my quilts have become gifts. I also make quilts and donate them for raffles. I get great satisfaction knowing that my quilts are being appreciated and used. Last year two quilts were shown in a local quilt show.

I am pleased that my daughter, Kim, is interested in quilts. They are not just an art form, but a way of life that should be preserved. I collect antique tops and blocks. My collection ranges in age from 1870 to 1930 – 40. I am currently a member of AQS.

Germaine Bold Kramer, Glendive, Montana

Have been a member of the Sacred Heart quilter's group for many years.

Erma Biro Kranstuber, Valley View, Ohio

Erma Biro Kranstuber was born in Cleveland, Ohio, January 26, 1923. Now resides in Valley View, Ohio. My people were the crocheters and also did a lot of embroidery.

With my children grown and married and my husband gone, I decided to try quilting. I taught myself and later took classes to learn more and improve various techniques. I prefer traditional patterns, hand piecing, quilting, Baltimore Album appliqué, stained glass, and creating my own designs.

Learned Brazilian embroidery and encouraged by friends, I started to teach it at age 70. Also enjoy teaching hands-on techniques with quilting, particularly with beginners.

I am a member of NQA, AQS, and am an active member of Ladies of Baltimore, Keep Us in Stitches Quilters, Western Reserve Quilters Anonymous, and North East Ohio Regional Quilters Council of Ohio.

Have received awards in local and national shows and was very proud to see my 4-Leaf Clover Quilt and pattern published in a national magazine.

Quiltmaker, like to add my own touches and design some of my own pieces. I made a quilt for a friend and entered it in a quilt show, it was my first pieced quilt. It won a blue ribbon.

Catherine "Cat" Kreder, Dallas, Texas

Fiber artist, teacher, program founder, historian, guild founder, collector, author, and quiltmaker. I am a native Texan with a BA degree in history and English literature, with a special education certification – secondary education, from the University of Texas – Austin, an associate certification in computer word processing from Brookhaven College – Dallas, a licensed veterinary technician from Texas A&M – Bryan, have a Master's degree in business management from the University of Texas in progress, and am an NQACT program candidate – pending certification 1995.

I consider myself a fiber artist and have done needlework since age 7, being skilled in needlepoint, crochet, knitting, tatting, crewel embroidery, quilting, and heirloom sewing (I am currently learning bobbin lace). I received my first ribbon at age 8, an honorable mention from the State Fair of Texas for a beaded and embroidered Christmas stocking. I continued to expand my needle art background and in 1974 I again won ribbons at the State Fair of Texas for my needlepoint pillows, in 1975 for knitted baby afghans, and in 1976 for crocheted baby items. Throughout the 70's and up to the mid 80's I concentrated on my professional career and the single parenting of my son, then in 1988 I was exposed to and now suffer from the "quilt pox." To date, I have ribbons in quilting, crochet, needlepoint, knitting, and crewel/beaded embroidery. (I have not entered anything in tatting, heirloom sewing, or bobbin lace, yet.)

I am a member of the American International Quilting Association, the American Quilter's Society, the Quilters Guild of Dallas, the National Quilters Association, the Quilters Guild of Arlington, the Cedar Hill Quilters Guild, and founder of The Silver Threads Project – April 1991, and the Quilters Guild of Grand Prairie – July 5, 1993. My memberships also include the American Needlepoint Guild, American Quilt Study Group, the Dallas Lace Society, the Embroiders' Guild of America, Inc., the International Old Lacers, Inc., the Quilters Guild of Mesquite, the Tatters Guild of Dallas, the Grand Prairie Arts Council, and the Dallas Heritage Society.

I am currently a candidate for certification in the NQA Teacher Certification Program, with an interest in their Judge Certification and the American Quilter's Society program for quilt appraisers. I also serve as the chairperson of the City of Grand Prairie, Commission on Disabled Services, and served on the City of Grand Prairie, Commission on Aging – 8/91 – 5/93. In December of 1994 I was approached by Governor Ann Richards to participate in the Federal Ombudsman program for senior citizens and in January of 1995 I became an Ombudsman Intern for the Area Agency on Aging serving in Dallas County, and specifically in the nursing homes located in Grand Prairie.

I am a Dallas Heritage Society tatting docent – Old City Park, a quilting and tatting docent for the Grand Prairie Independent School District, and teach quilting and the six other needle arts I have mastered through the GP Parks & Recreation department and at local quilt shops and area quilt guilds. Additionally in my spare time, I write articles for quilting and needle art publications, with six articles published this year, and have two books in progress – one on the Silver Threads Project, and one fictional historical novel.

My quilts are characterized by transparent, translucent, opaque, and rainbow coloring utilizing out of the ordinary fabric selection and with embellishments from related needle arts – tatting, crewel embroidery, bobbin lace, silk ribbon embroidery, crocheted laces, beading, and needlepoint. Patterns tend to be expanded and explored/modified traditional in nature.

Jan P. Krentz, Lemoore, California

Jan Poulsen Krentz, born March 7, 1955, is a graduate of the University of Nebraska, and married to U.S. Naval officer, Don Krentz. The mother of three children, she has lived in several states, Canada, and Japan.

Jan credits her mother, Joie Poulsen, for fostering a love of needle arts at an early age. She enjoys all aspects of quiltmaking: sewing, quilting, designing, teaching, and lecturing. Jan continually challenges herself with new techniques and methods in contemporary quilting. Jan has been an active member of the following quilt guilds: Thimble Thumbs Quilt Guild, Lemoore (CA), Valley Oaks Quilt Guild, Tulare (CA), Monterey Peninsula Quilt Guild (CA), Creative Textile Guild (VA), and Quilter's Unlimited, Fairfax (VA). She spreads knowledge and enthusiasm to every group, sharing ideas and skills between women in different regions of the country. Jan's quilt, "Spring Crocuses" appeared in the January 1994 issue of *Lady's Circle Patchwork Quilts*.

Audrey Krois, Southampton, New York

I am an artist working in the following two mediums – fabric tapestries and watercolor paintings. I find that I usually focus on one medium at a time because each medium consumes all my energy and attention. Being an artist, I have only created wallhangings of my own design. I like the freedom to create, to use dynamic design, to use whatever kind of stitching is appropriate and to use whatever techniques are needed. As a consequence, I have worked outside the status quo and have developed my own direction and focus. It is exciting now to see the direction of the quilting field in artistic design and the work draw closer to my own concepts. My wallhangings range from representational to abstract design. My work also includes various small fiber constructions, some three dimensional, some two dimensional. These small works are usually mounted in lucite boxes or in matted frames. My work is shown in national competitions and in galleries.

My professional affiliations have been with the Studio Art Quilt Associates, our local guild: The Eastern Long Island Quilters Guild, and the Southampton Artists Association where I have been on the board in a variety of positions including a term of the presidency.

It was of great satisfaction to me to have my patriotic quilt called "Liberty" acquired by the Statue of Liberty Museum on Liberty Island in New York City Harbor and included in their collection. Having incorporated the liberty image into the quilt, I feel it is very appropriate that the quilt is part of this historic setting.

Toni Kron, Guntersville, Alabama

Designer and quiltmaker. Toni Kron was born July 1, 1929, in Wellman, Iowa. She currently resides in Guntersville, Alabama.

Quilting is part of her heritage. As she works over the same quilting frames her grandmother used, she has a penchant for neatness. She began quilting in 1954. Since 1978, with her family grown, it has gradually turned into a business. She designs

her spread-type appliqué quilts making one of a kind. Toni's work is currently more in demand so she also works pieced quilt tops set together by an Amish friend after first choosing the design and material.

She has received numerous awards at local, state, and national competitions along with having a quilt in the MAQS collection. She is a member of NQA and AQS.

Awards received: Best of Show at State Fair and NQA Blue Ribbon, Blue Ribbon, Best Original Design, Viewers Choice on one quilt at Blue Ridge Competition; sale of quilt to MAQS.

Georgean M. Kruger, Shell Lake, Wisconsin

Quilter, designer, instructor, and collector. As an artist, quilter, designer, and teacher, Georgean began her journey into the world of quilting in 1984. She started sewing at the age of 10, first making and designing doll clothes. She began sewing for herself at the age of 12.

If asked how quilting has influenced her life, her reply would be that it hasn't influenced her life, it is her life. She finds the evening and early morning hours to be her most productive time for making quilts and designing patterns. Her husband swears she eats, drinks, talks, sleeps, and dreams about quilts. He is 100% correct. She has explored and taught many areas of quiltmaking both national and international, has been featured in the quilt magazines published by Chitra Publications, her students are encouraged that quilting should be fun. She enjoys collecting old fabrics and recycling neckties, chicken feed sacks, and handkerchiefs into quilts, these quilts are pieces of art that link to her past.

She is an active member of the Wild River Quilters and Piecemakers Quilting Guild of NW Wisconsin, also Minnesota Quilters. She loves making quilts and is fascinated with challenges and new techniques and definitely hooked on quilting.

I have had many special quilting memories, quilters' cruise, Quilters' Heritage tour, retreats, and many workshops. The most memorable experience, was my "Hook and Stitch" quilters' retreat held in Nestor Falls, Ontario at Allen's Crow Lake Lodge. Both husbands and wives attended a trout seminar, during our stay, the ladies quilted by the lake while the fellows fished trout on the lake, what a retreat! Published in Oxmoor Books and *Miniature Quilts,* and two small quilts displayed at Paducah, Kentucky.

Vi Kubas, Glendive, Montana

Member of Sacred Heart Church quilters.

Marit Lee Kucera, St. Paul, Minnesota

Marit Lee Kucera, a Minnesota native from International Falls, is a textile artist, primarily self-taught, who hand dyes cotton and silk yardage for quilters and for her own line of classic-inspired garments. For more than a decade, Marit has provided "atmospheric" (cloud-like) and "echo" (repeated patterns) hand-dyed fabric for quilters worldwide. Marit teaches dyeing, surface manipulation, and garment classes. In addition to the "artstanding" yardage and wearable art, she also creates humorous screen-printed designs with "artspoken" titles and poetic tales for t-shirts and cards.

Mary Jo Kurten, Marceline, Missouri

Mary Jo Kurten was born September 1, 1937, in Humboldt, IA, where she graduated from high school in 1955. With a liberal

arts degree and a major in English, she graduated from Drake University in 1959. She and her husband live in Marceline, MO, where both are employed by Walsworth Publishing Company. Mary Jo is also a field editor for AQS.

Involvement in a group-quilt fundraiser in the late 1970's made Mary Jo a quilter and quilt-lover for life. She opened a quilt shop in Fort Wayne, IN, in 1983 – later moving into an antique complex in Grabill, IN. Her husband's job moved them to Missouri in 1986 and took her out of the retail quilt supply business and back into editing, both full-time for Walsworth and part-time for AQS.

Mary Jo quilts for pleasure and relaxation and supports the industry by investing heavily in books and fabric.

Appliquéd and embroidered quilt: "Autumn in Central Park," Integrated Science and Art project, Marymont School of New York. Art teacher and quiltmaker, Barbara Ledig-Sheehan, classes seventh and eighth. Science teacher, Robert Lynum. Sold at auction in April 1995 for $7,000.

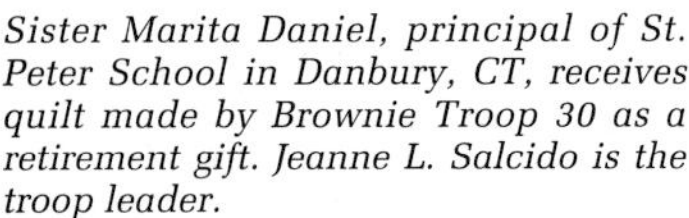

Sister Marita Daniel, principal of St. Peter School in Danbury, CT, receives quilt made by Brownie Troop 30 as a retirement gift. Jeanne L. Salcido is the troop leader.

Janet Grieshaber Lakin, Redmond, Oregon

In Kansas in the 40's and 50's I grew up in a family where the women quilted occasionally. I don't remember not doing needlework. Occupational therapy has been my profession since obtaining a Bachelor's degree from Kansas University and a Master's from San Jose State University.

With our son and daughter in college, my spare time is spent making small quilts, with the goal of making one of every kind, with every technique imaginable! These small quilts are machine pieced, hand quilted, and occasionally embroidered. I have finished over 50 in the past 5 years.

Martha M. Lane, Houston, Texas

I am married to Charles Lane, a wonderful man who supports my every endeavor. I have sewn all my life, starting with doll clothes, progressing to clothes making, ending up at quiltmaking. Quilting has allowed me to express all my creative ideas in a form that will last forever. I am a quiltmaker who likes to design on my computer. I have been fortunate enough to be able to count among my accomplishment having one of my quilts juried into the American Quilter's Society annual show, having quilts exhibited in several American International Quilter's Association annual quilt festivals, and having several of my quilts being awarded blue ribbons at various county fairs and other quilting exhibitions. I have also had a quilt published in the annual AIQA calendar.

The first time I entered the annual AQS show I was accepted and only now appreciate the magnitude of that accomplishment. Being there in person to see my quilt was a memory I will always cherish.

Maxi Lardiere, Ship Bottom, New Jersey

Collector, designer, quiltmaker, fabric maniac, and quilt book librarian. Arrived as an immigrant in the U.S. in 1961. Out of necessity started all types of needlework, saw a quilt show in 1990 in Ohio, and fell in love, attended more shows, workshops, seminars, and read books, books, books; taught herself lots of techniques. Now an avid quilter, she belongs to Pieceful Shores Quilters Guild in Manahawkin, NJ, and exhibits her work. Make

two of almost every project. One to give away and one to keep. Displayed in her house 100 year plus collection of family needlework, passed from generation to generation.

Making a baseball quilt for grandson, Matthew, with signed baseball on the front was one of her most memorable projects.

Wendy Lavitt, New York, New York

Author, curator. Curator: contemporary pictorial quilts for the Kimball Art Center – Park City, Utah.

Author: *Contemporary Pictorial Quilts, Labors of Love: America's Textiles & Needlework 1650 – 1930.*

Martha "Marty" Lawrence, Flint, Michigan

Fabric dyer, quiltmaker, freelance teacher, and author.

Marty was born on November 1, 1953, in Ferndale, MI, to Wilbert and Dolores Calhoun. Her maternal grandmother, Luella Farrell Armstrong Windover Way, a custom dressmaker, introduced her to the passion of sewing as a child. She married Brett Lawrence on 10/6/73, and has two daughters; Samantha Jane born 6/27/78, and Kerstin Jan born 5/27/82.

She graduated from Grand Blanc High School, MI, in 1971 and from University of Michigan-Flint in 1978 with B.S. vocational education. Between 1980 and 1984, she attended the business education graduate program at Michigan State University.

In 1978 Marty made her first quilt and began teaching part-time in an evening adult high school program. Between 1984 and 1987 she sold quilt crafts in Michigan. In 1985 she taught a quilt sampler class for the Stitching Post, Flint, MI.

The colors of hand-dyed quilts in national publications prompted her to follow the directions in a magazine article by Jan Myers-Newbury and she dyed her first colors – eight shades of sky blue in spring 1985. A Kentucky workshop with Kaye Wood, followed by local seminar and a motivating discussion about the budding quilt industry, led to the acceptance of an invitation to sell her initial dyed cloth yardages in fall 1985.

Marty registered the name Kwilts & Kloze and officially opened a fabric design and quiltmaking studio at home in 1986.

Freelance lectures began in 1987 during the county fair in Greenville, OH, and she entered a quilt at a regional show in Battle Creek, MI, and received a second place ribbon. Marty exhibited quilts on a random basis at regional and national shows.

In 1988 she taught her first national dyeing workshop at Ghee's Creative Sewing School in Shreveport, LA. Between 1989 and 1993, Marty wrote for the quilt magazine division of House of White Birches and *Quilting International*.

In 1990 she wrote *Vests to Dye For* after a guest appearance on Kaye Wood's PBS-TV show *Strip Quilting 3*. Kaye edited, published, and promoted the booklet. Marty wrote a dyeing and quilting booklet, *Skyskapes* after her guest appearance on *Strip Quilting 8* and *Quilting For the 90's*. This was self-published.

In 1994 she was predominantly hand-painting silk ribbon with the assistance of both daughters for local quilt shops, Davison Fabrics and Stitching Post in Flint. The ribbon is packaged as Rainbow Ribbon.

She is presently writing a surface design series for the National Quilting Association's, *The Quilting Quarterly*.

Jill Campbell McLean Le Croissette, Carlsbad, California

Born May 2, 1933, Australia. BA Sydney 1953, MSLS Drexel 1962. Married 1960, U.S. citizen 1967. Academic and special librarian; Australia, Britain, U.S. 1953 – 1981.

Specializes in contemporary quilts and wearable art. Member of AQS, AIQA, NQA, AQSG, (British) Quilt Guild, and local guilds.

Juried into Natural Impressions II, Santa Barbara, CA, 1995; Walking Canvas, Fullerton, CA, 1995; Guest lecturer Penasth Quilters, Wales, 1995.

Ann Leatz, Victorville, California

Ann Leatz was born on November 17, 1941, in a beautiful farming community in southwestern Michigan known as Dowagiac. She currently resides in Victorville, California, with her husband.

Ever since Ann can remember, she has loved fabrics and their total pleasures! Ann's first indoctrination to quilting came when her mom and aunts would make quilts to help keep them warm in those cold Michigan winters. They were wonderful, and Ann still has one left from those early days. She began quilting in 1960. Ann made her wedding quilt, and presented it to her husband on their first wedding anniversary. She has pursued her education in textiles and art; achieving degrees in both fields. She began teaching quilting in 1972, and today Ann not only teaches but travels to lecture, judge, and do workshops on a continuing basis. She has received many awards for her quilting locally and nationally. Ann has been published in various quilt publications, not only for her original quilting designs, but also for original counted cross-stitch designs. Ann was nominated for "Teacher of the Year" in 1992. Ann considers herself a quilt artist, always pushing the boundaries of the fabric, and trying new and innovative techniques. She is often invited to showcase her work throughout the country. Ann has served many compacities on art councils and quilt guilds all across the country. Ann was a charter member of NQA. Is a charter, and current member of AQS. Ann is a friend of MAQS. All that I do in quilting and its related fields, has not only been therapy for me, but for everyone whom I've ever taught or come in contact with. What a beautiful heritage we have!

Barbara Ledig-Sheehan, Bronx, New York

Designer, quiltmaker, and teacher. Barbara Ledig-Sheehan was born in Brooklyn, New York. She holds a B.A. from Marymount College, a M. Mus. from Manhattan School of Music and a M.A. from Goddard College. She is chair of the art department at Marymount School of New York. Barbara and her husband, John, reside in the Bronx.

Barbara began quilting in 1976 after taking a workshop with Barbara Danneman at Riverside Church. Since then, she has taught quiltmaking to numerous groups of adults and children. For the past ten years Barbara and her students at Marymount have made quilts in a variety of techniques which have been sold at auction at the school's annual Spring Benefit. Barbara enjoys making story quilts inspired by travel. These quilts are predominantly appliqué with patchwork and embroidery. She is a member of AQS and had two pieces displayed this year at the annual show. Her quilts are represented in several private collections.

In 1992 Marymount students and I made a Columbus quilt which was sold at auction for $15,000. It hung for a time at the State House in Albany, NY.

Marsha Lee, Rochester, New York

Born Dec. 14, 1966, in Brockport, NY, graduated from Victor High School in 1985, received a BA in psychology in 1990. Presently employed for NYS in the office of Court Administration. Began quilting when I was 17 years old. Presently a member of AQS, NQA, and the Genessee Valley Quilt Club. Eight members from the Genessee Valley Quilt Club are making a quilt for the Landmark Society in Rochester.

Carolyn Jarboe Leidecker, Symsonia, Kentucky

Quiltmaker. My interest in quilting began some thirty years ago. I was introduced to the art of quilting by two of my aunts. They had been quilting for many years and attended neighborhood quiltings frequently. It was by their love, encouragement, and patience that inspired me to keep trying.

My first quilts were made for my children. I designed a Dutch doll quilt for my daughter and an Overall Sam for my son. When they married they took their childhood quilts with them.

I felt honored when my daughter-in-law chose to display my son's Overall Sam quilt in the downtown business exhibits during the 1995 American Quilter's Society Show in Paducah.

Quilting is a heritage that we leave for our children and grandchildren. I have a few quilts that belonged to my mother, and my husband has a Double Wedding Ring quilt that was his mother's. These are displayed in our home with lots of fond memories. I feel our lives have been enriched and blessed by their presence.

My friend, Peggy, has been a great influence on my quiltmaking. She encourages me to strive for accuracy, neatness, and to take pride in the planning of my projects.

Quilting for me is a relaxing and rewarding hobby!

Diane Leighton, Yuba City, California

Diane is an enthusiastic teacher whose love of quilting is contagious. Since 1985 she has taught a wide variety of quiltmaking classes at Yuba Community College in Marysville, CA. Her lectures and workshops for quilt guilds have been popular throughout the state. In the March 1993 issue of *Traditional Quilter*, she was the feature teacher. Another magazine article written by Diane appeared in the *American Quilter* in the spring issue of 1995. She is active in the Valley Quilt Guild, having served two years as president, currently as treasurer. A strong supporter of quilting for community service, Diane is a willing participant as well as a leader in the quilting community.

Presently working as a registered nurse (after a 20 year hiatus in the profession), Diane is busy with classes and lectures finding much joy in infecting her students with her love and enthusiasm for quilting.

Chloe Trivett LeMay, Rock Hill, South Carolina

Born in Watauga Valley, Tennessee, 1917, currently residing in Rock Hill, South Carolina. Though I played with it a little, I did not start serious quilting until I retired in 1987. Since then I have made over 100 quilts and given most of them away. Have had articles published in *Quilt Magazine, Quilter's Newsletter, Quilting Today*, and others. In Knoxville, TN, I taught a "Modern Techniques in Quilting" class, made two local TV shows about quilting. Like most of all to do hand work, especially appliqué in silk, but also use machine piecing and machine quilting. Transplanted to Rock Hill, SC, in June 1994, to be with family.

Mary Lou Lembcke, Bloomington, Indiana

Judge, lecturer, teacher, designer, and writer. After painting for many years, I came across the world of quilting. In a second, I was hooked. Upon moving to Bloomington, Indiana, in Dec. of 1980, from Minnesota, I formed the local quilt guild. Today, I am very busy, teaching, lecturing, writing monthly quilt-related articles, and designing my own projects. I work mainly in embellishing crazy quilts and other projects. I depart from the usual crazy quilt, in that, I draw with my needle as an artist paints with the brush. I am not restricted by the fabric lines. I love the freedom and creative possibilities I can do working in this style. I am currently writing my ideas and methods down for a book. It is so thrilling to see my students become excited about discovering crazy quilting. From studio to the fabric shops; from the guild meetings to my small sewing groups. It is a wonderful world to be in.

My most memorable experiences includes starting a guild in Dec. 1980. I was thrilled in Dec. 1990 when my guild presented me with beautiful blocks to celebrate our 10th anniversary.

Lillian J. Leonard, Indianapolis, Indiana

Lillian J. Leonard was born October 2, 1922, in Indianapolis. At the age of 10 she began making embroidered quilt blocks featured weekly in the Indianapolis Star. A year later she started piecing a Grandmother's Flower Garden. After retiring, quilting became her hobby, her solace, and outlet for artistic creativity. She has won many ribbons at state fairs. Her quilts were judged at the Paducah AQS Show for ten years in succession. Her quilt, "Tranquility" is in the permanent collection of MAQS. Her speciality is appliquéd medallion quilts. She is a member of the Quilters Guild of Indianapolis.

Linda J. Lewis, Kailua, Hawaii

I live in the state of Hawaii. My husband and I sailed here in 1978 in a 32' sailboat from Southern California, via Mexico, the Marquesas and Society Islands. We have a son, b/1982 and a daughter, b/1985, and are very involved in their activities from school to sports. I am also very involved with my Brittany dogs, training in obedience, conformation, showing, grooming, and education.

My mother taught me to sew as a child. As I grew older I experimented with different types of needlework – embroidery and crochet lace, more often than not, making up my own patterns instead of following the exact designs of others. I discovered fabric paints in 1980, fooled around with block printing and hand printing and was hooked! At about that time I won a blue ribbon at a local country fair for a hand-painted western shirt.

I have been actively quilting since about 1988, and around that time joining the Hawaii Quilt Guild. I like doing my own thing following whims, ideas, and inspirations. I am fascinated by the traditional geometric pieced blocks, block names, and origins, as well as social aspects of quilting and quilters. Equally intriguing are the many cultural influences to draw from, Seminole, Japanese Sashiko, the colors of the Amish, and appliquéd molas, etc.

Although occasionally I make a bed quilt and pieces with more traditional techniques, patchwork, or appliqué, mostly my work is small, about 3" to wall size. Some portion of the piece is hand painted, usually the central motif, and then hand quilted in large, Sashiko-like stitches using thick black thread. I enjoy combining a hand-painted motif with patchwork, large stitches, and traditional quilting on the same piece. I also enjoy color and integrating my paintings with calicoes, cotton prints, and solids. Many pieces are embellished with small shells, buttons, and beads, some smaller pieces wearable as pins, some as everyday ornaments, and some are professionally matted and framed. (Usually framed in black to enhance the colors.)

My topics are influenced by everything, although I do draw a lot from my tropical surroundings – colors and culture. The light here is amazing and the colors are intense! I like to feel my work is bright and cheerful and am usually not satisfied until a piece "sings" to me upon completion. I exhibit regularly with Hawaii Quilt Guild. In 1990, my pieced Palm Tree block was a winner in the Palm Beach Post Tropical Palms contest. In 1991, my wall piece, "The Colors of Freedom," was a runner up in best use of color category in Piecemakers "Freedom of the Nations" contest. I have also done some pieces for Oxmoor House in *Scrap Crafts for all Occasions* and *Great American Quilts 1992*.

I also teach kids whenever I get the chance and have worked on projects with kids 4th – 8th grades. I've found that combining the hand painting and a larger quilt stitch with the quilt lesson is less intimidating for non-sewers, girls and boys alike. I love that quilting, as a woman's craft/art form, is fast becoming recognized as a valid form of artistic expression, appreciated and cherished by many!

Mary Jo Lewis, Battle Ground, Washington

I never dreamed I would become a quilter. Glenn, my husband of over 43 years, died in August 1991. As a snowbird in Arizona, Jan. 1992, a good friend urged me to take classes from a professional quilter, which I did for two months in Florence. I fell in love with the world of quilting and when I returned home I retired from operating room nursing.

Many talented instructors have contributed to my knowledge and I am grateful to each of them, for there is so much to learn. I sold my motor home and now share my quilt studio with fellow quilters of Battle Ground Quilt Group.

Passion for quilting has saved my mind in time of grief. Quilting is an art for me. I have two married sons and three grandchildren that benefit from my craft.

Amy L. F. Lindberg, Hayes, Kansas

Amy L.F. Lindberg was born July 31, 1963, in Concordia, KS.

She currently resides in Hayes, KS, with her husband. Amy has been quilting since 1980 when she started doing traditional quilts. Over the next several years she developed her own form of appliquilting. Her favorite part of the process is the quilting because then she is almost done.

She recently completed a commissioned piece for IMIA. She has shown quilts at Tactile Architecture, G Street Fabrics, GWU Library, Belle Grove Plantation, and other local shows in the D.C. area.

Amy is a member of AQS, BCQG, and three local groups in Hayes. Her sisters Tina Woodall and Jenny Hubbard also quilt.

Beverly Hicks Ling, Birmingham, Alabama

Quiltmaker, collector, teacher, and secretary of Quilt Alabama. Beverly Hicks Ling was born on January 2, 1954, in Maryville, TN. She has lived in Birmingham, AL, since 1966. Beverly attended college locally. Beverly lives in Birmingham with her husband, Ronald, and their son, Jared, 15.

A self-taught quilter, Beverly began her journey into the world of quilting in 1986. Beverly credits her great-grandmother's memory and the Lone Star quilts she made as her inspiration. The encouragement of others spurred her on in the beginning. Beverly loves traditional quilting and quilts. She loves to give new twists to tradition through color play and arrangement. Smooth, clean lines and appliqué are personal favorites. Beverly's work has won many awards locally.

In keeping with the spirit of giving that quilting represents, Beverly has introduced and taught quilting to many beginners. She was the co-founder of the Heart of Dixie Quilters Guild, where she served as president and newsletter editor for four years. Beverly is a charter member and secretary of Quilt Alabama. In 1993, she was instrumental in the formation of The Central Alabama Cut-Up Quilters and Night Owls. She has been a member of NQA and the AQS since the late 1980's. Received Best of Show – North Jefferson Quilter's Guild Show, 1990, in wall quilts. This was her first entrance in a show.

Beverly Taylor Link, Weaubleau, Missouri

My name is Beverly Taylor Link. I have been quilting since 1968. Prior to that time, I wanted to quilt, but didn't know how, since none of the women in my family did any quilting. What is surprising is that my sister, Dorothy Adamovich, her daughter, Kathy Van Buskirk, and my daughter, Melody Johnson are all quilters!

Mary Stuart Link, Roanoke, Virginia

Wife, mother of four children, needlework artist, designer, framer, and teacher.

Collector of antique quilts, lecturer, quiltmaker, guild member, and officer. Judge of needlework and quilting.

Jeanine Page Linn, Benton, Illinois

Quiltmaker and collector. Jeanine Page Linn, born Nov. 29, 1934, in Detroit, Michigan, youngest of seven children. In 1944 her family moved to "Walls Landing" a farm near Elizabethtown, IL. Attended a one room school at Tower Rock, graduated from Cave-in-Rock High School in 1952, attended SIU. Worked in Chicago for five years.

Jeanine and husband Charles live in Benton, IL. They have one daughter and two grandchildren. Her mother, Mary (Gustin) Page, taught her to sew and crochet. Interested in quilting but not having time until retiring from Old Ben Coal in 1990.

She has quilted Song Birds, Queen Anne Star, which is a whole cloth quilt, winning first place at Duquoin State Fair. Made a Christmas quilt on the serger for granddaughter, Courtney. Designed a wool quilt from family scraps. Designed a quilt from T-shirts that she won at road races. Embroidered phrases on the T-shirts, put silhouettes of her running friends on the border. Now quilting the Lone Star. She is a member of River to River Road Runners and AQS. Her name can be found in the quilters' walk bricks in Paducah, KY. Her quilts are registered with the State of Illinois Early American Museum. Won first place ribbon at DuQuoin, IL, State Fair.

M. Joan Lintault, Carbondale, Illinois

Judge, lecturer, teacher, designer, and writer. Born in New York City, 1938. B.S., State University of New York, New Paltz, and M.F.A., Southern Illinois University, Carbondale. Professor, teaches fibers and textile design, School of Art and Design, Southern Illinois University, Carbondale, IL. Lectures on various surface design techniques throughout the U.S.A.

Ms. Lintault enjoys making quilts and researching various traditional textile techniques that can be used in a contemporary way. She wants every process and technique to contribute to the content of her quilts so she dyes, hand paints, and prints her

---

own images and fabrics. In her quilts it is her objective to produce work that is inspired by nature. She is a teacher who is concerned that many traditional techniques are rejected because they are time consuming.

She was awarded an Illinois Art Council Fellowship in Crafts 1995, an NEA in 1974, a Fullbright Grant to research Japanese dyes and resist techniques 1984 – 85, and an Indo-American fellowship grant to research textile cooperatives and processes in India 1979 – 80. She has exhibited work in numerous galleries in the U.S. and abroad such as the American Craft Museum (New York); The Dairy Barn (Ohio); American Museum of Quilts and Textiles, San Jose, CA; Renwick Gallery in Washington, D.C.; Museu Da Arte Sao Paulo in Brazil; Maronie Gallery in Kyoto, Japan.

Connie Litfin, Carmel, Indiana

Connie Litfin was born September 28, 1946, in Rochester, NY. She currently lives in Carmel, Indiana, where she is employed at Quilts Plus. She is serving as president of the Quilters Guild of Indianapolis, Inc. She is also a member of AQS, Indiana State Guild, and Society of Old Quilters. She began quilting 12 years ago with a friend. Scrap quilts and old looking quilts as well as thirties quilts are her favorites. Her favorite block is a basket.

Catherine Noll Litwinow, Davenport, Iowa

Quilter, collector, lecturer. Catherine Litwinow is a fourth generation Iowa quilter. Quilting is a connecting thread to the past and a record of the present for the future. She holds memberships in AQS, NQA, AQSG, IQG, and MVQG. She teaches and gives quilt presentations to groups and guilds. Collecting and making quilts is a passion.

Her work has been displayed in art galleries in Iowa, Illinois, and Ohio. Some of her quilts were featured in the *Quilting Today* magazine. She helped register and document quilts for Iowa and Illinois and Cody Homestead research projects. Cathy demonstrates quilting at many local events. She has judged, curated, and advised quilt plays and shows.

Quilting accomplishments: Iowa & Mississippi Valley Quilt Guilds award winner; quilts at Quad City Art Council; private one woman show, Cedar Falls Art Gallery, Iowa; and Alma Gallery in Lima, Ohio. Helped with IL & IA documentation projects and chaired Cody Homestead documentation project.

Vicki L. Lockhart, Brighton, Tennessee

Vicki Turner Lockhart was born Feb. 10, 1959, in Calloway Co., KY. She presently lives in Brighton, TN, with husband, David, and daughter, Cheryl. Vicki's interest in art and needlecrafts led her to quilting in 1983. She has since won several awards for her quilts and wallhangings including Best of Show at the Mid-South Fair in Memphis. Her quilted clothing also earned blue ribbons there as well as placing Best of Show in 1989. In recent years, participation in nineteenth century living history has left Vicki little time for competitions but has been a great influence on her quilt work. In striving to re-create the spirit of the 1800's, she uses traditional patterns and fabrics in her current quilts. The Log Cabin and homespuns are favorites.

Nancy L. Losee, Fallbrook, California

Teacher, member of Fallbrook Quilt Guild, collector of old quilts. I have taught semester length beginning and beyond basics quilt classes for Palomar College, San Marcos, CA, 1987 – 91. My foundation of learning at The Quilt Patch, Fairfax, VA, 1980 – 83, was where teacher role models gave me the confidence and motivation to involve myself in teaching quilting.

The special memories I have of quilting are of my many quilt students who allowed me to be a part of their lives, sharing not only the learning process of making a quilt but also the joys and sorrows of their lives.

Martha Theobold Lowery, Greenwood, Indiana

Martha Theobold Lowery was born in Beech Grove, IN, on December 3, 1942. Graduated from George Washington High School in 1960 and Purdue University in 1965. Marti and her husband, Jim, reside in Greenwood, IN, and she is a Medicaid consultant for the state of Indiana.

She began quilting in 1977, when the *Indianapolis Star* and Block's Department Store co-sponsored their first of several quilt contests. The patterns were Ruby McKim's Flower Garden patterns. That first quilt won an honorable mention. Since that first quilt there have been many more quilts winning awards for her quilting at the Indiana State Fair, NQA, *Quilter's Newsletter*, Quilt America! and others. She is a member of AQS, The Quilt Connection, and the Quilters Guild of Indianapolis.

Bethyl Lueck, Jamestown, North Dakota

I have been quilting for several years and find it a thoroughly enjoyable social hobby. I can take it with me when I travel. I am married and my husband and I farm. Our two sons are both doctors, are married, and I have one, soon-to-be two, grandchildren to make quilts for. My niece and I enjoy our quilter's support group, encouraging each other in our projects.

I am past president of the Jamestown Quilter's Guild. I have taught several classes to our local guild. I have worked on our raffle quilt. I also belong to the Quilters Guild of North Dakota.

I have shown my quilts at our annual art show in Jamestown, ND, each December for many years. I have won ribbons at the Indian Summer Quilt Show and Conference in Fargo, ND.

Lois Elaine Lynn, Connersville, Indiana

Lois Elaine Lynn was born December 24, 1954, in Fayette County, Indiana, where she currently resides.

Lois started sewing at the age of 10 with her cousin when their grandmother showed them how to sew doll clothes. As the years progressed she had her clothes win high marks in junior high school and also be shown in their annual fashion show.

She made her first full-size quilt her senior year in high school after first making throw pillows. She subsequently made quilts for all her nephews, nieces, and friends' first borns for the love of it. She now sews, quilts, and crochets for the need of it, but still enjoys it very much. She also has taught several classes for beginning quilters.

Janet Zellman, Karen Price, Rhea Wiens, Zeta Williams & Anita Casey, Fresno, CA.

Roxanne McElroy, in her own unique way, challenges Pat Bishop, of Friendswood, TX, to make a quilt!

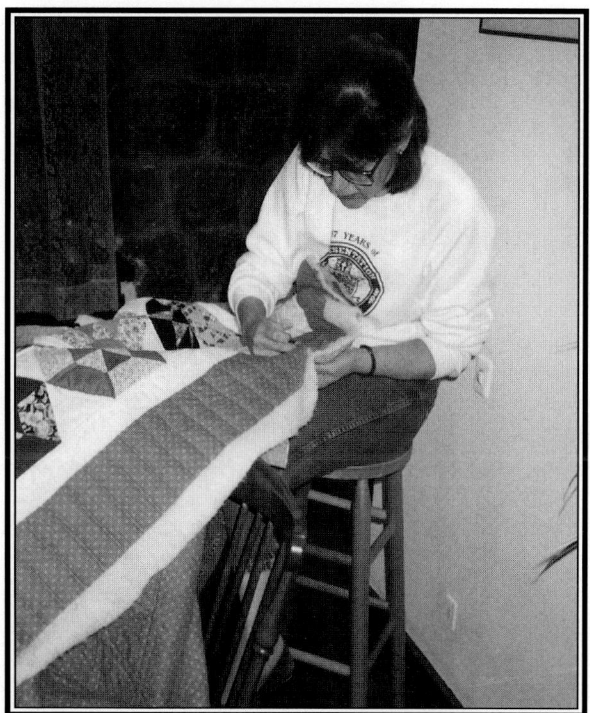

Lita Karlstrand working on "The Last Stitches," Madrid, Spain.

Nancy Elliott MacDonald, Carmichael, California

Quiltmaker since 1988. Completed more than 175 large/small quilts in 7½ years. Has exhibited and won awards at local, national, and international juried competitions. Led local guild project donating over 200 comfort quilts in two years. Contributed quilts to local guild and museum for fundraising projects and auctions. Was featured artist, River City Quilter's Guild Show '94. Attended Quilt Surface Design Symposium and National Quilting Association Short Course on Quilt Judging. Studied with major national quilting instructors. Work has been published in *Quilters' Newsletter Magazine*, *Art Quilt* magazine, and local newspaper magazines.

Patricia C. Magee, Mesa, Arizona

Avid machine piecer and quiltmaker. Wife of retired Navy pilot, Hugh Magee, mother of Laura, Bill & Heather. Raise and breed Scottish Fold cats. Writer, active computer user. Member of AZ Quilters Guild, AQS, North County Quilters Guild, and National Online Quilters. Internet address: BPMW75B@PRODIGY .COM, aka, "The Desert Squirrel."

Making cat quilts for fund raisers. Also hand quilting Grandmother's Flower Garden pieced by my mother and both grandmothers. Many thanks to my quilting mentor and dear friend, Suzie Sergeant of Bucks County, PA, for getting me hooked on quilting.

Kathy O'Meara Magnuson, Elmhurst, Illinois

Quiltmaker, collector, historian, appraiser, and computer designer. My techniques and tastes have evolved somewhat over the four year period since I discovered quilting. Originally a hand piecer, I now piece almost exclusively by machine. Much of my past work had been hand quilted; I'm currently experimenting with free-form machine quilting, embroidery, and surface design techniques. I still do traditional pieces, but increasingly tend to favor more non-traditional work and the use of unconventional designs, fabric, and color choices. I'm also

fascinated by the application of computers in quilting; I use various packages specifically designed for quilting and also software that wasn't created for this purpose. As a result of workshops I've recently taken, I've started creating my own fabric (as if I don't have enough already). Airbrushing, fabric dyeing, painting, and stamping are all very intriguing and provide me with the ability to add truly unique and personal elements to my work.

While my quilts have won awards and been published I think the satisfaction I've gained from group quilting projects is more memorable. I've been a participant in the ABC project; Quilting for the Kids; guild, church, and United Way raffle quilts; and a wide gamut of world-wide projects on the Internet, for friendship quilts and charitable purposes. I consistently find these group experiences rewarding beyond measure.

Cynthia Mahdalik, Stafford Springs, Connecticut

Born October 31, Stafford Springs, CT. Graduated Bay Path College, Longmeadow, MA. Married 30 years to Rudolph Mahdalik, my #1 supporter and my quilt show buddy. Have one daughter, Alana Jean.

Started quilting in 1980. A member of Ellington Country Quilters, Enfield Quilters, Greater Hartford Quilt Guild, Connecticut Quilt Search Project/historian. First quilt won best in show trophy, Hebron Harvest Fair, 1986. Currently very interested in feedsacks. Belong to a Log Cabin group and we meet once a month. Quilting is a major part of my life.

Ricki Lee Moler Maietta, Cogan Station, Pennsylvania

Originally from Mt. Orab, Ohio, I was raised in a family of sewing women. My maternal grandmother, Jessie Mae (Watson) Cremer, was the quilter. Her fabric was "surprise bundles" from catalogs, and I am sure it was the excitement of helping to open those bundles that started my interest in fabric.

My mother, Leona (Cremer) Moler, made an orange and brown

Lone Star entirely by hand as her first quilt. She often said, "Why didn't someone tell me to start with an easier pattern?" She continues to quilt, being interested in miniature quilts and watercolor wallhangings. She and my father, Donald Richard Moler, designed a quilt for my son, Richard in 1983. The quilt depicted "Herky the Beaver," a bedtime story my father told me every night for years, using animal characters from the creek and woods at the edge of town. This quilt was pictured in *Quilter's Newsletter Magazine*.

I made my first quilt in 1982. I am now active in the Tiadaghton Quilt Guild in Williamsport, Pennsylvania, a member of the Pennsylvania Quilters, the American Quilter's Society, and Quilt Restoration Society. My interests are the extremes – antique quilts and contemporary art quilts. I am developing a wallhanging design that takes its inspiration from the floral still lifes of nineteenth century painter, Severin Roesen. My original design "Star Trek" was featured in November 1992 *Traditional Quiltworks* magazine, and the same magazine has plans to run an article and pattern of an antique quilt from my collection sometime in 1996. I harbor the usual frustration of having more ideas than time, and intend to live to be 200 so that I may finish everything in my mind's eye.

Lyn Oser Mann, Lake Forest, California

Teacher, designer, and lecturer. Born and raised in Cleveland, Ohio, Lyn Mann was taught embroidery at an early age and fell in love with needlework. After receiving her Bachelor of Arts degree from Bowling Green State University, she moved to Southern California with her husband. Shortly after being widowed, she took her first quilting class in 1981 and was hooked. Lyn started teaching in 1987 and specializes in scrap quilts, the more fabrics the better. She is also known for her ability to put colors together. Lyn's love for her craft comes through strongly in the classroom. Lyn is an active member of Flying Geese, Orange County, and Beach Cities Quilt Guilds as well as Northern and Southern California council of quilt guilds. She was also past president of Flying Geese. She now lives in Lake Forest, CA, with her son, Damon, and two cats, Tela and Raz.

Honors include being the featured artist at the Irvine Fine Arts Center in 1989, and featured quilter at the Flying Geese quilt show in 1994.

Sheila Marie, Woodridge, Illinois

A self-taught crafter from an early age, Sheila was introduced to quilting in late 1989. Sheila's favorite aspects of quiltmaking are

designing and precision piecing, developing quilts of her own design, pieced and quilted by machine. Her approach incorporates simple lines, texture, color, and illusion. She has produced one-of-a-kind commissioned work with tucks and textures, and also delves into the realm of Escher with tessellating designs.

Sheila was born September 24, 1954, in Minneapolis, MN, and currently resides in the Chicago, IL, area. She holds degrees in pharmacy and business/marketing and practices pharmacy at a local hospital. In pursuit of quilting as her avocation, Sheila has taught and lectured locally and has served on the boards of her local guild and the IL Regional Quilters Network (IRQN). She is a member of Pride of the Prairie Quilters, Riverwalk Quilters Guild, IRQN, and AQS.

Ann P. Tutor Marks, Yuba City, California

Ann P. Tutor Marks was born May 23, 1939, in Miami, FL. Married in Tracy, CA, Nov. 21, 1958, raised two children, one daughter, one son. Sewing has always been a part of my life, making clothes, curtains, fishing gear holders, etc. I taught crafts to youth for years. I live in Yuba City with my husband, Bill. We both are retired after working many years. We have one grandson.

I made my first quilt blocks the first year I was married as my husband worked nights and went to college days. He purchased me my first sewing machine so I would have something to do when I got off work. I remember my grandmother's quilts and always wanted one for me to keep but I did not put my first quilt together till many years later. I started taking quilting classes through Yuba College night classes and met many other women who were interested in forming a quilting group of our own. I started the first quilt guild with a meeting in my home and a bank account for dues money and a post office box in January 1982. We started with only 9 members and in 1994 we had almost 300 members. In March, 1995 we held our 12th annual large quilt show which as usual was very successful. We all share our talents, ideas, and work together doing many good things in the community through our quilting.

My favorite quilts are crazy quilts. I do all types of quilting and enjoy it more than ever. Our guild assisted the Mormon church in putting on all types of classes in quilting so more people could learn all about quilting. I love the sharing part of quilting, such as our quilt show, teaching, and telling all about quilts.

I am so pleased people are more and more aware of quilts and what beauty, warmth, and pleasure they can bring. I stay very active in the local quilt group and I am a member of American Quilter's Society and the Northern California Quilt Council, and serve as chairperson for the Valley Quilt Guild.

Mary Ann Marman, Glendive, Montana

Stitched only patchwork quilts for many years as part of the Sacred Heart Quilter's Group. Now that I am retired, I have expanded into other forms of quilting. I am a beginner, approaching intermediate quilter! Won first prize at the county fair on my first quilt – the Lover's Knot pattern.

Gwen Marston, Beaver Island, Michigan

Author, teacher, quiltmaker. Gwen Marston is a professional quiltmaker, author, and teacher who has written twelve books, and produced a series of videos on quiltmaking. She has taught quilting across the United States and in Japan. She has been a regular columnist for *Lady's Circle Patchwork Quilts* magazine for ten years.

Her quilts have been shown in many exhibits throughout the United States and abroad. A selection from her collection of more than 240 small quilts has been exhibited by seven museums over the past several years. Her work is represented by the Tamarack Craftsman Gallery in Omena, Michigan. For 13 years Gwen has offered quilting retreats at her Beaver Island home on Lake Michigan.

Katie Pasquini Masopust, Santa Fe, New Mexico

I have been quilting since 1978. I travel throughout the world to teach and lecture on my personal style. I have gone through several quilting styles, and have written books on each: *Mandala Quilt Designs*, *Isometric Perspective*, and *Fractured Landscapes*.

Beth A. Mastin, Plymouth, New Hampshire

Collector, designer, quiltmaker. Beth A. Mastin was born in Sacramento, CA, January 27, 1966, but grew up in Plymouth, NH. Currently she resides in Plymouth, NH, with her husband and two children. She spent her childhood among quilts and quilt-making since her mother, Mary Emma Allen, operated a quilting business in their home and wrote articles about quilts and quiltmakers. Currently Beth is a stay-at-home mom and works on quilting projects in her home, making them for her family's use and for sale. She also collects old quilts, fabrics, and patterns, and is restoring some old family quilts.

Judy Mathieson, Woodland Hills, California

Quiltmaker, author, teacher. Judy has a B.S. in home economics from California State University, Northridge, and has been teaching quiltmaking since 1977. She lectures and conducts workshops throughout the United States for quilt guilds and conferences and has taught internationally in Canada, Japan, Australia, and Scotland. She exhibits regularly in national juried quilt shows and her work often appears in national quilting publications. She is certified by the National Quilting Association as a judge and teacher of basic quiltmaking. Her book *Mariner's Compass: an American Classic* was published in 1987, and *Mariner's Compass Quilts: New Directions in 1995*, by C&T Publishing. She lives in the Los Angeles area with her husband, Jack. They have two sons.

I have belonged to a quilting group of about 14 women since 1977. We call ourselves the Loose Threads. Each spring for the last six years we have gone on a wonderful retreat in the Santa Barbara area for about four days. Most years we have worked as a group to create a fund-raising quilt for one of our members who has a profoundly retarded child living in a community home. We all come home feeling closer to each other, refreshed by the spirit of involvement.

Merry May, Tuckahoe, New Jersey

Merry and her husband, Joe, share their home with their two teenagers (Sarah & Jim), two dogs, and two dozen chickens (who reside in their own little house!). Merry is "acknowledging those who have helped her" by serving as president of both the Tri-State Quiltmaking Teachers and South Shore Stitchers (local guild). She has been a regional coordinator for the American Quilt Study Group since 1992. She actively participates in monthly charity quilt workshops, and happily serves as a "walking encyclopedia" on many aspects of quiltmaking. She also likes to offer "a leg up" to others who are new to our industry, in order to help them succeed.

In 1994, sixteen years after making her first pillow, a hard winter and a husband recovering from surgery brought on "a major case of cabin fever." Merry decided there had to be a way to mass produce Flying Geese units. After a dozen or so icy trips to the library's copy machine, she produced a grid which could achieve her goal. She then jumped into the marketing world with both feet. One year later she officially introduced GRIDDED GEESE© during Spring Quilt Market in Charlotte, NC.

In April 1993, Merry was asked to make a presentation quilt for Virginia Gunn, the departing president of the American Quilt Study Group. The quilt included signature blocks from 65 notable quilters and quilt historians. It was also the last project which Merry shared with her grandmother, Elizabeth Evans, who had taught her to sew 30 years earlier. "Libby" passed away about 2 weeks before the quilt's completion.

Teressie May, Mt. Morris, Michigan

Teressie May was born January 27, 1932, in Ozan, Arkansas, graduated from Clow Training School in 1950. Teressie and her husband, David, live in Mt. Morris, MI.

She began piecing quilts at the age of 6, by observing her grandmother (Bell White) and stepmother (Rosie White). She began quilting before graduating from high school. Teressie has taken quilting classes but is mostly self-taught. She has taught quilting since 1977. She has taught classes, performed demonstrations, presented slide presentations, and set up displays in the following facilities: Senior Citizen Quilt Factory, Flint Community Schools, local churches, Flint Institute of Art, Flint Urban League, Michigan Historical Museum (Lansing, MI), and Crossroad Village (Flint).

She is a member of Flint Afro-American Quilters Guild which has held its 5th annual quilt show (1990 – 1994). She is also a member of AQS and Michigan Quilting Network.

Teressie is teaching her granddaughter, Teressie Davis, age 12, the art of quiltmaking. Designing and machine quilting are favorite parts of Teressie's quiltmaking.

Virginia Mayes, Alexandria, Virginia

Quiltmaker. One of my grandmothers made appliqué quilts and the other made crazy quilts. My mother didn't quilt, but sewed most of our clothes, and taught me to use the sewing machine at an early age. In elementary school I did crewel embroidery and sewed clothes. I made two tied comforters in college, but got hooked on counted cross-stitch in graduate school and did not quilt again until 1987 when I made a Triple Irish Chain for a friend's wedding gift. I have since finished 13 baby quilts for

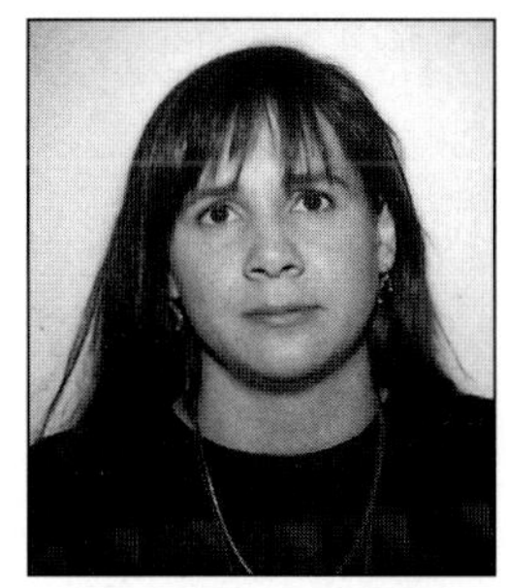

nieces, nephews, and friends. I am currently working on a Kaleidoscope quilt and finishing quilting an Amish Diamond in the Square. I am mostly self taught and do machine piecing, hand appliqué, and hand quilting. I have exhibited quilts in Virginia and New York.

Lynne McCaffry, Monroe, Wisconsin

Quiltmaker and teacher. The evening about 8 years ago that I walked into Sandy Wakeman's quilt class in Baldwin, Kansas, my life changed forever. Sandy is a gifted and enthusiastic teacher and I would guess that an extraordinary number of people who take her beginning quilt class continue to quilt for the rest of their lives. I was certainly hooked. My husband and I have lived many places following our careers (he in education and me as a librarian/researcher/historian) among them Indiana, North Carolina, Wyoming, and Kansas. Kansas was not my favorite place – as a northerner it was too hot and dry for me. But in Kansas, you can't sling a cat without hitting a quilter (I have beautiful cats and would never seriously consider slinging any of them) and I believe I was meant to be in Kansas for a while to acquire one of the loves of my life. I am now back "up north" and still quilting and teaching when the occasion presents. My love of history and of quilting complement each other well, and I hope to pursue both for many years to come.

My most memorable quilting experience was helping to launch the Maple Leaf Quilt Guild in Baldwin City, Kansas, and to serve as the secretary/historian/newsletter editor for the guild. A close second was teaching half the junior class at the local high school how to quilt and completing a raffle quilt with them.

Pauline G. McCall, Tampa, Florida

Born in Michigan in 1915. Studied art at the Chicago Art Institute and the American Academy of Art. Worked in design studios until marriage when I moved to Michigan. Became a floral designer for 10 years. Began 1st quilt "To My Daughter With Love" in 1975, a crazy quilt, five years in the making which covered her growing up years. 2nd quilt: "Coffee," silk screen and appliqué for my artist son who likes lettering, coffee, and brown colors. 3rd quilt: "Memories" for the Statue of Liberty Contest 1986 (was runner-up from the state of Florida). 4th quilt: "World Map" for a neighbor couple, he served on the S.S. Jacksonville. 5th quilt: "Garden Jewels" for American Flower Garden International Contest 1991 by The American Folk Art Museum in New York, Northern Tissue, and *Better Homes & Garden* magazine (one of 12 winners). 6th quilt: "Curwood's Castle and 11 Centenarians," 1994, a gift to the Historical Society in Owosso, Michigan. 7th quilt: "Salem, Massachusetts," 1995, appliqué and embroidery for my granddaughter, now in progress. I work independently and design and make each quilt.

Irene McCann, Clearlake, California

Irene McCann's family submitted the following biography as a special surprise Christmas present: Irene McCann is a 79 year old great-grandmother who has been quilting, to delight of her family for over 65 years. In the beginning, her quilts were a matter of necessity, times were hard and money was scarce. As time went on, her quilts became a treasure for anyone who was fortunate enough to get one.

Many people benefited from Irene's quilts. If a person was strong enough to fight off her daughter and daughter-in-law, they earned a quilt. Every new baby, wedding, anniversary, graduation, or other special event warranted a quilt, at least as far as family members were concerned. Rumor even has it that there were marriages just to get one of her quilts and custody battles when break up occurred.

Irene's favorite quilt is the Double Wedding Ring with the Dresden Plate running a real close second. She finally got to keep one of her own quilts (her daughter didn't see it in time) when she made a Double Wedding Ring for her own 50th wedding anniversary. Congratulations!

In most recent years, Irene began making quilts using pre-made scarves with the Harley Davidson design for charity events and motorcycle runs. These have helped to raise money for many a worthy organization and have become so popular with the local motorcycle clubs that she is booked up for years in advance. The riders enjoy the motorcycle motif and the idea of owning something that someone put so much love and devotion into.

We lost count years ago of exactly how many quilts Irene has made...far too many to count. We just know that any person who gets one feels a special kind of love and caring. A bad day is made better by cuddling up under one of these special quilts with a cup of hot tea. Even the smallest baby, and there are many wrapped in her special quilts, feels warm, safe, and protected. Yes, she puts love into every stitch. She claims her stitches are getting bigger these days but that just means there's more love in each and every one. We can never tell her in words how much her and her very special talent means to us, but from all of us, children, grandchildren, great-grandchildren, and the many others in homes and hospitals that have benefited. Thanks mom, we love you.

Janice L. Ferguson McClung, Jacksonville, Florida

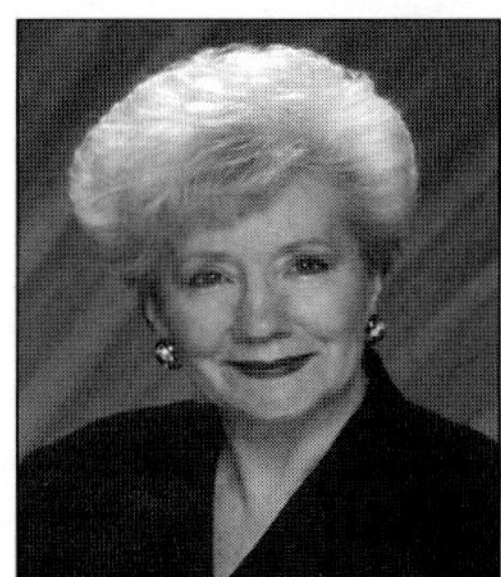

Quiltmaker and designer. As a girl my mother taught me to sew for pleasure and artistic release, after my husband died I made quilts to help support my family, the hobby expanded to wonderful heights yet remains my dearest personal joy.

A memorable quilting experience was when I was commissioned to make and design a quilt for Princess Beatrice of England. Featured in *Great American Quilts, 1988*; displayed quilts at West Virginia State Fair.

Jessie Wall McCoy, Decatur, Georgia

Jessie Wall McCoy was born March 6, 1921, in Virginia, but grew up in North Carolina. She learned to quilt from her paternal grandmother. College, marriage, birth of five children, 16 years as an overseas missionary, allowed no time for quilting. In the 60's quilting began to come back into her life and grew until, in retirement, it has become Jessie's number one activity. A scrapoholic and traditional quilter, she nevertheless likes to try new techniques, and makes all sizes and types of quilts. She quilts for the pure joy and fun of seeing the fabrics come together. Her works may be given to family or friends, never sold. Jessie belongs to her local guild, AQS, NQA, AIQA, and is a supporter of MAQS. She attends workshops and expositions in other countries and enjoys friendships with several international quilters.

Donna Shrout McDade, Middletown, Ohio

Author of 18 foundation piecing books, teacher, quiltmaker, and designer. Donna Shrout McDade was born January 19, 1940 in Middletown, Ohio. She attended Miami University. She is a secretary and computer operator. She and her husband, Paul, reside in Middletown, Ohio. Together they have six children and 18 grandchildren.

Donna has won around 200 ribbons with her many hobbies and cooking including a Best of Show in quilting. Some of the classes she teaches: English Piecing, Seminole, Foundation Piecing, Ruching, and Indian Ribbonwork.

Following shoulder surgery, she was unable to sew or quilt, so began designing foundation piecing patterns, eventually publishing more than 1,000 patterns in 18 books. Her work has appeared in: *Quilter's Quarterly, Lady's Circle Patchwork Quilts, Quick and Easy Quilting, Quilt World,* and *Miniature Quilts.*

Quilt guild membership: founding member and past president of Buckeye Blossoms Quilt Guild, current president of Oxford Piecemakers, Southern Ohio Snob Quilters, National Quilting Association, American Quilter's Society, Clinton County, and Ohio Valley.

Bobbie-Frances McDonald, Huntington Beach, California

Bobbie-Frances McDonald born April 12, 1945, has always done needlecrafts but only discovered quilting in Nov. 1990. In April 1992 she retired from nursing after 25 years so she could quilt full time. Although she makes contemporary wall quilts, she collects vintage bed quilts and consequently now enjoys quilt restoration and renovation also.

A member of AQS, NQA, Quilt Restoration Society, and Flying Geese Quilt Guild. She has won prizes at the Orange County Fair. She designed and made the appliquéd Victorian Farmhouse Block of the bridal quilt in Steven Spielberg's movie *How to Make an American Quilt* attributed to Anne Bancroft's character, Glady Jo. There are two generations of quilters in the family now that she taught her mother the art in 1994.

Ruth B. McDowell, Winchester, Massachusetts

Born in Washington D.C., June 8, 1945. B.S. in art and design, Massachusetts Institute of Technology, 1967.

In 1972, she began her quiltmaking career inspired by Ruby McKim's 101 Patchwork Patterns. She encountered the world of contemporary quilting in 1978, in the quilts of Nancy Halpern and Rhoda Cohen.

Ruth began to develop her skills as an artist and designer of quilt blocks. Her quilts were first featured in *Quilter's Newsletter Magazine* in 1982.

Since that time she has become a full-time professional quilt artist, leading an active career in teaching and lecturing nationally and internationally, and exhibiting and selling her work. With over 275 quilts to her credit, she is also the author of *Pattern on Pattern*; The Quilt Digest Press, 1991, and *Symmetry: A Design System for Quiltmaker's*, C&T Publishing, 1994. Featured also in the "Quilters Stars" video series.

Dierdra A. McElroy, Martinez, California

Designer, quiltmaker, and teacher. Dierdra A. McElroy was born in Denver, Colorado, August 10, 1966. Her corporate executive father helped her to experience and understand people of many customs and cultures as they moved around the world. She spent her childhood playing in every sport she could find with obvious impatience to experience to the maximum level. At the same time her creativity kept screaming for an artistic outlet. She would sit and draw for brief periods between sporting events but could never manage to sit still long enough to accomplish much.

After graduating from Texas A&M in 1991, she married and had a child, Victoria Renee. Her creativity came to the foreground while teaching junior high school French and gifted studies but it was not until her mother, Roxanne McElroy, recruited her to take over the mainland operations of her quilting business so she could be with her husband in Hawaii that DiDi's creative abilities really began to blossom.

Being a single parent and managing a busy office is time consuming but DiDi has managed to find time to develop her quilting skills to the professional level of her mother. She teaches needle-turn appliqué and hand quilting in California. She has the whole world to look forward to in quilting and as usual, she is impatient to experience it to the maximum degree!

Roxanne H. McElroy, Mililani, Hawaii

Author, designer, lecturer, teacher, and quiltmaker. Roxanne H. McElroy attributes her quilting abilities to the quilting genes she inherited from her grandmother, Gladys Charlotte Lee. She has been quilting since 1987 but came into it with hurricane force. Before her first year anniversary she had already formed her own pattern company, done her first lecture, and written her first article!

Roxanne lived in Tahiti for a number of years and brought back with her from that country not only award-winning quilting talents but the conviction that every effort made by anyone can be improved by having a party atmosphere – so she carries her own personal party around with her wherever she goes!

She is always looking for new ways to help her friends' creative growth. In 1994 she cut 2,000 squares of scrap fabric, glued them to 2,000 bamboo shish kabob skewers and stuck them in the front lawn of her friend in Friendswood, Texas. She challenged Pat Bishop to make a quilt from the fabrics and it turned out to be a wonderful experience for them both. Roxanne was born in Denver, CO, April 4, 1947, and grew up in Englewood, CO, but has spent her married life moving around the country with her corporate executive husband. She has enjoyed getting used to new routines and customs while living in Utah, Montana, Texas, California, Georgia, and Hawaii.

The Tahiti move, however, seems to have had the greatest influence on her quiltmaking. She teaches and lectures on the subject on a national level and has been featured at such illustrious events as AIQA Houston, AQS Paducah, and NQA. She appears annually at the Mid-Atlantic Quilt Festival in Williamsburg, VA, the Pennsylvania National Quilt Extravaganza in Fort Washington, Pennsylvania, and the Pacific International Quilt Festival in Santa Clara, CA.

Roxanne designed and developed the phenomenally popular Roxanne's Thimble and Roxanne's Quilter's Choice Pencils, which are both distributed internationally. She is a contributing author of three books and will have two of her own out on the market by 1997.

Maureen H. McGee, Lansing, Kansas

After a short time of making traditional quilts in 1979 – 80, I began collaborating with Sarah A. Dickson and making quilts from traditional patterns but with a definite contemporary look. We were strongly influenced at first by Roberta Horton's "Amish Adventure." The play of color, both bold and subtle, against black was very appealing to both of us.

We have been fortunate to have been awarded a blue ribbon at the AIQA show for our quilt "Cygnus X-1" and have shown at the AQS show as well as numerous quilts shows, particularly in Texas and Kansas. Our work has been featured in *Quilter's Newsletter Magazine, Patchwork Tsuchin,* and two books by Joen Wolfrom, the Lang Calendar, along with exhibits in the United States, Europe, and Japan. We were also chosen to make the raffle quilt for the AIQA show in 1990. We continue to collaborate and to grow as individuals in this artistic endeavor.

Susan McKelvey, Millersville, Maryland

Susan McKelvey is a quilt artist, teacher, and the author of several books on quilting. She has been quilting since 1977, and her work has appeared in museums, galleries, and quilt shows throughout the United States, as well as in magazines and books. She began her company, Wallflower Designs, in 1987 to design and produce unusual quilt supplies and patterns. In the days before quilting, Susan earned her BA in English from Cornell College and her MA in English from the University of Chicago. She has taught English in the United States and in the Peace

Corps in Ethiopia, from 1966 to 1968. She currently resides in Maryland with her husband, two golden retrievers, and two cats, while her two children are off at college.

Barbara McKie, Lyme, Connecticut

Designer, quiltmaker, makes imprinted products for quilters, and offers service of fabric transfer. Barbara Barrick McKie, from Lyme, CT, has been a quilter since 1971. Barbara graduated from Purdue University, took computer courses at Thames Valley Community College, and has an M.S. degree in marketing from Rensselaer. She was a professional quilter in the 70's. Seventeen of her quilts are featured in Time-Life Family Creative Workshop (Quilting and Trapunto), McCall's Contemporary Quilting, *The Complete Guide to Quilting* by Heard and Pryor, and *The New York Times.* Several galleries have shown her work. She taught quilting before becoming an automation consultant, but has just returned to professional quilting.

Utilizing her background, Barbara incorporates computer-printed fabrics in her art quilts, which often celebrate people and events. As a genealogist, she documents family histories through her quilts. Barbara owns Graphic Memories by McKie, a business offering fabric transfer service for photos and computer images. She also creates and sells imprinted items such as shirts and tote bags for quilters. She is a member of AQS and Shoreline Quilters Guild.

Cheryl L. Mercer, Macon, Georgia

A member of Patchwork Pals Guild & Georgia Quilt Council, Cheryl began quilting in college. A fund raiser & researcher with the Georgia Quilt Project for three years, she now concentrates on quilt restoration, design, commissions, and trapunto, despite working full time for the government. Her quilts have earned ribbons in many S.E. shows and have sold throughout the country.

A former Miss Teen-Age Macon and Miss Teen-Age Georgia, she frequently makes guest appearances at historic sites & tourist attractions in authentic 1800's outfits, demonstrating quilting to stimulate public awareness and interest. She participates in a round robin with other volunteer "historic quilters" around the country to share information and encouragement.

Carol Warner Mesimer, Boones Mill, Virginia

Born in Bardstown, KY, on June 27, 1955, Carol was taught an appreciation for handwork by her mother, Helen Mann Warner.

Her needlework talents include crochet, knitting, needlepoint, embroidery, tatting, and fine hand sewing. All this naturally led to quilting. A member of Star Quilters Guild, Lake Quilters, and The Baltimore Appliqué Society, she is on the board of the first two. She and her husband of 10 years have one son, Raymond, now six years old.

Carol is currently teaching quilting in the Mid-Atlantic region. Her classes include miniature Baltimore Album appliqué, 3-D ribbon flowers, 4-Patch Kaleidoscope, and more. She designs her own quilts, including her Baltimore Blocks. The silk ribbon embroidery work in the book *Unique Sewing Treasures* by Ginny Watson, was done by Carol. A pattern book for Carol's quilt, "Baltimore Baby" is in the process of being written.

Among the many projects that are currently ongoing, her personal favorite is her series of quilts titled "Quilting Against Cancer." The quilts are made and donated to families raising money to pay for cancer treatments. She has also worked on several raffle quilts for the various guilds, won many ribbons for her work, including reserve champion, grand champion, and twice winning best in show. She has been showcased on two local television shows, Channel 10's *Spirit of Virginia* and *Libby's This and That* with Libby Thompson on cable channel 12. A second feature on this show is scheduled for summer 1996.

Carol Meyer, Ruidoso, New Mexico

Born and raised in New York, Carol has lived most of her life in New Mexico. She is a registered nurse, married 30 years, has four grown children, and one granddaughter. She moved to Port Charlotte, FL, in 1991 and recently moved back to New Mexico part-time enjoying the best of both worlds.

Carol discovered quilting in 1979, became a professional in 1984, and was the New Mexico winner of the Great American Quilt Contest in 1986. She has won numerous awards at National Quilting Association, American-International, and many other shows around the country. Her work has been exhibited in Japan, Great Britain, and in this country at the Cornell Museum in Palm Beach, FL., Schweinfurth Museum in NY, State Capital in Santa Fe, NM, and the Woodlawn Plantation at Mt. Vernon, VA. In 1992 she had a one person art-quilt show at the Venice Art Center in Venice, FL.

Carol teaches at Cloth World stores throughout the southeast United States. Her specialty is pictorial quilts and she will be marketing pictorial quilt patterns shortly from her business in Ruidoso, NM.

Georgellen Mikkelson, Madison, Wisconsin

Georgellen Ouellette Mikkelson grew up in San Diego, CA, attended college in Missouri, lived in Kansas, Alabama, and Illinois, before moving with her family to Madison, WI. She has a B.A. in home economics education plus additional credits earned in art, design, studio art, and elementary education.

For more than 20 years Georgellen has been teaching, lecturing, showing, collecting, selling, and making quilts. Currently she enjoys selling/showing at art galleries, teaching/lecturing for guilds and International Quilt Festival. Each spring/fall she conducts tours to an Amish area.

She has displayed quilts at AQS shows, chaired an international show in Madison, was awarded an art grant in 1992, has been featured in several publications, and founded or is a charter member of 6 quilt guilds.

Bonnie Miller, Poplar Bluff, Missouri

Collector. My name is Bonnie Miller. I am a member of AQS. I am a quilt collector. I, as a beginner quilter and collector, have a love for this hobby that goes back to my mother, Mrs. Myrtle Hart. She made several quilts years ago and I inherited most of those when she passed away.

My mother left me with a special memory. As a child, I use to play under the quilting frame that hung from the ceiling in the farmhouse. I got to quilt when I was 8 years old. My stitches are still in that quilt today.

When I am quilting or going to purchase a quilt I feel like my mother is always there beside me.

Phyllis D. Miller, Murray, Kentucky

Phyllis D. Miller, from Murray, Kentucky, is a graduate of Berea College. She began quilting in the summer of 1968 and has since made numerous quilts and wallhangings. She is a quilt teacher

whose quilts have been exhibited and won awards on the local, state, and national levels. Her favorite parts of quilting are designing, choosing the colors, and deciding on an appropriate quilting design. She promotes using creative and innovative quilting designs to make every quilt unique. She makes both traditional and contemporary quilts often combining both ideas in one piece. Her book, *Encyclopedia of Designs for Quilting* will be published by AQS in 1996.

Phyllis has served as first vice president and assistant treasurer of NQA. She is an active supporter and member of the Kentucky Heritage Quilt Society where she is currently the museum and archives committee chairman and also served as president. Quilters' Day Out in Kentucky was started by Phyllis and has since become National Quilting Day.

Sharon H. Miller, Errol, New Hampshire

Married, mother, grandmother, nurse, social worker, Ph.D. Needle artist. Made a surprise Baltimore Album wallhanging for husband's retirement as district court judge; scene was of us and our two labrador retrievers hunting in Maryland. Now I am designing a Baltimore Album mourning quilt in memory of mother and four generations. The message will be of hope in finding a cure for breast cancer, which is intergenerational in the family.

Sandra T. Mitchell, Nocona, Texas

Born and reared in Texas. Mother of two and grandmother of three. Work full time as an office manager of an oil field construction company in our small town. I think I was born with a needle in my hand. Past president of Red River Quilt Guild in Wichita Falls, Texas, presently historian. Occasionally teach, especially dimensional appliqué.

Attending AQS show with my travel friends and seeing the delight on faces when I gave them a quilt I have made for them was a truly memorable experience.

Sibyl (Darling) Mizer, Breckenridge, Michigan

I'm 77 years old. I was married 54½ years and had two sons. Have five grandchildren, two step-grandchildren, three great-grandchildren, two step-great-grandchildren. During the early 1930's my girlfriend and I each started our first quilt. I was 12

years old and the pattern was a Wedding Ring. We moved from where we were living and I put my quilt away in a box. I finished making my quilt in 1939 and my grandmother, Whitney, helped me quilt it. I was married in 1940. During the first 30 years of my marriage I made quite a few quilts and baby quilts.

After retiring from secretarial work in early 1970's I decided I would make quilts. So far I have made over 130 quilts plus over 50 baby quilts, lap quilts, and doll quilts. I quilted all of them and over half of them I handmade the top. I've also made and quilted for other people.

During the 1950's I visited my great-aunt Caroline Herlings, she was getting ready to move and she had a quilt with an orange background and six dark blue snowflakes. She had a blue ribbon from the Detroit State Fair in 1916. I purchased the quilt for $15 and in the 1980's it was appraised for $950. This quilt is my pride and joy and I have one cut out to appliqué.

One year I made a large handmade pink quilt. There was so much quilting on it that when I was through I said I wouldn't make another unless I would get $800 for it. I received a blue ribbon from the Saginaw Fair and I had it appraised for $800. There is only a few of my quilts that anyone has helped me quilt.

I belong to a quilting club. We quilt twice a month, from October to May each year at the Lakefield Township Hall. Our group of quilters has gone to the Saginaw Michigan Fair each year and we quilt. Have lots of memories. We used to have a van and we gals would all ride in it. One time I was overloaded. There was 11 of us in the van. I told them not to tell my husband. I've entered my quilts in the Saginaw Fair and received ribbons on them.

When I first started to quilt I made goofs. One time I wanted to make a diamond quilt and I didn't have a pattern so thought I would just cut one. I did and when I sewed them all by hand the diamond didn't lay smoothly so I had to take it all apart. After that except a flower garden that I didn't sew correctly I used my head. Getting them sewn by hand and having to unrip them is not a lot of fun. It causes one to think before acting.

I enjoy the old patterns and have made a lot of different ones. This coming winter I'm really going to make quilts.

Rose Momsen, Puunene, Hawaii

Quiltmaker of contemporary art quilts, designer, and community college teacher. Born in 1958 in Washington, D.C., Rose now lives on the island of Maui, in the state of Hawaii, where she is an assistant professor in the fashion design department at Maui

Community College. A self-taught designer, she attended University of California, Santa Barbara (BA, film studies, 1976) and California State University, Dominguez Hills (MA, art history, 1993 – 95).

Rose likes the graphic design elements of quilting, especially the mix of painterly effects and modern art styles in the art quilt movement. She has been sewing since childhood, but only started quilting in 1984. She exhibits with the Maui Crafts Guild, and has been juried into numerous local and national art shows with her contemporary Hawaiian quilts and her Afro-American-style pieced wall quilts. Rose wants to teach content-based quilting classes to incorporate both personal issues in quilting design as well as the adaptation of traditional multi-ethnic sewing styles. Received Quiltfest USA '94 juror's ribbon.

Emmy Adrian Moore, Decatur, Illinois

Emmy was born May 1, 1953, in Decatur, IL, and grew up in Clayton, IL. She graduated from Millikin University, Decatur Memorial Hospital School of Nursing, and executive MBA program at the University of Illinois. Emmy works as director, maternal-child nursing at Decatur Memorial Hospital. She is married and has two sons.

Emmy began sewing at age 5, but did not start quilting seriously until 1988. She has completed more than 22 bed quilts for relatives, many quilt tops, wallhangings, baby quilts, table runners, and lots of work in progress. She especially likes scrap quilts and is working on a series of charm quilts.

Emmy has been a regular entrant in the Decatur Quilt Festival, Rockhome Gardens Quilt Show, and Decatur Area Arts Council, "On My Own Time" program. She has earned blue and red ribbons and viewer's choice honors.

Cornelia Morgan, Corpus Christi, Texas

Married, retired teacher, needlewoman, watercolorist, adult Sunday School teacher, choir member. Quiltmaker, wearable art designer, workshop leader within local organization, Coastal Bend Quilt and Needlwork Guild.

The first year of my retirement I organized a group of church women to create a fundraiser quilt. "Stacked Bricks" was the chosen design. Church members brought "bricks" of cotton

fabrics in dark clear colors. Learning together, correcting mistakes, and solving problems cemented friendships and tested our committment. What had been scraps in February became a king size quilt by bazaar time in November. The $2,070 raised furnished an adult classroom.

Dr. Joyce Mori, Morgantown, West Virginia

Author, designer, quiltmaker. Joycelyn I. Mori was born September 10, 1942, in Ottawa, IL, and now resides in Morgantown, WV. She graduated from Beloit College (B.A.) and the University of Missouri (M.A. and Ph.D.) She works full time as a freelance writer, book author, and quilt teacher. She received an N.Q.A. grant to study the use of Native American designs in quilts. This research is ongoing.

She likes to combine her academic training in anthropology (major in North American Indians) with her quilting; and several of her books deal with using Native American design motifs for quilting patterns, appliqué designs, and new piecework pieces. She is currently doing surface design with dyes and fabric paints. Her quilts have appeared in galleries and various quilt shows including AQS.

Janet R. Morin, North Brookfield, Massachusetts

Designer, volunteers organizer, and coordinator for charitable organizations. The mother of five adult children and three grandchildren, I've been a bookkeeper and a crafter all of my life. In 1991 I started a "quilting school" in my home to teach hand sewing and quilting – an experiment to see if there was a need. Indeed there was. It has taken over my house and my life. I love sharing what I know about sewing and quilting with the girls, ages 6 to 76, and more keep coming every week!

In my classes, I design the templates based on what my girls need to make based on pictures they see or ideas they have. The sizes vary according to need, from mini stuffed animals to king size quilts. My classes can be as small as two students or as large as ten. All of the work is hand done.

Making queen size Cross & Crown quilt for church raffle; crib quilt for a leukemia patient; and pictorial wallhanging for town library's 100th anniversary are my most memorable projects.

Anne C. Morrell, Windsor, New York

Anne C. Morrell was born in 1948. A native of Bucks County, Pennsylvania, Anne also has duel citizenship in Canada and divides her time between her home studios in Windsor, NY, and Margaree Valley, Nova Scotia.

Since 1972, Anne has created over 270 quilts mostly as commissions for private homes, businesses, and public places. She also designs wearable art and soft sculptures. The focus of her work is pictorial appliqué featuring nature, the environment, life, and historical events. A member of quilt and art organizations in both countries, Anne has won numerous awards at shows.

When not making quilts, Anne is busy teaching out of her home studio or at guilds, conferences, and children's and women's groups. She is also known to sneak out of the studio to enjoy her other interests including gardening, biking, hiking, riding, fishing, and cross-country skiing with her husband and two sons.

Carrie Morrison, Fort Worth, Texas

Carrie Morrison was born March 24, 1907, in Hunt County, Texas, and now resides in Fort Worth. She started quilting at about 8 years of age. She remembers quilting in order to have warm bed covers and also remembers her mother saving a quilt to have to donate to neighbors who'd been burned out of their homes. Her favorite pattern is the Tulip pattern and favorite colors are red and blue.

Peggy Durbin Morrison, Corinth, Mississippi

Peggy Durbin Morrison was born November 15, 1948, in Bardstown, KY. After relocating many times due to her husband's job, she now resides in Corinth, MS. She has always enjoyed all types of needlework but quilting is her favorite. She prefers the traditional patterns, and is currently working on an Irish Chain, a sailboat, and a Grandmother's Flower Garden quilt. She is a member of the Batting Brigade Quilters in Florence, AL, NQA, and AQS.

LaVera Moss, Cannonville, Utah

I love quilts! It's very interesting what you can create from scraps of cloth. I was born in Cannonville, Utah, a town of 150 dear souls, have lived here most of my life. My ten children have lives of their own so I can spend my time as I choose, since I live alone now. I learned quilting from my mother, Alice, as she pieced from shirttails and other articles of leftover clothing. I love piecing and quilting for selling or making quilts for friends and family. My children especially like the denim ones with the pockets left on.

Sandra Goss Munsey, Norfolk, Massachusetts

Lived in Rye, NH, and Medfield, MA. Husband, Donald T. Munsey Jr., two daughters, two granddaughters. BA in government, University of New Hampshire; MPA, Northeastern University. Analyst, state and federal government; lecturer, Suffolk University. Held elected/appointed positions in town government. First woman to serve on Medfield Board of Selectmen.

Directed Medfield Quilt Document Project, 1st in MA; Secy, MASS Quilts, MA Quilt Project. Lecturer, teacher, quilter, exhibit curator. Rhododendron Needlers QG (founder); Narragansett Bay QA; New England QG; New England Quilt Museum; AQSG. Interest: quilt history; Hawaiian and outline embroidered quilts. Finding a hidden date on a Civil War quilt; sharing new excitement about a quilt, its story and spreading the word in lectures and articles are favorite quilting activities.

Joyce Murrin, Orient, New York

Designer, maker of one-of-a-kind art quilts: large and small, many with nature inspiration.

Born with identical twin, Jean Disbrow (Evans), August 6, 1939, Benton Harbor, MI. Lives with her husband, Charles, overlooking the lighthouse at Orient Pt., NY. Sons: Charles P., Michael, and Stephen.

Teaches her techniques nationally. Loves an artistic and techni-cal challenge! Has made quilts with twin, Jean, and others. Helps promote quilts and quiltmaking through area exhibitions. Born creative!

Joyce's quilts have won many awards, are published, exhibited in one woman, group shows, and in major juried shows as Visions Quilt San Diego, Tactile Architecture, AQS. Quilts are in private collections and the MAQS.

Nancy Leith Musser, Avalon, New Jersey

Nancy Leith Musser was born August 10, 1936, in Philadelphia, PA. She currently resides in Avalon, NJ. Nancy graduated from Lansdowne-Aldan High School, graduated from West Chester University, and attend-ed Pennsylvania State University for graduate studies in elementary edu-cation.

Nancy comes from a family of quiltmakers. In a treasured 1900 photo her grandmother Kegel and great-grandmother Applegate were shown with their quilting group in Nuremburg, PA. Their quilts are Nancy's treasures too. Nancy's mother and aunts often quilted in the family home. Nancy began her quilting 20 years ago. She lectured and taught quilting in Pleasantville, NY. Her favorite sampler quilt has been shown at shows in Ocean City, NJ, and Meriden, CT.

Janet Myers, Carmel, IN

A native of Tennessee, Janet and her husband, Gary, live in Carmel, Indi-ana, close to their three grown chil-dren and grandson.

An avid quiltmaker, collector, and lecturer with a passion for the history of quilts and their makers, and a stu-dent in the preservation of quilts.

A special quilting project in which I've participated for the past four years has involved making quilts for women to have free mammograms and to revise awareness that mammograms can save lives. I've made four quilts from queen size to wall size, each having a message from the quilt world. Quilters care, and because they care, they show their support in helping me make these quilts. How lucky for me to have won awards for these projects!

Barbara McKie, Lyme, CT, working on AOL Exchange quilt for Progressive Opera. Picture shows computer setup used in transferring images to fabric.

Hook and Stitch quilters' retreat in Nestor Falls, Ontario. The ladies quilted by the lake while the fellows fished. (photo courtesy of Gorgean M. Kruger, Shell Lake, WI)

Left to right: Rose, Mary, Loma Tippin, and Sibyl Mizer working on a quilt at the Saginaw Fair. (photo courtesy of Sibyl Mizer)

Paula Nadelstern, Bronx, New York

Author, quilt artist, teacher, lecturer. Paula Nadelstern's award-winning, kaleidoscope-inspired quilts have been showcased on the covers of *Quilter's Newsletter Magazine, American Quilter, Quilting International,* and in many books, magazines, TV shows, and exhibits both nationally and internationally, including Quilt National '95. Awards include Artist's Fellowship from the New York Foundation for the Arts '95, and New York State winner of the first and second Great American Quilt Contests. Curated Citiquilts, a composite exhibit of quilts, photos, and text for the Museum of American Folk Art (1991). Author of *Quilting Together: How to Organize, Design, and Make Group Quilts* (Crown '88), *Color Design in Patchwork* (Dover '91), and *Kaleidoscope Quilts* (C&T, in-progress). Co-creator with Marilyn Henrion of Quilt-O-Rama: The Board Game Where the One with the Most Fabric Wins. Member of the Manhattan Quilters Guild.

Ann Bodle Nash, Bow, Washington

I have been deeply involved with quilts for the past seven years as a buyer and seller, collector, quilt show coordinator, quilt guild member (Quilter's Anonymous), retail store owner (Creighton's Quilts in La Conner, WA), and as an appraiser of quilts and quilted textiles, certified by AQS. Married (husband Rick), with three children, living on beautiful Samish Island along Puget Sound. As a retail quilt and folk art store owner I have exposed many to the delights of quilts from Pennsylvania to Washington, old to shockingly new, Amish made to grandmotherly made and even Hmong.

The joy of receiving certification as an appraiser by AQS and making such wonderful friends in the process (those Yahoo girls) has been a wonderful experience.

Lana C. Neal-Clark, Indianapolis, Indiana

Quiltmaker and teacher. Started quilting in 1989, do program with lecture and slides "History and Mystery Quilting." I teach quilting at my home on weekends. My specialty is English piecing.

Belongs to Working Wonders Bee. We share a lot of happy times together.

Helped with Indiana State Museum to get Indiana Quilt Registry together. Indianapolis Quilt Guild has a show every two years; I participate in their training workshops.

Dianne Nelson, Sioux Falls, South Dakota

Quiltmaker. Dianne Lee Smith Nelson was born June 21, 1943, in Norfolk, Virginia, and resides in Sioux Falls, South Dakota.

She began quilting in 1978, and has taught quilting at a local fabric shop. Her first quilt was for her parents 40th anniversary.

She enjoys floral appliqué and traditional patchwork. Most of the quilts she's made are bed sized, for her family and friends. She also has made many wallhangings.

She is a current member of AQS; a member of the Sioux Falls Quilters Guild, of which she is a past president; and member of the Minnesota Quilters Guild.

She sews and quilts weekly with a small group of friends. One of her memorable experiences was making baby quilts for the intensive care unit at a local hospital.

Dorothy Nelson, Del Rio, Texas

Quiltmaker. My belief that quilts should be shared, not stored, is popular with my family and friends.

The Piecemaker Quilters of Del Rio being chosen to create Val Verde County wallhanging was most memorable.

Dolores Nielsen, Glendive, Montana

Have been a member of the Sacred Heart Quilter's Group since its formation in 1984. Worked on the centennial quilt (Montana's centennial in 1989).

Josephine Niemann, SSND, St. Louis, Missouri

Designer, quiltmaker, author, and lecturer. Josephine Niemann, SSND, was born in Effingham, Illinois, February 20, 1939. Her mother, Cecilia, taught her to sew doll dresses when she was young, then her own dress when she was 12. She entered the

religious community, the School Sisters of Notre Dame. She taught art, English, and religion in secondary schools in Missouri, Illinois, Iowa, and Sierra Leone, Africa. After more than 20 years of teaching, Jo began a second career designing vestments and banners for her community's ecclesiastical department. She began quilting around this time in 1983.

Many of the liturgical vesture and banners she designs incorporate quilting techniques. In her spare time, Josephine makes bed quilts – many are original designs. She has a Master's degree in art from the University of Notre Dame and has served as chairperson of the Art Commission of the St. Louis Archdiocese and is a member of AQS and the Thimble and Thread Quilt Guild of Greater St. Louis. Her work has been published in *American Quilter, Modern Liturgy, Environment and Art Letter,* Jill Liddell's book *Patchwork Pilgrimage*, and in *Great American Quilts.*

Emily Nipp, Amarillo, Texas

My career as a passionate quiltmaker began in 1988 when a friend suggested a beginning quiltmaking class at the local community college. The "bug" bit me hard! I now average making a quilt a month in addition to teaching several classes at Rt. 66 Quilt! here in Amarillo, Texas. My quilts have been shown (and won awards!) both in Amarillo and in neighboring states, and several are on display in the shop where I work and teach. Future plans include entering quilts in some of the bigger shows nationally. My favorite quilts include a large dose of appliqué, and I really enjoy the current trend toward "folk art." I teach several classes locally including a perennial favorite called the "block of the month" quilt where students are provided with fabric, pattern, and instruction. Several of my students have won ribbons for their work! In addition to teaching beginners the basics of hand appliqué, piecing, and quilting, I am also an avid machine quilter (teacher and advocate). Garments and invisible machine appliqué round out my repertoire. My husband, David, and I have five children.

Fran Norris, Woodridge, Illinois

My name is Fran Norris, I will be 46 at the end of this year. I have been married to Paul for 26 years and we have three great sons, Jeff, Steve, and Brian. I was born in Chelsea, a Boston area of Massachusetts. A company transfer moved us to the Midwest town of Woodridge, Illinois, 19 years ago, and here I found my interest and love for quilting.

I have been involved in making blocks for quilts through a quilt club, school projects, raffles, and gifts, but have not made a quilt for myself yet! My first two projects (1981 – 82) were a 5 x 7 grandma quilting at a table framed block for my mom and an interlocking square pillow. In 1987 I designed an 18" x 18" block for the quilt club (Faithful Circle) contest, "A Tribute to the Amish." It incorporated handmade stencil and stenciling, padding, appliqué, and hand quilting. In 1991 I designed a Wedding Rose Pillow as a gift. It was all hand quilted with natural and colored threads with gold accent thread worked throughout the design.

Ann Clare Novak, Dewey, Arizona

Teacher, author, and quilter. Ann celebrated the Bicentennial by creating her first quilt in 1976. From 1987 to 1990, as a member of Quilt-Ed, she helped create materials to encourage Arizona teachers to combine classroom quilting with language arts, math, and history. Ann won the *Better Homes and Gardens* Blue Ribbon Quilt Award for Patchwork at the 1991 Arizona State Fair.

Ann's most memorable quilt was "Mimbres Showcase." An Indian friend wanted a quilt of ancient Mimbres Indian animals that were found painted in round bowls. Ann's challenges were: putting rounded designs into a square quilt, finding a controllable fabric paint, and using unusual construction techniques. A poster was made of the quilt.

Quilt Retreat in Front Royal, VA, with the Fairfax Chapter of Quilters Unlimited.
Left: Mary Grace Ronan. Right: Jan P. Krentz.

Hallie H. O'Kelley, Tuscaloosa, Alabama

Designer and maker of quilts. Received a B.S. in home ec. education and M.S. in applied art from Iowa State University. Screen printing became my specialty.

Made first quilt in 1980; to date have completed more than 100. The design of my quilts includes screen printing and/or hand-dyed fabrics as an integral part. Have participated in several workshops at Arrowmont School of Arts and Crafts in Gatlinburg, TN. Author of book *Screen Printing for Quilters*. Do workshops on screen printing.

Received first, second, and third place awards at AQS shows; best-of-show and blue ribbons at other national shows.

Anna Oberlander, Norwood, Massachusetts

Anna Oberlander, a partner in Quilt Escapes, Inc., is an experienced travel coordinator who has arranged and conducted hundreds of bus tours and cruises for over two decades. The tours, for the last five years, have been dedicated to quilters, friends, and family who were soon hooked after seeing all the great quilts, wallhangings, and clothing in such places as Williamsburg, VA; Lancaster, PA; Paducah, KY; etc. The other side of Quilt Escapes is spending an entire weekend just quilting, going home with a finished top or a piece of clothing completed. A daughter accompanied her mother on one of our weekends, assuring us that even though she brought material and a sewing machine, she was going to read and hike for the weekend. She never left the table and completed a vest. Another phase of our tours are day trips to local stores and shows.

Anna was born in Norwood, MA, a many-crafted person (sewing, ceramics, stenciling, and quilting), and is a member of the RNQG, ECQA, AQS, NQA, and looks forward to meeting many more quilters from all over the country.

Becky Olson, Paradise, Utah

I began quilting in Berkeley, CA, in the early 1970's. Moved to Kentucky in 1979, I opened a quilt shop in 1982, and in 1985 became a Bernina dealer. The shop was sold in 1992 when I moved to Paradise. I wrote *Quilts by the Slice* in 1992, the second edition was published by Chilton, 1995. I have taught both nationally and with Japanese and French students. Presently working on Hand Pieced Heirlooms (Japanese Hand Piecing). I am currently the chairperson for the American Heritage Quilt

Festival. I operate Thimble and Thumb which specializes in pre-washed, precut quilt kits, and an extensive assortment of patterns. I am a quilt appraiser and plan on being certified by AQS in 1996. I am working on teacher certification through NQA.

An area of special interest is to excite new quilters on the possibilities in quiltmaking for them. My primitive appliqué classes have started many on the path to fine appliqué. My expertise lies in hand piecing as well as "slice and dice" (rotary cutting and sewing). I consider myself an expert in quilt drafting and design, on paper and computer.

Carol Kidwell Orona, Morro Bay, California

Quiltmaker. Carol Kidwell Orona resides in Morro Bay, CA, with her husband, Armando. She first became interested in quilts while teaching her fourth graders about pioneers. Reading as much as she could about quilt history, she decided she must be a part of keeping this tradition alive. She enrolled in her first quilt class in 1988.

Becoming a skilled quilter seemed impossible while teaching full time. Now retired, she quilts daily, takes various classes and enjoys her involvement with the Schoolhouse Quilters, a group of five elementary teachers who meet monthly.

Giving away her quilts to special friends has given her the most pleasure. Although she designs quilts to enter in shows, her first priority is to complete a new quilt each year for her first grandchild, Jake Ryan. This family tradition began with a quilt given on the day of his birth and now each birthday. She hopes these quilts will be passed down to his children.

Erna O'Shea, Bronx, New York

59 year old grandmother. Born and raised in NYC. Soon to be a resident of Keene, New Hampshire.

Erna has been quilting since the mid 1970's. She quilts by hand

and machine, for fun and profit. Erna works with traditional patterns and regardless of original intent, usually produces a scrap quilt.

Kathryn H. Ott, Highspire, Pennsylvania

Designer and quiltmaker.Kathryn Jane Holsinger Ott was born January 16, 1937, in Altoona, PA, graduated from Brentwood High School (Pittsburgh, PA), and from Juniata College (Huntingdon, PA). Currently she resides in Highspire, PA, where she serves as church organist in addition to her full-time job as computer programmer with EDS (Electronic Data Systems) on the Bethlehem Steel account.

A fourth generation quilter, Kathy began piecing when she was 5 years old, but didn't get hooked on quiltmaking until the early 1970's. She prefers designing wall quilts composed of squares, triangles, and strips that can be easily sewn on a machine.

Kathy is currently a member of AQS. Several of her wall quilts have been displayed at Quilter's Heritage Celebration in Lancaster, PA, and her family's four generation quilt collection was displayed for two months at Juniata College.

Mira Loy Ott, Cannonville, Utah

My name is Mira Loy Ott, born June 17, 1934, in Tropic, Utah, living there until moving to Cannonville, Utah, January 21, 1983. When I learned to quilt as a child taught by my mother, we used leftover scraps from articles of hand-sewn clothing. My mother always allowed even the youngest to quilt, never removing our stitches. The magic of the quilt was in the recognition of family members' articles of clothing, Dad's old shirt and Mom's apron.

AQS staff, Bonnie Browning and Libby Boswell, answer questions at the workshop registration desk, AQS Quilt Show, Paducah, KY.

Kern County Museum Quilters, Bakersfield, CA.
Back: Ann Brewer, Shelley Reese, Marian Anderson, Ann Kline, Florence Christy. Front: Myrtis Bailey, Pauline Brandt, Doris Nash.

T & T Quilters, admiring "1,000 Pyramids" quilt, Mountainside, NJ. Left to right: Jan Cunningham, Rita Mears, Evelyn Hill, Thelma Murphy, Bennie Ungerman, Susan Armbrust.

Quilters anxiously await the opening of the AQS Quilt Show, Paducah, KY.

A visit to the Museum of the American Quilter's Society is on the agenda of quilters throughout the year, Paducah, KY.

Photographer, Richard Walker, captures the prize winning quilts on film during the AQS Quilt Show, Paducah, KY.

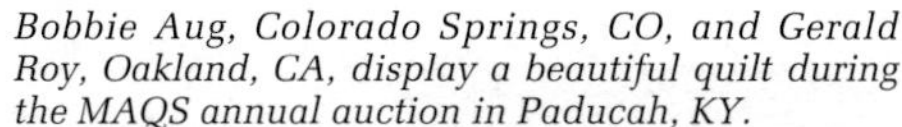

Bobbie Aug, Colorado Springs, CO, and Gerald Roy, Oakland, CA, display a beautiful quilt during the MAQS annual auction in Paducah, KY.

Quilters gathered at the Miniature quilt display, AQS Quilt Show, Paducah, KY.

Pamela Mary Simonetto Pampe, Miami, Florida

Pamela Mary Simonetto Pampe was born March 6, 1951, in Gary, IN. Graduated from the University of West Florida, Pensacola, FL, in 1974, and attended San Diego State University for post-graduate work while teaching at the secondary level in history and English.

She began quilting in 1979, with interests ranging from the techniques of the craft to the tales behind the quilts and quiltmakers themselves. She attained certified appraiser status in 1994 from the American Quilter's Society. Pamela is a member of the Professional Appraiser's Association of Quilted Textiles, Southeast regional coordinator of the American Quilt Study Group, a friend of the Museum of the American Quilter's Society, the National Quilting Association, the Ocean Waves NQA chapter in Miami, and the Quilt Restoration Society.

Pamela teaches quilt restoration, preservation, and conservation. She has been able to contribute to on-going knowledge in the field of restoration with her own writing for the Quilt Restoration Society and by being sought as a resource by individuals and museums after Hurricane Andrew devastated personal property, particularly quilts, in 1992.

Holding awards on her own quilts, in both traditional and innovative categories, Pam continues to explore all areas of quilts and quiltmaking. She lives in Miami, FL, with her husband, son, and daughter.

Esther Small Pancho, Rolling Hills, California

Esther Small Pancho was born June 4, 1925, in New York City, she attended public schools in Harlem, and received her degree in home economics education from New York University.

She began teaching in 1950 and taught in Brooklyn, NY, AZ, and CA.

Her early interest in quilts began when as a young child, she was kept warm during the bitter cold New York winters with heavy wool patch quilts which were made by her great-grandmother, Agnes, who was born a slave in Florida.

As a young teacher working with the Tohono O'dom Nation, formally called Papago, in Arizona, she met a colleague, Addie Morgan, who came from Oklahoma and brought many beautiful quilts in her trunk. Esther copied one of the patterns and made her first quilt. Since 1965 she has been making quilts and enjoying her role as quiltmaker and teacher. Her special interest is obtaining historical data that relates to early and subsequent African-American quiltmakers and their quilts.

She is influenced by people and places encountered in her travels. From her West African trip, colorful bright cotton pieces are used with traditional American patterns. Designs from baskets, instruments, and masks are seen in her original quilts.

Esther has two daughters and four grandchildren and is currently a member of the African-American Quilters of Los Angeles and resides in Rolling Hills, CA.

Anita Parker, Philadelphia, Pennsylvania

MBA degree, Philadelphia College of Textile and Science; program director for my guild, Quilter's of the Round Table. Quiltmaker since 1989; started with miniatures and progressed into quilt designing; wearable arts; dollmaking under the name "Three Sisters Doll Creations," with my sister, Sharon Speller; and teaching young students and seniors with my "Patchwork Partner," Josephine Scott Countley.

1. Three Sisters exhibits custom dolls at East Coast juried doll shows. Examples: Headhouse Square, Philadelphia; Resorts International Hotel, Atlantic City; Black Doll Show, Wilmington, Delaware. 2. Quilts and dolls exhibited at the Afro-American Historical and Cultural Museum, Philadelphia. 3. "Patchwork Partners," taught silk ribbon embroidery at 3rd Annual African American Quilter's Conference and Retreat, Bowie, Maryland.

Jean Parker, Harrisburg, Arkansas

I began my quilting career in 1985 when I went to work for a community action agency as coordinator of a craft group based in Jonesboro. It was my responsibility to sell the items that were handmade by the women and men in their homes. We specialized in making quilts — making at least 10 quilts a week, we filled orders, selling the rest at craft fairs. Then we sold the Double Wedding Ring for $175, and a Postage Stamp for $275.

In 1988, I purchased the craft store from the agency, calling it The Nettleton Quilt Station. In 1993, I moved the store from Jonesboro to the community I live in and it is now called Nettleton Quilts. We have a small quilt club, called the Cozy Quilt Club, that meets the second Monday of each month.

Charlotte Patera, Grass Valley, California

Author, designer, quiltmaker, and teacher. Charlotte Patera was born in Detroit, MI, in 1927. She spent her early years in Ohio, later working in Detroit, Chicago, and San Fransisco as a graphic artist. Later she switched to needlecrafts, producing ideas for magazines. She made her first quilt for her first appliqué book for Better Homes and Gardens, published in 1974. Since then quilting has been her main focus. Her study of the Kuna Indians' molas has influenced much of her work. Her quilts have been exhibited widely and have won many awards. She has taught at the Houston International Quilt Festival, AQS, and around the USA since 1979. She had two books published in 1995: *Mola Techniques* (AQS) and *Schoolhouse Appliqué* (C&T). She is striving for status as an art quilter, though she still likes to do and teach decorative and ethnic appliqué.

Acceptance in Quilt National '93, and awards in Paducah and Houston are memorable achievements.

Patricia Patterson, Oakland, California

Quiltmaker and collector. Born May 18, 1935. Graduate of University of California, married, two children, and three grandchildren.

I began quilting in 1970. I have made 77 quilts. I lived 5 years in the Middle East and taught quilting to an international group. I made crib quilts for five Arab babies. I now volunteer at the American Quilt Study Group in the library. I am also a member of the "Stitch & Bitch" group and also East Bay Heritage Quilters. I have 15 antique quilts, 9 which were made by family members: my mother, grandmother, and great-grandmother.

In 1992 I was included in Nancy Cameron Armstrong's study of "Desert Storm" quilts. I was living in Abu and during the bombing made a Hovering Hawks Missile quilt, which I later donated to the Boise Peace Quilt Project.

Charlotte Helstern Paugh, Greenville, Ohio

My introduction into the world of quilting came about as a result of realizing in retirement I just didn't need all those clothes I was making. No place to wear them, as every day to the office, which I did for nearly 30 years.

After moving to a retirement village, I attended one of the annual quilt shows of the local quilting club, and learned they met regularly each month in the main facility of our complex. I joined this group for a number of years and became hooked on quilting.

Most of all of my quilts are made and designed for a specific individual or occasion. Participation in as many workshops and classes as possible keeps me abreast of all that is new and exciting in this challenging hobby. I will not live long enough to complete all the ideas for quilts that keep swimming around in my head. That is why most of my work is machine pieced and quilted. Quiltmaking has become a wonderful substitute for dressmaking and I have applied my dressmaking skills to some blue ribbon wearable art ensembles.

Elizabeth D. Pauley, Westtown, Pennsylvania

Elizabeth (Beth) Pauley (November 3, 1940) grew up in Chesapeake City, MD. She lives in Westtown, PA, with her husband, Ted. Together they have raised four daughters. Beth graduated from Hood College in Frederick, MD, in 1962, with a B.S. in home economics. In 1987 she graduated from West Chester University, West Chester, PA, with a Master's degree in education, counseling option, and in 1989 with a Master's degree in health care administration.

Beth teaches home economics at Springton Lake Middle School in the Rose Tree Media School District, Media, PA. She is a quilting teacher certified by the NQA and teaches at A Patch of Country in Chadds Ford, PA, and for quilting groups. She lectures on a variety of subjects including making friendship quilts, judging quilt shows, and improving quilting techniques. She is a quilting judge certified by the NQA and is qualified to judge master quilts.

Beth's quilts have received numerous awards in local, regional, and state fair quilt shows. She is a past president of Brandywine Valley Quilters and currently serves as chair of the Documentation Committee whose goal is to document quilts made in Delaware County, PA. Beth is a member of the NQA and AQS.

Joyce B. Peaden, Prosser, Washington

Quilt designer and seamstress. Pieced my first quilt, a "Devil's Claw," as a distraction to the Battle for Iwo Jima, February 1945. Began serious piecing again in the mid-1970's.

I am a quilt historian, and a teacher of quiltmaking techniques. I am the author of *Irish Chain Quilts, A Workbook of Irish Chains and Related Patterns*, (American Quilter's Society 1988), and historical and technical magazine articles. Articles include "Donated Quilts Warmed Wartorn Europe," and "The Multicolored Geometric Pieced Sails of Mindano and the Sulu Archipelago," *Uncoverings 1988* and *1990* (American Quilt Study Group). "Donated Quilts" was published again as a chapter in the book *Quiltmaking in America: Beyond the Myths* (Rutledge Hill Press, 1994).

I particularly enjoyed being co-designer with Gloria Harries of the "Bountiful Harvest" quilt made by the Horizon Quilters Unlimited of Yakima Valley, first place in the Chapters Row Division of the 21st Annual Show of the National Quilting Association, Inc.

Roslyn Rowley Penk, Renton, Washington

Wife, mom, and have a degree in fine arts. Teacher and designer of 39 original Mystery Quilt Patterns. Published Oatmeal Originals Patterns. Quiltmaker of whatever strikes me. Favorite activities include: a trip to the Sisters quilt show with my mom and grandma (3 generations of quilters); getting two quilts into the Association of Pacific Northwest Quilters Show and enjoying the friendships I've made through quilting.

Gai Perry, Walnut Creek, California

Author, teacher, and quiltmaker. I discovered the art of quiltmaking in 1981. One day I took a beginner's quiltmaking class, just for the fun of it, and I fell in love! Six months later I closed the antique shop I had been running, and have been happily quilting ever since.

In 1985 I began teaching at some of the local shops and quilt seminars throughout California and Oregon. My focus was on the effective use of color and fabric in traditional quilts. In 1990 I developed an original style of contemporary quilt design that I call "The Art of the Impressionist Landscape." I have written a book on this subject titled *Impressionist Quilts*, published by C & T Publishing Co., Lafayette, CA.

Molly M. Perry, Drummond Island, Michigan

Quiltmaker and photographer focusing on nature themes. BS animal science and BS in communications, Michigan State University; current MBA candidate, Lake Superior State University; professional career as historical museum director and museum consultant. Researched Michigan's Upper Peninsula quilts and quilters funded in part by grants from the Lansing, Michigan, Capitol City Quilt Guild and the National Quilting Assoc. Active member of Michigan Quilt Network and Keeping the Piece Quilt Guild.

Alice M. Person, Greenwood, Indiana

Alice Manlove Person was born in Richmond, IN, on November 18, 1940. She is a graduate of Richmond High School, Purdue, and Indiana Universities. She is currently a middle school teacher in Indianapolis. She and her husband, David, live near Greenwood, IN.

Alice is a charter member of the Quilt Connection Guild. She has organized charity events, taught classes, and edited the newsletter. She currently is guild historian and bee chairman. Alice is a member of the Indiana State Quilt Guild and AQS. Appliqué, hand quilting, and making quilted clothing are among her favorite quilting activities.

Bonnie Peterson-Tucker, Elmhurst, Illinois

Bonnie Peterson-Tucker was born in 1955 in Illinois. She was raised primarily in the suburbs of Chicago but also attended

high school for a year in Zaire. Her undergraduate degree is from the University of Illinois and she received an MBA from DePaul University. She currently resides in Elmhurst, Illinois.

After a career in marketing, she started quilting while in Tallahassee, Florida. Much of her work is motivated by her life experiences. Some of it is philosophic, geographic, or political. She tries to express visually, with fabric, some of the changing concepts, ideas, and dreams in her life. She uses the creative process to work out, organize, and communicate her questions, frustrations, and goals. Some of her wallhangings look like collages of fabrics and ideas. She uses fabric words, photographs, newspaper articles, yarn, and beads in her work.

She received an Artist Fellowship Grant Award from the Illinois Arts Council and has exhibited her work throughout the country.

Libby Dubois Pettit, Indiana, Pennsylvania

Quilt artist and quilt teacher who expresses social issues through quilt art. Libby Pettit's quilt art combines her southern heritage, formal education in fashion, artistic flair, and intense interest in history. Her signature pieces, dramatic period fashions designed and presented in the quilt motif, reflect a degree in fashion from Stephens College. One of Ms. Pettit's most recent pieces is Anita Hill Meets "Justice."

Liz Piatt, Orinda, California

I was born in Columbus, Ohio. I graduated from Ohio State with a B.A. I married a physician and we had one daughter and three sons. We have lived in the San Francisco Bay area since 1959.

I have been creating fabric art since 1975, and have been in many juried shows across the United States. I like to make original innovative art quilts using hand appliqué and hand quilting, painting, machine work, etc. I also like to do informative descriptive quilts of an area, the history of a certain region, the animals in a certain area, etc. all backed up with much research. After my family which now includes grandchildren, art quilts are my first love. I like working with fabric because there are no limits – anything is possible.

Doris V. Pickhardt, Whiteland, Indiana

All aspects of the quilt are exciting to me. After quilting on

Mother's quilts while in junior high, I didn't get started on my own until a few years ago.

I didn't see Mother's quilts, or didn't pay attention, until they were in the frame so my actual knowledge of quilt construction was nil. Having made small pieces and only two bed-size quilts I consider myself a novice. The importance of friends who have been generous in sharing their knowledge has been invaluable to me.

I helped make a baby quilt for a friend's first child, and our quilt guild has made several raffle quilts. I was fortunate enough to win one, a Sunbonnet Sue quilt.

Barbara G. Pietila, Baltimore, Maryland

Barbara G. Pietila, born March 11, 1942, lives in Baltimore, MD, and is a fiber artist and the mother of three. Barbara has quilted for 20 years beginning her career as a maker of traditional quilts.

In the mid 80's she moved to Moscow where she lived for four years. In order to continue quilting in a country where quality cotton fabrics were all but non-existent, she began doing appliqué with the fabric scraps left over from the stash she had taken with her. She discovered she loved appliqué and now produces pictorial quilts depicting African-American life.

Barbara teaches quilting, does research on African-American quilts, and exhibits her work across the country. She is currently national coordinator for the national asssociation of African American Quilters, president of the African American Quilters of Baltimore, and holds membership in NQA and AQS. Her work has also been featured in two quilt books.

Marilyn Johnson Pilkey, Canyon Country, California

Pilkey, Marilyn Johnson, 1947 – . B.A., Calvary Bible College, 1968, biblical studies; B.A., The Master's College, 1985, English literature; graduate studies Cal State University, Northridge, theater arts; workshops, American Conservatory Theater, London Academy for Music and Dramatic Arts, 1993. Member of AQS, American Craft Council, TAFTA, SAQA, Friends of Fiber Arts, Surface Design Association, Santa Clarita Valley Quilt Guild. Tailor/costume designer/dollmaker, 1972 – 75. Teacher (English/theater) 1975 – 95. Quilting since 1980, largely self-taught; studied color with Michael James. Has shown widely in the U.S. Maintains a studio in Canyon Country, California. Signature pattern: "Winding Ways" (also called "Wheel of Wonder" and "Wheele of Mysterie" in Quilts of Illusion).

Elaine Plogman, Cincinnati, Ohio

Elaine Huninghake Plogman was born December 7, 1938, in Cincinnati, OH. She received her BA in art from Edgecliff College of Xavier University in Cincinnati where she still lives.

Since 1976 Elaine has been making the innovative pieced wall quilts for which she is known. Most of her designs start with a manipulation of original block units. She has received many compliments for her unusual fabric combinations. She is pleased to share with students her design and fabric selection skills.

Elaine's work has been included in four of the eight biennial Quilt National exhibits and in all four of the AIQA sponsored Quilt Expo Europa conferences as part of the *Quilter's Newsletter* competitions, Karlsruhe, Germany (1994), Hague, Netherlands (1992), Odense, Denmark (1990), and Salzburg, Austria (1988). Her quilts have appeared at most of the AQS annual quilt shows in Paducah, and in 1994 her entry was awarded first prize in the Professional Wall Quilt category.

Daniel Plyler, Mason, Michigan

Daniel R. Plyler was born April 16, 1949, in Rock Hill, South Carolina, and currently resides with his wife, Linda, and dog, Maggie, in Mason, Michigan. While Dan has never stitched a single stitch, he is an important part of the quilting world. He is the "behind the scene" support; moving furniture, setting up tables, and preparing his house for his wife's quilting students. He cooks for some classes and does the dishes after potlucks. He graciously accepts exuberant ladies into his home. Dan is there to help set up quilt shows and take them down. He travels out of state to take his wife to a fabric shop she "just has to go to," and he knows vacations will include trips to fabric shops. He helps extensively with household chores so Linda has more time for creative activities. Most importantly Dan supports his wife with praise and is proud of what she does. Dan has even been known to help layer a quilt and offer opinions on color selections. All this is done in his spare time as he is a postal employee, operates his own business, and is restoring his 150-year-old farmhouse. Linda says she owes her quilting freedom to Dan.

Linda L. Plyler, Mason, Michigan

Linda L. (Webb) Plyler was born June 12, 1953, in Lansing, Michigan. Currently she and her husband, Dan, reside in Mason, Michigan. A graduate of Michigan State University, Linda is the postmaster of Shaftsburg, Michigan.

Linda teaches quilting in her home studio. Her main area of expertise is in appliqué. Her prize-winning quilts range from the precise Baltimore Album to the free and whimsical folk art. In 1994 she was selected as an honored teacher of Baltimore Quilting at the Baltimore Quilt Revival in Lancaster, PA. Linda is a member of AQS, Lansing Area Patchers, and Capitol City Quilt Guilds.

In the future she is looking forward to teaching her young nieces the joy of quilting. As preschoolers they are already intrigued with Linda's extensive fabric collection and want to examine fabric every time they come to visit.

Linda feels she owes her quilting freedom to her supportive husband, Dan.

Linda M. Pool, Vienna, Virginia

Linda Marie (Leaman) Pool was born October 5, 1952, in Lancaster County, PA. She currently resides in Vienna, VA, with her husband, Don, and four children. Linda is a quilt teacher and lecturer and has been working with Jinny Beyer Hilton Head Quilting Seminar for eight years.

Linda learned to sew at the age of eight but only started quilting at the age of 24. Her grandmother, from Lancaster, PA, quilted for the Mennonite Sewing Circle and for herself for most of her life. Linda decided to try quilting because of her grandmother's dedication to the art. She sent for a pattern from *Better Homes and Gardens* magazine not knowing the difference in piecing and appliqué and got an appliqué. This is where her love of appliqué began.

Linda loves to design and create and is good with color. She quilts in a wide range of patterns and styles and loves a challenge. Linda is known for her three-dimensional portrait quilts and most recently for her "The Bride" quilt. Linda also makes crafted ornaments and other accessories for sale. Her daughter, Stephanie, 16, is following in her mother's footsteps and is now making her third quilt.

Linda was the Virginia state winner in the Great American Quilt Festival for Memories of Childhood in 1989. Also for the Discover America contest in 1991, and was judged and invited to make a quilt for the fourth Great American Quilt Festival, in 1993, in New York City. She has exhibited in NQA, AQS, AIQA, Quilt Europa, and many other local and invitational shows. Her quilts have been published, on numerous occasion, in magazines such as: *Traditional Quiltworks, Traditional Quilter, Quilting for Christmas, Family Circle, Lady's Circle Patchwork Quilts* and *Quilt Crafts, Quilting,* and *Quilting Today, Miniature Quilts,* AIQA, NQA, and AQS magazines and brochures. Her quilts have also appeared in several books printed for the Great American Quilt Festival and three of Jinny Beyer's books and Linda herself appeared on Jinny Beyer's video, "Palettes for Patchwork."

Mildred Jeanne Poore, Overland Park, Kansas

Mildred Jeanne Enfield Poore (known as Jeanne) was born June 25, 1942, in Washington Co., KS, just outside Morrowville in her maternal grandparent's home. She spent her school days in Kansas City, KS, and currently lives in Overland Park, KS.

She remembers both her grandmothers and great-grandmother quilting and completed her first full-size quilt at age 13. She joined her first guild in 1986, the Starlight Quilters Guild, for which she has served as secretary, vice president, workshop chairman, and president. She also belongs to the Nitetime Needlers, Kansas State Quilters Organization, Missouri State Quilters Guild, and AQS. She also works with the Quilters Unlimited Showcase. She gives lectures and teaches workshops to guilds in the area including both Missouri and Kansas State Guilds, teaches at local shops, teaches for the Johnson County Parks and Recreation Dept., and gives talks to school groups.

"My belief is that quilting is a way of life for me. It is an integral part of me and my home. I have a quilting project in the front room either in my rocker when I am not in it so it is always close at hand to be worked on or next to me on the quilt rack where it comforts me with its presence."

Leona Popiel, Glendive, Montana

I am a member of the Sacred Heart Quilter's Group, since its formation in 1984.

Cheryl L. Porter, Hong Kong

Quiltmaker. Born in Ohio and raised in Kansas and Michigan. Earned BS in mechanical engineering at Univ. of Michigan, MS in industrial engineering at Purdue, and MBA at Univ. of Dayton. Employed with AT&T in Ohio, New Jersey, Illinois, Tokyo, and Hong Kong. Involved with quilting guilds and/or local shows in last 3 locations after beginning to quilt in 1991. Active member of Girl Scouts for over 35 years, and have taught quilting/needlecraft. My interest was inspired by several cross-stitched and embroidered quilt tops inherited from my grandmother and great aunt. While primarily a machine quilter, I am carefully hand quilting these pieces to complement craftsmanship already woven through fabric by the ancestors from whom I inherited my love of needlework.

Marcia Potter, Denver, Colorado

Born in Lansing, Michigan, in 1950, Marcia Potter, currently resides in Denver, Colorado. Marcia has a B.S. from the University of Colorado and an MBA. from the University of Denver. She is employed as comptroller for Signet Partners, a real estate services firm in Denver.

Marcia took a beginning quilting class at Quilts in the Attic, a Denver quilt shop, in 1974. Since that first class, Marcia has completed over 20 bed-size quilts. Marcia prefers traditional patchwork patterns and is particularly fond of star patterns. She attempts to sew every day and usually works on three or four quilts simultaneously.

Marcia is a member of several local quilt guilds and participates in a bee and a dollmaker's group.

Ruth Potter, Snohomish, Washington

Designer and quiltmaker. I was inspired by Katie Pasquini and Margaret Miller. I started quilting seriously in 1987. I like to do original work but fall back into traditional on occasion. I love collecting unusual fabrics. I am a member of QA, AQS, and MAQS.

Joy Avon Press, Godley, Texas

Joy Avon Curtis Press was born October 7, 1948, in Harrison, Arkansas, graduated from Lead Hill High School, Lead Hill, Arkansas, as salutatorian in 1966. She currently resides in Godley, Texas, and is employed as an information system specialist for Lockheed, Fort Worth, Texas.

My mother, Mary Ethel Wade Curtis, made quilts out of necessity. We would help tack the quilts on a frame hung in the living room. We would have to re-cover older quilts that were torn but were required. It was not uncommon to have five or six quilts on the bed. They would be so heavy we could barely move but we stayed warm. Our house only had a wood-burning stove in the living room and Daddy would not let us keep a fire at night, he was afraid the house would catch fire.

My grandmother, Nina Mae Downes Wade, made quilts for all of us grandchildren and her great-grandchildren. Her favorite pattern was Trip Around the World. She made a lot of postage stamp quilts. My son, Michael Len King, has one which we treasure. She always had quilts in progress and would cut out an entire quilt, label it, and place in a box until she was ready to make it. Her quilting frames hung in her living room and now they hang in mine.

I wanted to please her with my first quilt in 1973. I made a king size Nine-Patch quilt out of my dress scraps. I quilted it with double thread without a quilt frame and used an old blanket for the batting. I did not pull my knots through to the middle! When

I took it home to her to see, she sure was disappointed and was not shy about pointing out my mistakes. She gave me several lessons and an unquilted doll quilt to study as a pattern. I still have it just how she gave it to me. I love to look at her perfect seams, how she pressed the seams and how the little squares all matched. I wish I had taken more time to learn from her. Hopefully, I will have a daughter-in-law someday to teach how to quilt and grandchildren to give my quilts to.

My quilting has improved over the years and in 1992 I started my own business. My primary product is my own hand-dyed fabrics. My goal is to continue to expand my business, plus teach quilting and sewing to others.

Nancy Marsh Price, Santa Fe, New Mexico

Nancy Marsh Price, born Lansing, MI, Dec. 11 1942. Graduated from Michigan State University 1965, home economics and elementary education. Resident of Santa Fe, NM, for 25 years.

As a child I played under my grandmother's quilting frame. Around the age of 16 I begged her to teach me to quilt, and she gave me my first quilting book. In 1974 after our son started school, I began to quilt in earnest.

At first I taught quilting to Manos Encantadas De Santa Fe of the Embroiderers' Guild of America. In 1985 they recommended me to Santa Fe Community College to succeed Mary Woodard as their Community Service quilting instructor, where I taught eight years.

My special interest lies in the blocks, tops, quilts, fabrics, and patterns of the 1920's and 1930's. All my quilts are made from a historical perspective and either reflect my family's study of genealogy or commemorate a specific event or person. I also have made ecclesiastical banners for my church. I am a member of AQS and Northern New Mexico Quilters' Guild.

Merl & Fay Pritts, Mt. Pleasant, Pennsylvania

Merl Edward Pritts born Sept. 8, 1948, in Mt. Pleasant, PA. Essie Fay Hays Pritts born Oct. 23, 1955, in Seymour, IN. Merl and Fay met at the Mt. Joy Church, in Mt. Pleasant, PA, where Fay's father was the minister. Fay learned quilting from her grandmother, Essie Girl Hood. Fay started quilting May 1983, she started by making quilts for her three nephews. In 1987 she started quilting for customers. In the past 12 years, she has quilted 59 quilts. She made some of the tops along with her husband, Merl. He cuts all the material and does the machine piecing. Merl has pieced 25 tops in the last 5 years. Jan. and Feb. 1995

Merl learned to hand appliqué and machine quilt. He made his first wallhanging and is working on a miniature quilt. Fay is a member of AQS and the Mt. Joy Women's Fellowship Quilters. Merl and Fay entered local shows in 1992 – 1994 – winning many top prizes. 1994 Fay entered the AQS show and won Best of Show with her "Wild Rose" quilt. Their quilt "Elizabethan Woods Variation" was accepted at the 1995 AQS show. They make one show quilt a year. They are booked up doing customer's quilts until the summer of 1998.

Betty Wood Prochnow, Bellevue, Nebraska

Collector and quiltmaker. Betty Wood Prochnow has lived in Bellevue, Nebraska, for 35 years. Attended the University of Nebraska at Omaha. Married for 49 years, three children, and one granddaughter.

She taught quilting during the 1970's and 1980's at OFFUTT Air Force Base, Nebraska. Currently a member of AQS, NQA, Nebraska Quilt Guild, Omaha Quilt Guild, and Braided River Quilters. Her interpretation of an 1860 quilt made in Bellevue Territory of Nebraska won viewers choice, best of show, best large quilt, best appliqué, and best quilting at the Omaha Quilt Guild 1995 show.

Earlleen Losey Proctor, Cartersville, Georgia

As a wife, mother, and grandmother, I'm new to quilting though I have known since I was a young girl that someday I would make a quilt of my own. As a registered nurse working full time, with a family, I never felt I had the time to quilt or more clearly the time to learn to quilt.

Two years ago, my love for quilts led me to a quilt show where I met Sue Rupf and several days later became a member of Allatoona Quilter's Guild and the North Georgia Quilt Council. My first project was a Pineapple wallhanging and I was hooked! Since then I have finished little but learned so much. My first full-size quilt is a personal design and to be a gift for my daughter. My most memorable quilting experience was my first trip to the American Quilter's Society in Paducah, KY; so many quilts, so much fabric, so many wonderful dreams.

Jane Pronovost, N. Vassalboro, Maine

Jane Maria Pronovost was born September 12, 1941, in Norwalk, Connecticut; graduated from Mt. St. Agnes College in Baltimore,

Maryland, in 1963; married Jack in January of 1967; has two daughters, Alisa Antonia born 10-21-70, and René Rosemary born 3-20-73; and for the last 25 years has resided in North Vassalboro, Maine.

She began quilting in September of 1979 and has created 32 quilts as well as contributing to more than 20 group quilts.

In 1980 she began teaching quilting to friends. In 1982 she joined the Waterville Adult Community Education staff where she continues to teach today. She describes herself as a quilt teacher who specializes in teaching beginning quilters how to tap into their creative skills. Over 400 students have completed her classes. She has also taught at Yardgoods, the local quilt shop, and for the Colby College enrichment program.

All the quilts she has produced have either been given away or sold so two years ago a friend came over and helped her piece a quilt-in-a-day, "Trip Around the World," for her own bed.

Teddy Pruett, Winter Garden, Florida

Teddy Pruett, was born Barbara Elaine McMahon, a native Floridian. She began quilting in 1974, making nearly 100 quilts to date. She is a member of AQS, AQSG, CQSG, NQA, PAAQT, and several guilds, and has been a dedicated part of the latest quilting revival. Certification as an appraiser has led to a busy schedule of lectures, judging, and traveling, for learning as well as teaching.

Teddy states, "I am delighted to be a part of the world of quilts. It seems destined – I can't imagine anything I would love more. I'm particularly pleased with the new research and historical aspect. My schedule doesn't allow for much sewing lately, and I miss it terribly, but there are rewards to appraising and lecturing. It is always a thrill to be able to date, identify, and value a quilt for owners who haven't a clue. The appreciation on their faces, both for my knowledge and for their quilt, makes the sacrifices worthwhile."

Linda M. Publicover, Mansfield, Massachusetts

Quiltmaker and teacher. My first quilt was made for my oldest daughter in 1977. I started teaching quilting in 1984. Although I teach mostly quick machine piecing and machine quilting, on my own I prefer designing and working with as many different fabrics and colors as possible. Being involved with Quilt Escapes which conducts many quilting and quilt-related weekends and tours, has been a very exciting and rewarding experience. I especially enjoy teaching on the weekend quilting trips,

the energy levels and enthusiasm of everyone are so high.

I have had quilts exhibited locally and nationally, but challenges are intriguing to me. I have designed quilts including our local guild's raffle quilt, and have been involved with quilts for charity.

Florence E. Purcell, Dix Hills, New York

Quiltmaker, collector, and teacher with primary interest in traditional and reproduction quilts. When I retired from my position as director of Student Services, I desperately sought some creative activity to fill the void. Happily, I discovered quilting. Since I was a non-sewer I had to learn not only quilting skills, but also hand and machine sewing techniques. Despite my frustrations, quilting has given me many hours of pleasure. Fortunately, my three grown children, and my husband, also retired, are appreciative of my activities. Especially so are my grandchildren who are often the recipients of my projects.

It was a source of great satisfaction when we involved a group of Girl Scout leaders in producing Aids baby quilts.

Evansville, Indiana, quilters starting on Round Robin quilts.
Joyce Dillon, Mary McLean, Rethal Ball, Helen Deig, Margaret Blair, Susan Allen, Linda Reese, Rose Vanness, Judy Kaiser.

Ladies of Mississippi Valley Quilter's Guild at Walnut Grove Pioneer Village, Scott County Park, Iowa, demonstrating quilting.
Evelyn Maxell, Cathy Litwinow, Carol Boomershine, Frances Fostrom.
(photo courtesy of Cathy Litwinow)

Kathleen Keeble Qualia, Corpus Christi, Texas

Author of magazine articles and patterns. Designer, quiltmaker, guild member, guild librarian.

Kathleen's most memorable projects include: making my grandchildren's first quilts, working on the guild's community projects quilts, and my quilt that won first place – for most mistakes!

Members of greater Ann Arbor Quilt Guild, MI, working on "Safe House" quilts.
Left to right: Chris Menney, Lise Newland, Pat Ingersall, Saundra Weed, Patty Harbowy.
(photo courtesy of Saundra Weed)

Siskiyou Piecemakers Quilt Guild members check their 1993 Opportunity Quilt.
Donna Goodland, Dorothy Meamber, Harriet Houston, Betty Carrier, Bea Woodland.
(photo courtesy of Idabel Crowell Montague, CA)

Six quilters from Quilters Workshop of Tampa on train in Switzerland on tour with Swiss Quilters.
Grace Edwards, Garnet Edmonson, Lita Swindle, Barbara Kawalski, Merideth Wilmath, Alice Rodby.

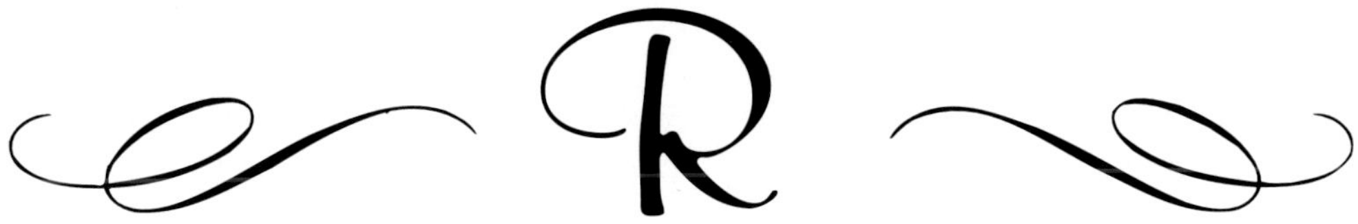

Kelly L. Racop, Lawrenceville, Illinois

Kelly L. (Whitlow) Racop, was born on June 5, 1966, in Tippecanoe County, IN. She currently lives in Lawrence County, IL.

It was in 1991 after she moved to Illinois and started attending the Ladies Fellowship of the Allison Prairie Church of the Brethren, Lawrenceville, Illinois, that she began quilting. Early on she was doing hand sewing but after a few weeks, one of the ladies showed her the basics of getting started as a quilter. A few other young women were coming with little experience, so a beginners quilt was put in. There were four beginners and a few regulars who worked on this quilt. She loved doing it and now has put together and quilted one of her own. She is presently quilting one for someone else. She is proud to be doing a craft that her grandmother knew and practiced so well.

Danita Rafalovich, Los Angeles, California

Danita began quilting in 1977 as an artistic outlet offsetting her deep involvement in the botanical world; she has a Bachelor of Science in biology with a major in botany. Currently she is working on two quilt series: one reflecting her years living in Japan and the other her humorous perspective of life through her rubber stamp art quilts.

Author of numerous articles published in America, Japan, and England, co-author of the book *Backart, On the Flip Side*, quiltmaker and rubber stamp artist. She teaches and lectures throughout the U.S. and Japan, where her award-winning quilts are exhibited.

While living for a year in Tokyo, and then in central Japan for 10 months in 1995, she traveled, taught quilting, visited quilters, and bought folk textiles. One of her many popular lectures is call "Quilting Adventures in Japan."

Betty Baker Ramey, Grayson, Kentucky

I was born in Greenup Co., KY, into a family of quilters. I am a retired teacher married to a retired principal who makes dulcimers. We have one daughter who is a librarian. I am a quiltmaker and a quilt keeper. I exhibited my work at the main library in Cincinnati, OH, in 1994.

Yetive Denton Ramsey, La Porte, Texas

If a generation is plus or minus 25 years and a person has an heirloom quilt that's been in the family six generations, consider the age of the quilt. And if a person is born in 1911 and has been doing needlework since she was four or five years old and making quilt tops and quilting since she wasn't much older, just think how many generations she's been creating quilts.

Yetive Denton Ramsey is living her "fourth generation," cherishing her "six generation" quilt and still using her piecing and quilting talents to make beautiful things that will endure generation after generation.

Yetive was born in Arkansas, Sydney Yetive Denton at Carrollton, Carroll County, January 28, 1911. Her Kentucky ancestors settled in Arkansas before 1820. Another ancestor settled in what would become Arkansas as early as 1812.

The first child of Tilford "Tiff" and Cora Sydney "Syd" Farris Denton, she was named for her mother and the Princess Yetive, a fictional character in books by George Barr McCutcheon, *Graustark* and *Prince of Graustrak*.

Yetive grew up in a two-story house built before 1900. Her great-grandmother, Dorcas Sophia McCracken Payne Sneed, lived with Yetive's family until her death in 1915. This ancestor, activity curtailed by a horseback riding accident, sat knitting and sewing. As she passed the time creatively, Yetive observed her and learned. At an early age she was able to piece Nine-Patch blocks by hand and produced a regular sized quilt.

Because of her mother's health, Yetive and family moved to Texas in 1916. They settled in Winnie where her dad worked in her Uncle Charlie Farris's general merchandise store until around the end of World War I when both parents took tests to become postmasters. Her mother took Yetive to work with her in the Red Cross room. Here Yetive participated in the war effort ripping flat felled seams that were not to standard. She also knit a pair of socks for a soldier. Her mother took off the heel and toe for her since she lacked experience reading directions.

As soon as Yetive could reach the pedals on her mother's White sewing machine, she pieced enough Nine-Patch blocks to make another full-sized quilt. This time she learned to pull the threads in the fabric to cut the pieces accurately.

During the early 1920's, Yetive's family moved to Daisetta, an oil field boom town. She finished Hull-Daisetta High School at age 17 in 1928. Home economics was her favorite subject. While in high school she did most of the family sewing. All this practice helped her produce a quilt that won first place at the 1936 Jefferson County Fair in Beaumont. This quilt, pieced in a broken star pattern, is a replica of the six generation quilt.

Yetive earned a Bachelor of Science degree in home economics from Sam Houston State Teachers College, Huntsville, Texas. She was the first vocational homemaking teacher at Crosby High School and helped plan, build, and furnish the Homemaking Department. Later she moved to a class A school at Alice, Texas, and organized its first homemaking classes and planned and furnished the first cottage there.

After marrying R.G. Ramsey and living in California at the beginning of World War II, the couple returned to Texas and Carl Allan, a son, was born in Beaumont.

R.G. joined the Marine Air Force. Yetive moved back to Daisetta with Carl Allan to be near her parents. At Hull-Daisetta she planned and furnished another new homemaking cottage to teach in. After a divorce, Yetive returned to school, earned a Master of Education degree and taught in the La Porte schools. Her teaching career spanned 32 years. Her 1971 retirement was caused by hearing loss.

During her 24 year retirement, Yetive is achieving success in the field of genealogy. Her homemaking vocation has become an avocation. She continues to sew, knit, crochet, piece tops and quilt, design, and do other needlework. She has knitted or crocheted 53 Afghans, 10 shawls, 11 hats or caps, many baby things, rugs, and pillows. With needlepoint and bargello stitches she's made pictures, 10 chair seat covers, 2 cedar chest cushions, 12 pillows, and plans to do more. She has also hem stitched a linen tablecloth with napkins. She has sequined and beaded 100 balls for her Christmas tree, crocheted a tree skirt, and crochets 100 plus Easter eggs for friends, children, and charity annually. For her son she has also made a felt trimmed, beaded, and sequined net Christmas cloth, designed luncheon mats to match his China pattern, and satin stitched an "R" on 8 mats.

Yetive still makes her clothes. She has saved and collected enough scraps for several more quilts. Yetive has also quilted with a church group and was a member of Shoreline Art League, La Porte, until it disbanded. Yetive has won many awards with her needlework aside from the sixth generation quilt replica, a version of the Broken Star pattern with fine quilting. Participation in juried art shows of Shoreline Art League alone brought

her these awards: 1986, 1st place, white on white bargello pillow; 1987, 1st place, wearable art for a linen cape with crazy quilt piecing, crewel embroidery, and crochet trim; 3rd place, fiber, petit point picture, Lady in a Hat; and 1988, 2nd place fiber, needlepoint pad for cedar chest, original design.

In 1986 Yetive made a replica of her 1928 prom dress featuring hand-painted fuchsias to wear to Shoreline Art League's Arty Party and Auction, the theme: Prom Night. She donated a biscuit "quilt" for the auction that added $250 to the scholarship fund.

The "Prom Night" dress was not Yetive's first attempt at heirloom sewing. In 1964 for La Porte's Diamond Jubilee, she designed an 1889 black, silk taffeta dress and incorporated an authentic boned collar of the period, a legacy from her mother-in-law. This garment won the most authentic design award. In 1992 at La Porte's centennial celebration she won a comparable award with the same gown.

Yetive's fondness for the cape that won the 1987 Shoreline Art League award is understandable. Needlework and genealogy are her passions. In this garment she combined the two by using bits and pieces of heirloom scraps and clothing, including lace from a treasured family wedding dress, and other sentimental trims for embellishment.

Yetive also taught piano for years. Her first earning paid for her sister's dancing lessons. Her work in other art media includes etched metal, copper tooling, water color, enameled jewelry, and ceramics.

Among other quilts and coverlets Yetive has made are: a 1943 ABC quilt for her son and several more baby quilts; a king sized Cathedral Window quilt; two reversible quilts, an original design utilizing quilted polyester crepe squares and "crazy quilt" embroidery; three double sized crazy quilts, one featuring manufacturer/store labels; another accented with lace and the third having jewel colors on black velvet; a queen sized quilt, "Aunt Minnie's Butterflies," a family appliqué pattern using all different butterflies on an unbleached background; a king sized "Aunt Minnie's Butterflies" similar in color choices but exhibiting an original (Yetive's) quilting design; eight biscuit "quilts" various sizes, Afghan to queen, assembled in polyester men's ties and fabric scraps including velvets in Round the World pattern, each coverlet requiring from 1,000 squares to 2,000 squares, and tacked instead of quilted; another king sized quilt, white on white, made from Yetive's son's flight shirts and featuring her original quilting design, butterflies and hearts; and other regular sized quilts including: 1) "3-D Nine Patch" in cotton polyester with original border quilting, 2) "Sea Gull" in cotton polyester with quilting, 3) "Jacob's Ladder" in quilted cotton polyester and 4) "Be a Square" in quilted cotton polyester.

Yetive is energetic and never idle for a moment. Her life is filled with not only plans and hope, but with accomplishment. She is always looking forward. In her words, "One of God's greatest gifts to me is allowing me to live more than four score and ten years so I can reflect and remember His many other gifts. If I live to be 105, I'll never accomplish all that I have planned. Blessings come much faster than I can count for which I am thankful."

Dallas Reed, Indianapolis, Indiana

Teacher, designer, quiltmaker, and lecturer.

Born in Scott Co., VA. Knew quilting as a child. Quilting since 1976, he has made over 100 quilts. Past president of Quilters' Guild of Indianapolis.

While teaching a quilt class at Indiana University-Purdue University Indianapolis, a beelette was formed that does only special projects. Since 1992, at least one quilt has been in a frame. The quilt is either auctioned or raffled and the proceeds go to a scholarship fund for a homeless or battered woman. A nursing career will put her in a position, where she will never be homeless or battered, again. The blocks are given, in lieu of travel expenses, by members of different Indiana Guilds, whenever Dallas Reed speaks. The guilds are always very generous. The beelette, known as The Class Act, has co-chaired National Quilting Day in Indianapolis for three years. In 1995 The Quilters Guild of Indianapolis gave away 251 quilts to 10 different charities.

Dorothy Ann Reed, Olympia, Washington

I, Dorothy Ann Nash Reed, caught quilt fever in 1976, when the American bicentennial celebration inspired me to try quilting as a way to use all those sewing scraps. Gift quilts for my three children and other family members provided opportunities to try new quilting patterns and techniques. I continued quilting through the last 19 years and today make mostly seasonal wall quilts. I am fascinated by new techniques I have not tried yet and try to include at least one in each project. Membership in the Blockbusters Quilt Group of Olympia, WA, has brought quilting friends into my life. My hobby will always be quilting because of the joy I get from the process of quilting, the accomplishment and pride I feel when a quilt is complete, and the love I express by making and giving quilts.

Lillian M. Reed, Taylorsville, Illinois

Lillian Reed was born April 21, 1938, and resides in Taylorsville, IL. She learned to quilt from her mother, Mary Durbin. Her first quilts were the Pineapple, Double Wedding Ring, and the Flower Garden. Then she made the Tumbling Star for her son, Glenn Reed Jr. It won viewer's choice at the Taylorsville

Chili Fest out of 114 quilts.

A great fan of country music singer, Garth Brooks, she heard a song of his titled, "Against the Grain," and was inspired to do something different. So she designed and handmade the "Musical Calliope" quilt. Quilting with metalic thread on ivory broadcloth with peach, teal, white, and gray. This giant carousel horse called Calliope, with sparkle in its eye, appears to come alive to the sound of authentic calliope music, that is concealed in a hidden pocket. Calliope won 1st place in the Christian County Fair, and 5th in the Illinois State Fair, and second place, viewer's choice, in the Decatur, IL, quilt show out of over 300 quilts. She and her quilts are well known throughout central Illinois. She would like to thank God for her many talents.

Linda Lee DeCou Reim, Vineland, New Jersey

I have a 21 year old daughter and I take care of a paralyzed man. I have a BA in elementary education and a 4th degree black belt in Goju-ryu Karate. I teach karate and arnis five days a week and compete in tournaments along the East Coast in weapons and kata (forms). I've been quilting since January 1991; have made 6 lap and wall quilts, 10 large baby quilts, 10 full-king size, and 14 quillows (quilts that fold into a pillow) for my friends and family. I have three king-size tops ready to quilt. I enjoy old patterns and I love using yellow. I have entered quilt shows and one of my quilts is featured in *Traditional Quiltworks* #41. I love hand quilting while listening to R. Carlos Nakai.

I made my mother an album quilt; a family tree where each person sent me their material for their block. Also included special events, pictures of my parents' wedding day, family, etc. I have "lost" two of my quilts to my daughter. One I didn't want to give away, so she volunteered to keep it in the family. The other one I was told was on her bed for a year, therefore it's hers.

Virginia M. Resnik, Rochester, Vermont

B.A., M.A. communications. Newspaper reporter, writer for 17 years before launching machine quilting business. Also a painter, photographer, bird watcher, walker, snowshoer.

Owner of Vermont Custom Quilting, a mail-order machine quilting service offering personalized quilting for quilters and artists. Because I live in a tiny town in the Green Mountains, I'm a

solitary quilter. My mail-order business lets me help others complete their works, and gives me the contact I need with other artistic people to stir my own creativity.

———

Speckman and taking a class from Deidre Amsden of England.

———

Sherri T. Reynolds, Sarasota, Florida

Quiltmaker, president of local guild for past two years (Friendship Knot Quilter's Guild) in Sarasota. Have been sewing since 8 years old — self-taught in Girl Scouts. Skills have progressed to quilting. Recently into trapunto and stippling and crazy quilts.

Very first quilt received 3rd place ribbon, 2nd place on 1995 quilt, organized the guild to make quilted wall quilts for Habitat for Humanity new home owners.

Ruth Rhoades, Toccoa, Georgia

My quilting interest began when I took a quilting class at Greenfield Village in Dearborn, Michigan, in 1978. Being part of a quilt club when we moved to Arizona furthered that interest, and I started a guild in Michigan where we lived for the summers. Later when we moved to Georgia, I organized a guild there.

I have participated in five documentations, have an antique quilt pictured in *Grand Endeavors* (Arizona's documentation quilts book), and have an original quilting design shown in *More Feathers and Others Fancies*. In 1991 I started a quilting retreat in Toccoa which has proven to be quite successful.

I particularly like old fabrics, and have a feed sack collection of 3,944 samples of varying sizes. I have pursued some research into feed sacks and am the author of the feed sack chapter in the proposed book on Georgia's documented quilts.

———

Jane F. Richter, Rock Valley, Iowa

Collector and quiltmaker. Jane just retired after teaching school for 32 years, so now she can devote full time to quilting.

Have made dozens of quilts both hand and machine quilted.

Memorable highlights are: quilting cruise with Doreen

Suzanne Mouton Riggio, Charleston, West Virginia

Suzanne Mouton Riggio was born Dec. 5, 1932, in St. Martin Parish, LA. She and her husband, Donald, live in Charleston, WV, where she was a musician and college administrator.

Her third career, quiltmaking and lecturing, began at retirement in 1990. A prize-winning quilter, she has exhibited in major shows, museums, and galleries in the U.S. and Japan. Several of her quilts are commissions; others are in private collections. She is published in several magazines and books.

———

Ashleigh Lynn Roberts, Brookville, Ohio

Ashleigh Lynn Roberts, born 1988, has already started a quilt collection. If allowed she will sleep on the floor to keep a quilt on her bed and would spend her allowance on fabric. She started playing with fabric as soon as she could sit in a high chair. She could sleep through any noise, except the least movement of the sewing machine. Ashleigh is a quiltmaker in the making.

———

Sharee Dawn Roberts, Paducah, Kentucky

Sharee Dawn Roberts received her Fine Arts Degree in Art/Textile Design from San Diego University. She has received national and international recognition for her high fashion quilted clothing and special machine art techniques.

Sharee was the recipient of awards in the American Quilter's Society Fashion Show, including two grand prizes, and has placed first in the Fabric Fantasies Fabric Festival at Bazaar Del Mundo two years in a row. She has been a fashion desginer for

the Fairfield Processing Fashion Show for 1988, 1989, 1990, 1992, and 1994, and for the current 1996/97 International Diamond Fashion Show. Her clothing has been shown in galleries and exhibitions throughout the United States, Japan and Europe. Sharee has been a contributing editor for *The American Quilter, Creative Needle, Sew News, Ribbon Magic,* and *Threads* magazines, and has designed a line of appliqué patterns. Her first book, *Creative Machine Art*, published by AQS, was released in April 1992.

Sharee has also contributed to many other books in the field of sewing, including, *The Ultimate Visual Guide to Quiltmaking, Easy Machine Quilting, Step-by-Step, The Experts Book of Sewing Tips & Techniques*, and is currently co-authoring a book of Wearable Art due to be released by Doheney in 1997.

Sharee travels extensively, giving workshops and lectures nationwide to various quilt and sewing related symposiums, and has been invited to Japan and Australia to give machine art seminars.

She owns and operates *Web of Thread*, which is a retail and mail-order business specializing in decorative threads for the Needleartist.

Jackie Robinson, Durango, Colorado

Teacher, author, publisher, shop owner. Began quiltmaking in 1978 with the completion of family Depression-era quilts. Involvement blossomed in 1982 upon opening "In" Stitches, a quilt shop in suburban St. Louis, MO. Created quilts and taught classes there. Authored first of nine books in 1988. Sold shop in 1988, and moved to Durango, in southwestern Colorado, to open a new shop, Animas Quilts. Continued writing books, forming a publishing company in 1991. Publishing company expanded in 1993 to publish works by other authors, and now has 18 titles. Books written by Jackie Robinson are: *Chains of Love, Star Gazing, Perennial Patchwork, Weaver Fever, Quadcentrics, Tessellations, Dining Dazzle, Animas Quilts,* and *Quilts in the Tradition of Frank Lloyd Wright.* Has made over 250 quilts. Highlights in quilting career: first book, *Chains of Love*, published in 1988. Faculty, International Quilt Festival, 1992, 1993, 1995. Faculty, Northern Lights Quilter's Escape, Denali Park, AK, May 1994. *American Patchwork & Quilting* article, Feb. 1995.

Marilyn Robinson, O'Fallon, Missouri

Mary Conner Robinson was born January 23, 1953, in St. Louis, MO. I've always been interested in needle work. I learned to embroider at 7 years of age. My first quilt took me 10 years to make. Once I finished, I was so inspired I began quilting for others. For the past 10 years I've been self-employed, teaching, lecturing, and designing for magazines.

The work I am most proud of, is a quilt I designed and made for Purina Mills 100-year anniversary. This quilt hangs in their St. Louis headquarters.

My favorite techniques include appliqué, trapunto, and stipple quilting. I've also found that quiltmaking is an excellent medium for that creative urge.

Connie Rodman, West Fargo, North Dakota

My quilting career began very early in life when I would play house under the quilt frame while my grandmother was quilting. I joined the Quilter's Guild of North Dakota in 1986. My aunts and my daughters belong to the same guild and we share our love of quilting, it is a family affair. My expertise and preference is appliqué and hand quilting. I am married, I am a secretary, and am working towards my B.A.

I have taught classes, been raffle quilt chairman, bazaar chairman, member at large, and conference committee member for many years.

I have won the guild award for two of my quilts and teachers choice award. In 1994, I won best of show Overall Needlework at the Red River Valley Fair. I have shown my quilts at several art exhibitions with my quilting group.

Rudee Ann Rodriguez, Corydon, Indiana

Rudee Ann Rudd Rodriguez was born April 10, 1945, in western Kentucky, and grew up in Trigg County.

Rudee Ann is an arts educator with 28 years of teaching experience, ranging from grades K – 12, including seven years as university crafts design instructor.

She is a member of the Delta Kappa Gamma Society International of women educators, and a charter member of AQS. Her work

has been exhibited in juried shows as far away as International Quilt Expo Europa II, Denmark, and as close as the J. B. Speed Art Museum's "Eight State Annual Juried Exhibit: Crafts," Kentucky.

She originated and directed the Capitalizing Designs Quilt Project, an arts project with support of the Indiana Arts Commission and National Endowment for the Arts. She and her husband especially enjoy international travel, ethnic foods, and browsing in markets and bazaars for arts and crafts.

Jean Roesler, Clifton, Colorado

Author: *Rectangular Quilt Blocks*, teacher, owner of Cotton Crossing mail order fabric. "Celebrating the Cowboy with Quilts" museum exhibit.

Catherine Louise Mears Roler, Indianapolis, Indiana

Catherine Louise Mears Roler, born August 22, 1952, has spent most of her life in Indianapolis, Indiana. Her love of needlework began at age eight with embroidery, continued to sewing clothing and household accessories, and graduated into quilting in the early 1980's.

She favors hand piecing and hand quilting but also does machine work. Her color palette is soft but sophisticated, usually including pink or a variation in much of her work. Many of her quilts are gifts to family and friends, and one of her pieces is in a private collection.

To date, she has created about 50 works ranging from six inches to queen size. She is a member of Quilt Connection Guild in Greenwood, Indiana; Indiana State Quilt Guild; and American Quilter's Society.

Scarlett Rose, Anderson, California

Author, designer, teacher, and quiltmaker. Scarlett Rose began

quilting in 1976 and began designing her own quilt patterns in the early 1980's. She has entered her quilts in various competitions and won numerous awards. One of her patterns, Star Bright, was published in 1992 by *Quilt World Magazine* in a special issue, titled "Blue Ribbon Quilts." Two quilts, "Autumn Leaves" and "Stars and Their Fans,"

were published in *Great American Quilts* 1993 by Oxmoor House. Her first book, *Celtic Style Floral Appliqué*, was published in 1995 by the American Quilter's Society. She has an array of designs planned for future books, some continuing in the style of her first book, as well as other patterns for different kinds of quilts. She has taught, lectured, and judged since 1986.

Judie Rothermel, North Canton, Ohio

Author, collector, fabric designer, miniature quilts and full size. Judie Rothermel co-owner with her husband, Bob, of the Schoolhouse Quilt Shop, in Canton, Ohio, has been teaching quilting for the past nineteen years and has been collecting antique fabric for nearly that long. For the past eight years through a collaborative effort with Marcus Brothers Textiles, Inc., she has been sharing her passion for old fabrics and nineteenth century quilts with others.

Using her personal collection of nineteenth century textiles as a guide, Judie designs and colors at least four fabric lines for Marcus each year. All of the fabric collections are of 100% cotton, and produced in American mills. Her first line produced in 1987, was a huge success. The line was called "Centennial Collection." Since then she has produced many notable fabric lines, such as "Discover America," "Aunt Graces Scrapbag," and most recently "Hyde Park," "Fox Hollow," "Renaissance," "Baltimore Album Prints," and "Peppermint and Sassafras," and "Textures." Each line has a theme, and is coordinated to work together, or with previous lines. Running the Schoolhouse Quilt Shop has inspired Judie to collect, study, design, and write. Each new project seems to have been a response to a personal interest, a trend in the shop, or the desires of her customers. Her knowledge of antique fabrics resulted from extensive reading, and studying fabric collections in institutions such as: the Shelburne Museum in Vermont.

Miniature quilts and appliqué are a time consuming interest for Judie and part of her teaching at the Schoolhouse. Judie is well known for her two miniature quilts, one full size made of four-inch blocks, and the other full size miniature quilt, made in five inch blocks. Both have been featured in quilting publications.

In addition to this, Judie has been writing pattern books for miniature and appliqué quilts. Most recently she has been producing books to promote the use of her fabric designs in quilts. The latest of her books entitled *Renaissance,* and *Baltimore Album Prints,* have been released. In these books Judie shows what she has done with the fabrics she has designed.

Judie also designs and sells a line of kits, from full size to miniature, through her mail-order catalog, and at major quilt shows across the country, traveling with her partner and husband, Bob, her biggest promoter.

Aunt Graces' Scrapbag is probably her most popular line at the moment. A wonderful line of 1930's reproduction prints, that look so perfect, that it is hard to tell they were printed in 1990.

Judie and Bob have three children, a daughter, Dana, and two sons, Christopher and Rob. Plus three grandchildren, Cole, Greer, and Macy. "The graphic patterns and craftsmanship of the best antique quilts compel people to stop and take notice, but it is the fabrics, charming, colorful, and imaginative, that makes the quilts so enduring. I have a great response to the fabrics I design, from people like myself who really like the look of old quilts."

Barb Rourke, Houston, Texas

Born November 24, 1933, wife of Tony, mother of Jim, 30; Mary, 28; Carleen, 26; Honoria, 25; and Tom, 21. Retired from So-Fro fabrics. Avid reader, enjoy going to plays, and listening to country and western singers.

I love to sew and especially enjoy making wedding dresses. Only in the last few years have I been bitten by the quilting bug. I like making the quilt top more than the hand quilting part. I always have several projects going and in the last few years completed several lap quilts. I really enjoy working with fabrics and intend to be active for many years to come.

Kathryn J. Rouse, Racine, Wisconsin

Quiltmaker and designer. Kathryn Rouse started quilting in 1980 when her best friend had her first child. Although she had no quilting experience, a quilt seemed like the most loving gift she could offer and she made a simple Log Cabin baby quilt. In 1983 she took a class at the local technical institute from quilt teacher, Geneva Watts, and learned the many different techniques in making a quilt from start to finish. Since that time she

has concentrated her efforts on making full-sized quilts interspersed with a handful of baby quilts.

Her sixth quilt, an original design of appliquéd flowers alternating with a traditional Russian sunflower pieced pattern, was chosen as the $10,000 national 1st place winner of the 1994 Land's End/Good Housekeeping All American Quilt Contest. Land's End's Coming Home division commissioned a group of Amish quilters to make a limited number of reproductions of this quilt, "Sunflowers," for sale through their catalog.

A former Montessori teacher, Kathryn enjoys volunteer work, gardening, traveling, and reading, as well as quilting. She lives in Racine, WI.

Nancy Rowley, Post Falls, Idaho

Quilt historian, member of AQSG, quiltmaker, designer, author, teacher. Wife, mother of 7, grandmother of 14, Master's degree in textile and design. Nancy is currently living in Hungary.

Published *Oatmeal Originals Patterns.* Enjoys research work in quilting; presenting a paper on Red Cross Quilts at AQSG; and making quilts for my family.

Mary Ellen Rucker, Issaquah, Washington

Mary Ellen Rucker was born in the heart of America (Missouri) into a large and loving family. We did not have quilts but my mother sewed practical items, mostly clothing for herself and me. She taught me to sew at an early age for which I have always been grateful. I won a city wide award in my junior year in high school from the DAR for the most outstanding garment of that year. It was my prom formal. I had a wonderful sewing teacher all throughout high school who taught me to always try to do my best work.

The years rolled by and I mostly made garments, then my career kept me too busy to sew. This was in the '60s and '70s. By the '80s I began to need something tangible to balance my work in the computer industry so I began to sew again. At that time I became interested in quilting. I saw some of Yvonne Porcello's work in California which deepened my interest.

I have been making quilts and garments since then. Also in the last few years I have been able to purchase some nice small quilts. Now I have a collection of about 100 quilts and hang as many as I possibly can in my home. My husband thinks we live in an art gallery.

Making and collecting quilts has become almost a full-time occupation for me. I was able to retire last year to enjoy this craft. Recently I won a first place award in our guild's show for a quilt which was made using the paper foundation method. I have begun to teach this method locally. I have just made a queen-size quilt (my largest yet) for our motor home and am in the process of quilting it on my Bernina sewing machine. When we travel in our motor home we stop at many quilt stores along the way and even plan our trips so we can go to quilt shows.

I must say that living here in the Seattle, WA, area has many benefits for quilters. I belong to a very active guild and to several small quilt groups. One group in particular has helped me to explore and develop my skills. Our instructor, Marilyn Doheny, seems to be able to inspire and guide us to each be more creative and experimental. We are currently working on a project where everyone will have a contemporary quilt when we finish. I have begun a newsletter for the group to document our work.

In summary, I am one of those people who doesn't usually enter contests and am not published, but simply thoroughly love the world of quilts in all its forms!

Margaret McNutt Rudd, Cadiz, Kentucky

Margaret McNutt Rudd was born September 9, 1919, in Graves County, KY. Margaret began piecing quilts while in elementary school. Her mother, Curnellia Newson McNutt, taught her to quilt and to card cotton for the batting.

Quilting was put aside in 1937 while Margaret earned B.S. and M.A. degrees from Murray State University; married Rudy Rudd in 1938; served seven years as home economist with Farmer's Home Administration; gave birth to a daughter – Rudee Ann in 1945; and, retired in 1983 after 31 years as a school administrator with Trigg County Schools, Cadiz, KY.

Margaret enjoys the prestige of being the first member of the American Quilter's Society. She is a member of Delta Kappa Gamma, a life member of the National Education Association, an active member of Cadiz Baptist Church, a founding member of quilt groups in Eddyville and Princeton, and an active member of Trigg County Quilters.

Margaret was a 1930's teenager when everyone was poor. She learned to crochet, knit, tat, and play the piano because neighbors taught her without charge. Now, her home studio is open one night a week for music, one night for quilting, when who-so-ever will, may come and learn. She freely volunteers at school. Her driving thought is, "Freely ye have received, freely give."

Cecelia Ruddy, Glendive, Montana

I have been a member of the Sacred Heart Quilter's Group for many years, since 1984.

Ruth Rudeen, Ridgecrest, California

Quiltmaker, teacher, designer, machine quilter. I started quilting during childhood. Over the years I became immersed in lap quilting, preparing numerous quilt tops and teaching this method at the local fabric store. Carpal tunnel converted me to machine quilting. I design new patterns, make tops, do machine quilting professionally, teach others, and am a member of the High Desert Quilt Guild and AQS.

In 1983 I initiated a one day quilt seminar in a church auditorium, showed 70 quilts, and shared information on techniques and the best equipment to use.

Jeffalone Brantley Rumph, Flint, Michigan

Quiltmaker. Jeffalone Brantley Rumph, a native of Europa, Mississippi, was born October 17, 1929. A graduate of Alcorn State University, with a BS in home economics, is a retired teacher of 33 years.

Quilting was a necessity, once chores and homework were completed. At an early age, I began piecing and hand quilting. 12 years ago, I began taking classes and quilting again. Since that time, making numerous quilts, the Log Cabin became my favorite pattern.

Co-founder of the Flint Afro American Quilters Guild (1989), we exhibit quilts and teach classes. Six of the guild members' quilts (including one of mine) traveled with the MSU Museum's traveling exhibition, across the U.S. In 1994, I received the National Council of Negro Women, Inc.'s Historical Heritage Award, "Women Who Make it Happen," for keeping our heritage alive through quilting. Presently, I am a member of the American Quilter's Society and the Michigan Quilters Network.

Helen Sue Rupf, Kennesaw, Georgia

Brought up in Kentucky, married a Kansan, three children. Made first quilt top at age 9. Always interested in hand work.

Like scrap quilts and have collected some. Have been president of Allatoona Quilter's Guild for two years, 1994 and 1995. Member of the Georgia Quilt Council and also a member of East Cobb Quilt Guild. Have taught beginning quilting and machine appliqué.

Mary Russell, San Luis Obispo, California

Mary Russell designed for Fairfield Fashion Show in 1992 and in 1993; AQS/Hobbs Bonded Fibers Fashion Show, 1991. Mary's clothes are published in *Fiberarts Design Book Five*; *Michaels Arts & Crafts*, Spring 1993; *Wearable Art For Real People* by Mary Mashuta. Russell is a member

of Network of Wearable Art; American Quilter's Society; National Quiltering Association; a charter member of San Luis Obispo Quilt Guild. Born April 1, 1950, she lived in Shandon, CA, during her childhood. Taking after her mother and maternal grandmother, she started quilting in 1975. Her hand quilted items often contain a symbol which is the same as her cattle brand. It has been passed down through the generations from her paternal great-grandfather.

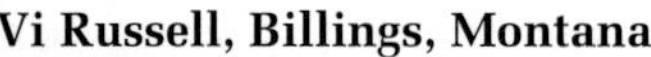

Vi Russell, Billings, Montana

Married 26 years, three sons. Owner of "Quilt Virus" and specializing in machine stipple quilting. Co-owner and quilt pattern designer for "In Sew Deep."

Jean Louise Ryder, Arvada, Colorado

Jean Louise Ryder was born October 26, 1952, at the Rhine Main Air Force Base in Frankfurt, Germany. She grew up in Idaho and attended Idaho State University before moving to Denver, CO, where she works for the USGS, specializing in computers.

She began quilting two years ago and just can't seem to stop buying books and fabric. She mostly prefers traditional designs and fabrics. She makes and designs quilts for the pure pleasure of creating something beautiful, but hasn't the time or interest in competitions which strive for perfection.

She dreams of making dozens more quilts to give to family and friends and to enjoy in her own home.

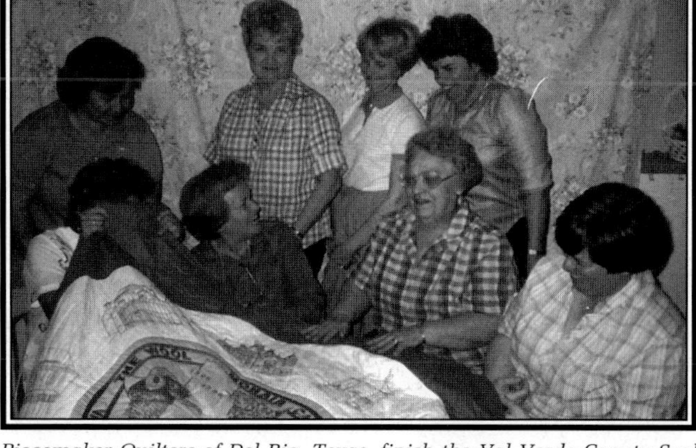

Piecemaker Quilters of Del Rio, Texas, finish the Val Verde County Seal wallhanging.
Front row, left to right: Rosie Calders, LaNelle Cross, Dorothy Nelson, Mary M. Reed.
Back row, left to right: Sylvia Smith, Sue Hill, Ada Sullivan, Dee Woodward.

Documenting a Pieced Rose quilt at Cody Homestead, McCausland, Iowa.
Donna Furrow, Donna Lanman, Cathy Litwinow.
(photo courtesy of Cathy Litwinow)

Quilters enjoying hand dyeing fabric.
Left to right: Emma Canto, Carol Shoaf, Kathy Fawcett, Larayne Cunningham.
(photo courtesy of Carol Shoaf)

Marie Salazar, Union, Kentucky

Quiltmaker, teacher, lecturer, curator, author. Wife, mother of five grown children, grandmother of 15 grandchildren, and an inactive registered nurse. As a child I learned to do and enjoy various forms of needlework including sewing. After my youngest child was in school I took a quilting class at a friend's shop and my involvement in quilting now consumes a great part of my life.

A founder and president of the Licking Valley Quilters; charter member, president, treasurer, chairman of The Museum & Archives Committee of The Kentucky Heritage Quilt Society; president and quilt heritage chairman of The National Quilting Association; board member of Quilters Unlimited; member of American Quilter's Society and American Quilt Study Group.

Most memorable quilting experiences: co-curating in 1986 "The Stained Glass Connection," an exhibition of stained glass quilts and stained glass windows; and being president of The National Quilting Association during the controversy between the quilt world and The Smithsonian Institution. Most enjoy collecting oral histories of quiltmakers.

Jeanne Lakatos Salcido, Danbury, Connecticut

Designer, quiltmaker, and owner of Tesselations, Fine Quilt Design. I have always loved the peace and creative pleasure of working with fabric. This, along with my love for writing and music combine to form the establishment of "Tessellations, Fine Quilt Design." I have taken the concept of tessellations one step further with the combination of my three loves — music, writing, and sewing into one creation. Each of my acoustical quilts is symbolic of special aspects of the person's life who is receiving the quilt. Then, I include a poem or prose explanation of the design.

One memorable quilt was a lap quilt I made for my mother, Pearl Lakatos, who was dying of cancer. She enjoyed it a lot before her death on June 23, 1993. Another creation was a quilt my daughter's Brownie troop made for a dedicated nun who served as principal of St. Peter School in Danbury for close to 20 years.

Mary Ellen Sample, Key Largo, Florida

Born May 16, 1952; Highland Park, MI. Grew up in Livonia, MI, and graduated from Franklin High School in 1970. Currently resides with husband, Tony, in Key Largo, FL, since 1980 and summers in Greenbush, MI.

Sewing has been an ongoing hobby since Mary Ellen was the age of 9. Originally making Barbie clothes she rapidly progressed to producing all of her own clothing. Quilting began approximately 10 years ago through the efforts of her sister, Beth Donaldson (quilt book author, teacher, and organizer of Northern Michigan Quilter's Getaway), as way to do something that would be enjoyed by both of them. Although her tastes in fabric have evolved in the past 10 years, Mary Ellen is still drawn to scrappy quilts and is an avid fabric collector.

Currently, Mary Ellen offers many classes in quilting at Island Country in Key Largo, Florida. She is an active member of the Florida Keys Quilters (treasurer), Ocean Waves in Miami, and Empty Spools in Oscoda, Michigan. Mary Ellen also belongs to four small quilting bees in Florida and Michigan. Currently she is writing a book on appliqué along with producing a monthly newsletter for the Florida Keys Quilters.

Muriel Sampson, Fargo, North Dakota

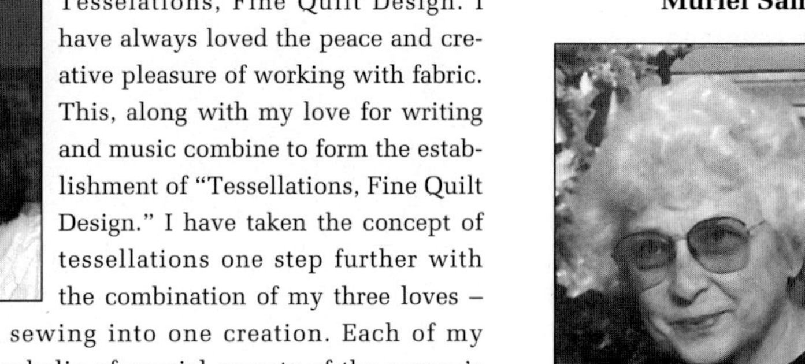

I was born Oct. 11, 1920, on a farm about two miles east of Colfax, North Dakota. When I started first grade, it was the first year the school had a nine-month school year. I graduated from high school in 1939.

I entered nurses training in 1940, and graduated from the then St. Lukes Hospital School of Nursing, Fargo, North Dakota. Had my R.N. certificate before I graduated. I was married after graduation and worked in hospitals wherever he was stationed so had many areas of experience opened to me. He became a quadriplegic after a plane crash so my experience came to good use. When a person asked him about how he felt about the many quilting projects he said he approves of it. When he sees what some women do, he can't complain, at least he knew where I was and what I was doing. I worked for several years at a clinic and a hospital, and was also active in many health-related clinics and research in the medical field which was really rewarding.

I began quilting when I was 9 years old, from used clothes, scraps, making Nine-Patches. My first quilt (complete one) was done when I was 13 years old, a full-size Flower Garden. I do both hand and machine sewing and prefer quilting on a frame. Wall quilts are done lap style or on a hoop. Of late, I've enjoyed appliqué. It's such fun to be with a friendship group so there is lots of experience with different styles of work to do.

I taught a group in Whapeton, N.D. Had about 100 students in all. They became very hooked, so a guild was formed, Three Rivers Quilters. This was a happy time. I also taught a class (stained glass) the first time our Fargo Guild offered classes with the quilt show; it was such fun. Our Indian Summer Show and Conference has grown tremendously since that time. I still teach. I'm active in our local group (QGND), Town and Country Quilters, Three Rivers Quilters, and a member of North Star Quilters. Spend one day a week mission quilting and my house is filled with projects from planning stage, the "in" program, to binding, and quilting needed. Quilting is a rewarding time, a quiet time of meditation for me. Many thoughts and prayers for people are stitched into each quilt. I'm so thankful to have been given this gift and talent to use for myself and others. I have three children, six grandchildren, and three great-grandchildren. A "Muriel Sampson Day" by the Three River Quilters, the governor's mansion quilt, was a joy to help make.

Candace Mixon Sanders, Arkoma, Oklahoma

I was born in Fort Smith, AR, and currently reside in Arkoma, OK. I have been sewing since the age of 9. My grandmother was a quilter. I collect antique fabric, quilts, and buttons. I took AQS appraisal course and assisted the curator of Old Fort Museum in Fort Smith on a quilt project.

I am an active member of Belle Point Quilters Guild in Fort Smith, the Arkansas State Quilters Guild, Oklahoma State Quilters Organization, AQS, and AIQA. I love trying new techniques as well as making old standards. I make quilts and clothing, many as gifts and donations. Occasionally, I teach a class or host a guild program.

My specialty is designing and making wearable art. I won first place in 1993 and 1995 in the Arkansas State Quilters Guild Fashion Show. I have also won some local ribbons. I like attending quilt shows and retreats and meeting the best people in the world – fellow quilters!

Auriel Oram Sandstead, Sterling, Colorado

Auriel learned to sew at her maternal grandmother's (Mary Stanley) knee. By the time she was 12 years old, she had pieced enough "durable" Four-Patch blocks for her first full-size quilt which was then quilted with her grandmother. The joy of working with fabrics and of quiltmaking has never faded.

Auriel is still a traditional country scrapbag quilter today, who hosts a Keota, CO, quilting retreat each June and again in August for quilters who appreciate the grassroots heritage away from the commercialism of the 1900's. She has had retreats since 1982.

For more than 15 years Auriel has shared with family and friends her "prairie patched medallion" quilting patterns that are an outgrowth from the Mary Stanley quilt collection that is representative of four generations of quiltmakers in one family. Many of her prairie-patched medallions are continuous thread quilting patterns that predate the computer continuous thread patterns of today. She was the originator of the Mary Stanley Quilt Collection that brought together quilts owned by 35 people for an exhibition in Keota, CO, in 1977, 1979, and 1981.

She served on the steering committee for the Colorado Quilting Council, served as Colorado Quilting Council charter president, and in 1988 became the first person entered in the Colorado Quilters Hall of Fame. She is a lifetime honorary member of the High Plains Heritage Quilters, a group that encompasses quilters from Colorado and Nebraska. Auriel is a qualified teacher and an experienced judge in Colorado and in Florida.

Merrilyn San Soucie, Newmarket, New Hampshire

Designer, quiltmaker, and teacher. A lifelong resident of NH, one of seven children, began sewing as a child. Graduated from the University of New Hampshire and taught for twenty years in public and private schools; presently pursuing a long-time dream of working at fabric art full time.

Accepted for two shows in 1989 – AQS Annual Show and New Hampshire League of Craftsmen Annual Juried Show; began studio sewing classes for children. Published in *Great American Quilts*, 1992.

Awarded an Individual Artist Fellowship from the New Hampshire State Council on the Arts in 1993; and the following year accepted by the State Council for the Arts in Education Artists' Roster which brought a 30-day fabric art residency in Barrington, New Hampshire. Accepted by a state jury to join New Hampshire League of Craftsmen.

Lisa Satermo, Fargo, North Dakota

My mother sent me a book on how to quilt when I was living in Germany for 3¼ years. I didn't know how to quilt but I knew more than the other Army wives and I started to teach them classes on quilting in our Wives Club. When I returned home I joined the Quilter's Guild of North Dakota and have continued with my quilting for the past four years. I enjoy appliqué and especially dimensional appliqué as well as making miniature quilts. I am married and have two children and I work as a legal secretary. I have taught classes, have been education chairman of our guild and chairman of our Indian Summer Quilt Show and Conference.

I have won many ribbons at our guild show. I enjoyed a trip to Paducah, KY, in the spring of 1995 going to the AQS Quilt Show.

Rosemary Scheppers, Holts Summit, Missouri

Rosemary Scheppers, born Nov. 16, 1926, in Jefferson City, MO, lives in Holts Summit, MO. Learned to quilt when I was a child from my mother, Emma Hager. Like to make all kinds of pieced quilts and like a challenge in a pattern. Design whole cloth patterns. I have made quilts for our three children and three grandchildren and am teaching our granddaughter to piece blocks. Wish I had kept a record of all the quilts I made for babies, anniversaries, weddings, and gifts.

I belong to AQS and MO River Quilters and quilt weekly with the Sew'n Sews at church. My quilts were entered in numerous quilt shows and have won ribbons.

Diane Rode Schneck, New York, New York

Quiltmaker, teacher, designer, fabric shopper, consultant. Originator of "The Phabric Phantom." Writer, editor, publisher of *New York Unraveled*! newsletter for fabric shoppers.

Margaret Schucker, Rancho Palos Verdes, California

Margaret is from Canada and moved to Southern California in 1960, after graduating as a registered nurse. She and her husband, David, and four grown children continue to reside there. She began sewing at an early age and can't remember a time when she wasn't involved in some form of needlework.

In the mid 1970's she began quilting and soon was teaching quilting classes for all ages. In 1980 Margaret co-authored with Evelyn Anderson, the book *A Miniature Patchwork Christmas*. Together they gave classes at quilt guilds, seminars, and stores,

as well as having booths at many shows. From 1979 to 1993 Margaret was employed as quilting instructor at Los Angeles Harbor Junior College. She is currently employed at Treadleart in Lomita as class coordinator and continues to teach many classes. Designing quilts and wearable art pieces are her favorite pastimes and she has won numerous awards for her work.

Vera L. Schuster, Corpus Christi, Texas

I have always loved quilting. As a child my mother and grandmother taught me how to piece and make quilts. As I grew older a friend taught me how to appliqué. I also appliquéd pillow cases and sold them. I made my first quilt at the age of 12. School and work left no time for quilting. After several years I was married to Bill, who became a minister. We have six children and nine grandchildren, who also love quilts.

I have made many other quilts, wallhangings, and banners in the past 30 years. I also taught quilt classes for 15 years or more. During that time our Coastal Bend Quilt Guild was organized and I became the first president. I have also entered some of my quilts and wallhangings in quilt shows and won several ribbons. I love quilts of all kinds and will continue to stitch them.

Marianne Elisabeth Schwers, Leominister, Massachusetts

If there is one theme that unites my adulthood during the past 15 years since graduating from Cornell University, it is creative challenge. I graduated in three years as a Dean's List student and member of the Omicron Nu honarary society from the school of human ecology, forever seeking creative expression in print, and "artistic expression."

It wasn't until 1988 when I began quilting, that I discovered my passion. My grandmother, taught me to embroider when I was 8. When I was 12, she taught me to sew. Years later, it was quilting that captured my imagination. Quilts were not a part of my family heritage but they had always intrigued me. In quilts I found the excitement of color and pattern combined in a pictorial window. Each quilt displays a point in time in a woman's life where her experiences unite in cloth to form a remembrance.

My life hasn't been the same since the night of my first quilting class. That night I learned that I, too, could create these fabric keepsakes. What has followed has been an "independent study" in the art of quiltmaking, under the instruction of some of the nation's foremost quilt instructors including Marsha McCloskey, Harriet Hargrave, Michael James, Elly, and Jinny Beyer.

What keeps me interested and excited is the fabric and that there is always another quilt to make. It is not necessarily new to the world but it provides a challenge to my skills and involves finding solutions to a new set of problems. There are avenues and venues to explore. Currently, my fascination is with reproduction fabrics and traditional patterns of the 1800's. This has led to my authoring and publishing of a newsletter, *Quiltiques*®, which focuses on the specialized interests of devotees of antique quilts and textiles. As a fabric lover, I also founded Vintage & Vogue, a retail/mail order company specializing in distinctive fabrics, including reproduction prints, Vintage, as well as the very finest in the "vogue" of today.

My most memorable quilt is one which I started the month my youngest son was conceived, worked on throughout our pregnancy, carried to the hospital, and completed during his first year of life. Each of the 12 calendar blocks induces a recollection of that precious time. My most important quilting memories will always include my mother, who after a life devoted to education, decided to pick up the needle in her sixties so as to have something we could do together. Every year we have a wonderful quilting weekend at the Quilter's Gathering, leaving children and husbands behind for four fun-filled days. The thread of quilting has been woven into our lives, binding our hearts even closer, leaving a legacy of love for family and each other.

Susan Chernan Scovern, Perrysburg, Ohio

Susan Chernan Scovern was born November 13, 1945, in Natrona, PA. Susan and her husband, David, reside in Perrysburg, Ohio. During the late 1960's Susan assisted fashion conscious customers worldwide as an international customer sales representative for Vogue-Butterick. The 1970's brought her two children and raising them became full-time.

While fashion, fabric, and pattern have always been a major factor in Susan's life it wasn't until 1982 when she accidentally stumbled upon quilting while seeking 100% cotton fabric for a skirt. Besides making and modeling her wearable art, her quilts have been shown locally and nationally. They have been awarded best of show and people's choice. Her quilt, "Spring Blooms in My Winter Cabin," appears in Nancy Pearson's book *Floral Appliqué*.

Susan's graphic art designs with a quilting theme have been used by NQA and Kaleidoscope of Quilts for promotional items. She feels quilting has given her the opportunity to explore her creative abilities and, besides that, it's fun.

Susan Elizabeth Harris Seater, Raleigh, North Carolina

Born in 1949, grew up in NJ & New England. Attended Brown University '71; Ph.D., 1978, biology. Married John J. Seater, children Elizabeth, 1977; and Robert, 1979.

Lived in PA 1974 – 81, NC 1981 – present. Quiltmaker & designer, 1978 – present. NC Quilt Documentation Project volunteer, 1985. Capital Quilters Guild, 1986 – present. Steering Committee for NC Quilt Symposium in Raleigh, 1991. Uncommon Threads, 1991 to present.

Zetta Pinkstaff Sellers, Flat Rock, Illinois

Zetta Pinkstaff Sellers was born July 18, 1925, in Lawrence County, Illinois, where she now resides.

For many years she admired the quilts that her mother and her aunt had done over the years. Many of those quilts are displayed in her home, and each of her four children have received a quilt from their maternal grandmother. When she retired from the business world in 1991 she was able to realize one of her dreams, learning how to make a quilt. She joined the Ladies Fellowship of the Allison Prairie Church of the Brethren, Lawrenceville, Illinois, and they helped her realize her dream. She has worked on many different patterns with these ladies, Dresden Plate, Log Cabin, Fan, and Wedding Ring. She has completed one Shoofly quilt on her own for her grandson. Currently, she is putting together quilts for two other grandsons, pattern is the Windmill.

Rebecca Selph, Corpus Christi, Texas

Married, nurse, mother of two boys and one daughter. Became interested in quilting after two accidents that required surgery and staying home.

Member of Coastal Bend Quilt & Needlework Guild. Quilt and fabric collector, designer, quiltmaker, bee member, historian, researcher for CBQ & NG.

Enjoyed working on ABC quilts, Ronald McDonald quilts for cancer children, won Wal-Mart quilt block contest for three years and won national one year. Worked on quilts for women's shelter, Texas Aquarium, and Botanical Garden, all donated by CBQ & NG.

Shelley Senteney, Greenwood, Indiana

Shelley Renee Senteney was born August 19, 1967, in Shelbyville, IN. After earning her B.A. degree from Franklin College in 1989, she now lives in Greenwood, IN, with her husband, Michael, and sons, Adam and Aaron.

Shelley learned to quilt from Wanda Black, who taught co-workers during lunch breaks. As a member of the Quilt Connection Guild since 1992, she has been secretary and co-chairperson of "Sew Day." Shelley is currently the newsletter editor, and is involved in a travel bee, a round robin bee, and the "Lulla-Bee." She is also serving as newsletter editor for the Indiana State Quilt Guild.

She was awarded grand prize winner in a Pretty Patriotic Projects contest in the July/August 1995 issue of *Crafting Traditions*. Shelley titles her entry "Bargello Glory!" which is a quilted wallhanging of the U.S. flag.

Marilyn Ruth Senyk, Charleston, South Carolina

Designer, quiltmaker, and collector of fabrics. Mary Ruth Senyk, born on Long Island, NY, currently resides in Charleston, SC. Marilyn is the very first quilter in her family. Most of her quilts are her own original contemporary designs and bold colors, her specialty. Winning many ribbons, she is very competitive and has had a quilt accepted into the 1994 Hoffman Challenge. Marilyn participated in a Swiss-American-French Challenge. The quilts were exhibited in Europe. Her piecing, appliqué, and quilting are all hand stitched and she has a very large collection of fabrics from her travels. A member of Cobblestone Quilters Guild, Charleston, SC, and AQS.

Saundra Seth, Running Springs, California

Saundra Seth was born March 16, 1951, in Los Angeles, CA. She currently lives with her family in Running Springs, CA.

She began quilting in 1990 after experimenting with numerous forms of needlework. Of course, once she began quilting, it dominated her life (as well as every available space in the house). In 1991 Saundra began dyeing fabric for her quilts and in 1992 began teaching and lecturing. One thing led to another and "Pieces of Dreams," her hand-dyed and original pattern business, was born. She now spends her time designing fabric and patterns and traveling for lectures, classes, and shows.

In 1995 Saundra was featured on the *Simply Quilts* TV program on HGTV. She is currently president of the Busy Bear Quilt Guild, and has helped design several opportunity quilts including the Bear Quilt shown at the close of the quilting program on which she appeared.

Carolyn B. Shay, DVM, Indianapolis, Indiana

Carolyn Marie Bloem Shay, DVM, was born February 24, 1952. She and her husband live in Indianapolis, IN, where she practices veterinary medicine. Carolyn took her first quilting class in 1992, and in 1993 joined the Class Act Bee. She is also a member of the AQS, NQA, and the Quilter's Guild of Indianapolis; serving as guild secretary in 1995.

Carolyn is primarily interested in contemporary design and the use of color; elements shared by her two favorite art forms, quilting and watercolor painting. Also, her love of animals has a major impact on much of her design motif. In her involvement with quilting, Carolyn is most proud of her association with the Class Act Bee. The majority of the group's time is spent on donation projects, with a strong dedication to community service.

Irene P. Shepard, Gautier, Mississippi

Born in Dallas, Texas. BA at Southern Methodist University, M.A., University South Alabama. Taught Spanish and lived in Texas, Cuba, and Mississippi until retirement.

Quiltmaker since 1984. Member of ACQG, Mobile, Alabama. Quilt Bees and Magnolia Quilters, Gautier, MS, and MSQG.

Bettye J. Sheppard, Evansville, Indiana

Bettye June Watson Sheppard was born June 18, 1946, in Evansville, Indiana. She began her teaching career there as a first grade teacher.

Bettye credits her grandmother for her love of quilts and fondly remembers sleeping on a palette or featherbed covered with

quilts. Her first quilt was a hand-painted cross-stitch completed during her high school years. She loves traditional patchwork, scrap quilts, and the color orange.

Her greatest love of quilting comes from teaching. She has worked with school districts to incorporate quilt-making into their curriculum through art, math, and history classes. She has taught throughout the United States and overseas and has been instrumental in starting several guilds. In 1988 Bettye's husband, Vic, retired from the Navy and they moved to Evansville where she opened The Quilter's Barn – in a 100-year-old barn! In 1990 she was nominated for the Teacher of the Year from the *Professional Quilter* magazine. Bettye enjoys working with a variety of groups and currently teaches throughout the Tri-State area. The Barn sponsors a weekend retreat twice a year called "Quilting in Harmony." She currently belongs to the Raintree Quilters Guild, AQS, MAQS, and KHQS.

Bettye says, "Finishing a personal project is always a thrill, but seeing what my students have accomplished is even a greater thrill! My most memorable quilting experiences have come from learning throughout my travels that quilting is universal and I can think of nothing more rewarding than to know that I have passed on tradition.

One of my most memorable quilting experiences took place during a tour of duty in the Philippines from 1980 through 1983. I was teaching for the naval base at Subic Bay and a pilot contacted me to see if I could teach him to quilt. Right away I thought this would be a great challenge and could just picture this developing into something bigger and better, perhaps an entire flight crew quilting as they flew from one continent to the next! That phone call began a wonderful and memorable three year experience that will last forever.

My experience started off as I left the security of the American base and went into the city of Olongapo to meet Mama Paa and several Filipino women. They lived in a small four-tiered home on the bank of the river that separated the base and the city. The river was the sanitation plant for the city as well as a source of food for the people. Our studio was the top level closest to the road. It contained several benches, a table, a few storages areas, and a treadle sewing machine. Upon my request a chalkboard was nailed to the bamboo pole in the middle of the room so I could explain things better by drawing them. There were swing-out wooden windows on the backside of the room and I quickly learned how wonderful it was to have them open so we could see and listen to the monsoon rains.

Our beginning supplies were very limited, there were no rotary cutters, matts, gridded rulers, and definitely no Ginghers! The lack of quality supplies didn't hinder the enthusiasm. Using ordinary rulers, yardsticks, and safety scissors each woman made their first quilt block. The blocks were assembled into a baby quilt and the Rockin' Rock quilt shop was established. Upon completion of that first quilt we had a party. The room was cleared, ice and soft drinks were purchased and Mama Paa quickly brought up from the kitchen a large pot of camodes (pronounced ca mode ee) and sugar. I was offered the first serving. They looked like yams or sweet potatoes but I wasn't really sure. Everyone else was served and they all waited for me to take the first taste. Very carefully I took a small bite of the item and every woman in the room started laughing, covering their mouths, turning their backs to me so I couldn't see their faces. I kept saying, "What's so funny? Why are you laughing so hard?" Finally, Gloria, Mama Paa's daughter told me that the Filipino superstition is that if you eat skin of the camode it causes you to go crazy and now they all knew why I was so crazy! We all had a good laugh!

Over the next 2½ years there were many, many more wonderful stories and memories made in that small studio on the riverbank. The women were extremely creative and adapted to quilting with ease. They quilted for the American women on the bases and developed a cottage industry for products to be sold in their country. For many of these women quilting became a means of support for their families.

It has now been 12 years since I left the Philippines. It saddens my heart to know that our American bases are no longer there, that others will not have the opportunity to experience first hand what I have. Each day something reminds me of time spent there, a story, a friendship, a particular quilt block or pattern and I know that through quilting I made a difference. No, the pilot never learned to quilt himself and the vision of a quilting flight crew never developed, but many, many memories did!

Carol S. Sherrill, East Granby, Connecticut

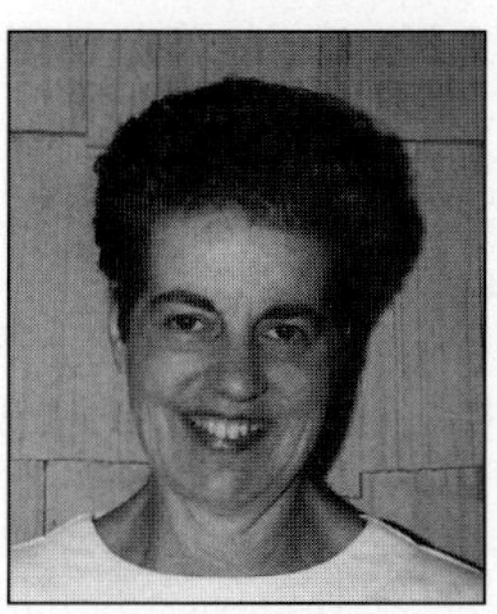

Quiltmaker. I am a retired dietitian, with a B.S. degree in foods and nutrition from the University of Massachusetts. Having a home economics background, I have taken many sewing courses and sewed my own clothes for years, often drafting the patterns. I began to quilt in 1985, and soon it took precedence over all other crafts and sewing projects.

I am a member of the Farmington Valley Quilt Guild, which I helped form, the Greater Hartford Quilt Guild, New England Quilt Guild, the American Quilter's Society, and the Gran' bees Quilters. I have done a little teaching, taken some blue ribbons, and held offices in some of the guilds. I like doing white on white quilts, miniatures, and new quilts made to look old.

Helping to form a new guild and having a miniature quilt shown in a book published by Chitra Publications are two quilting highlights.

Ann Shibut, Richmond, Virginia

I began quilting in 1957. For 25+ years I was self-taught, but since joining a quilt guild I have learned from many quilt teachers. I like piecing, but prefer the freedom of appliqué. I have made over 100 quilts. One was included in *Great American Quilts*, 1989. I had quilts pictured and an article in *Lady's Circle Patchwork Quilts* magazine. In 1990, I was commissioned by Simon & Schuster Pocket Books to make a small quilt to be pictured on the jacket of a romance novel. I teach and lecture about quilts to organizations.

I am a member and past president of the Richmond Quilters' Guild, a founding member of the Virginia Consortium of Quilters, and a charter member of the American Quilter's Society. I am a subscriber to Quiltnet.

Carol Ann Chavez Shoaf, Richland, Washington

Carol specializes in hand appliqué using needle-turned methods. She creates fabrics through marbling and other dying processes. Her workmanship in piecing and quilting is very precise.

Co-author of *Marbling Fabrics for Quilts*, is a pattern designer and co-owner of *Legacy In Stitches*, a company that sells elegant appliqué patterns, small doll patterns, and hand-dyed and marbled fabrics. She has won blue ribbons at the Arizona State Fair and various awards in Alabama. Her work has been exhibited in various galleries and has been in several magazines. She worked on the Arizona Hall of Fame Quilt.

Jill Shustoff, San Francisco, California

I am a fourth generation San Franciscan. I am 42 years old and am married with two grown daughters. I have always enjoyed needle craft, however, quilting has just been introduced into my world of sewing. I have always appreciated quilts and find them fascinating. Quilting has given me great healing, especially since both girls are now away from home.

I am a beginning quilter. My first quilt was made for my parents who celebrated their 44th wedding anniversary. I have just entered it in a show. I was honored to be among approximately

40 women who worked on the quilt to celebrate the United Nations 50th Anniversary. Although I only had a small part in its making, I became so proud to be involved and to see such a task completed. This was truly a memorable quilting experience for me.

Eleanor H. Sienkiewicz, Washington D.C.

Author, teacher, fabric designer. Elly's love of quilts and her initial instruction in making them came from those West Virginia relatives whom she has visited with a comforting regularity all her life. Degrees from Wellesley College and the University of Pennsylvania led to seven years as a social studies teacher. Then, at home with her growing family, Elly began to teach quiltmaking in 1975, and wrote the first of her 10 books on Baltimore Album quilts and appliqué, *Spoken Without a Word*, 1983. Her nine books *Baltimore Beauties and Beyond, Studies in Classic Album Quilt Appliqué* began with Volume 1, published by C&T Publishing in 1989. The Baltimore Album Revival show put on by C&T Publishing in 1994 to showcase quilts made from my books is a treasured memory.

Ami Simms, Flint, Michigan

Ami Simms first learned to quilt in 1975 while conducting research among the Old Order Amish for her thesis in anthropology at Kalamazoo College. She is the author of *How to Improve Your Quilting Stitch, Invisible Appliqué, Every Trick in the Book, Classic Quilts: Patchwork Designs from Ancient Rome, Creating Scrapbook Quilts*, and *How Not to Make a Prize-Winning Quilt*. She conducts workshops and presents lectures on various aspects of quilting and is the originator of the WORST Quilt in the World Contest.

Carol L. Smith, Elverta, California

Quiltmaker, guild member, and organizer. Organized! In a word, that is Carol's contribution to quilting in the Sacramento area. Charter member of River City Quilters Guild since 1977. Served on board of directors first 13 years; 11 parliamentarian, 1 v.p., president in 1988. Helped write by-laws and procedures. Quilt check-in and out chairperson 17 years.

In 1990, started quilting business, Granny Smith's Quilts (in addition to full-time job with city of Sacramento). In 1993,

organized Industrial Quilters Network (IQN) in Northern California; the group meets three times per year. Started TLC Quilters with two friends to make community service quilts. Also added three quilting retreats per year. President of River City Quilters Guild, 1988, Sacramento, CA. Made quilt to accompany me to U.S. Space Academy, May 1993; signed by fellow team members; resulted in "Right Stuff Award," Huntsville, Alabama. Presented 25th Anniversary Quilt in passenger talent show on m.s. Noordam, June 14, 1995.

Chris Smith, Newport Beach, California

Quiltmaker. New to quilting in 1994 through memory quilt participation, I became an avid quilter fast, finding in quilting a peacefulness, creativity, and soulful spirituality so lacking in today's society at large.

Member of America On-Line Quilter's Forum.

Cynthia Smith, St. Augustine, Florida

Self taught quiltmaker; wall pieces based on the tradition of quiltmaking; special interest in Names Project.

Finalist in 1995 MAQS "New Quilts from Old Favorites," Log Cabin quilts.

Janet Eastman Smith, Fair Oaks, California

Quiltmaker, wearable artist, and teacher. Janet Eastman Smith is a prolific and talented quiltmaker and wearable artist, as well as a teacher and lecturer. Janet's focus is on non-traditional quiltmaking. She often creates theme quilts and garments utilizing a traditional block design in unconventional ways. Her quilts and garments have earned her a variety of

awards, but she believes a quiltmaker should create from the heart and soul; awards are incidental.

Louisa L. Smith, Walpole, Massachusetts

Louisa L. Smith was born Jan. 12, 1943, in Batoe, Indonesia. She now resides in Walpole, MA. Educated in the Netherlands, she moved to the United States in 1960, and was immediately drawn to quiltmaking. She has been teaching and lecturing since 1981. After managing Quilts Ltd., a shop in the Boston suburbs for over a decade, Louisa is now a partner in Quilt Escapes Inc. This group arranges weekend quilting retreats as well as quilter's excursions to various parts of the country to visit the nation's top shows. She is a member of the New England Quilters Guild, AQS, NQA, AIQA, Studio Art Quilt Assoc., and past president of her local guild. Her quilts have received awards at local, regional, and national shows. Other honors include nomination for Outstanding Achievement as a teacher in Baltimore style by C&T Publications and a feature in *International Quilting Magazine*. Celebrity signature quilt was designed for the Shannon McCormack Foundation, with goals including a cancer hospitality house.

Louise B. Smith, Dalton, Georgia

Louise B. Smith was born July 12, 1928, in Craig, Colorado, and moved to Georgia in 1943.

Louise attended a church quilting class in 1969 and discovered quilting! She has attended available classes from nationally known quilters. She was commissioned to make quilted wallhangings of the four Georgia logos for the State Tourism Dept. She does commissioned work, attends craft fairs, teaches quilting classes at Dalton College, and quilts for others. She has won several cash awards and many ribbons on her work.

She is a member of AQS, Northwest GA Travel Association, and is president of the Handcrafter's Guild of NW Georgia. Louise quilted three quilts for the Georgia Quilt Project to give to the Olympic flag bearers in Atlanta, 1996.

Nancy Smith, Lake Forest, Illinois

Nancy Adrian Smith was born September 5, 1959, in Quincy, IL. She currently resides in Lake Forest, IL. She graduated from Millikin University in Decatur, IL. She has two daughters, and works

with her husband in their market research company.

Her first quilt was a hand-appliquéd baby quilt, made in 1978 from a Vogue pattern. She has completed 2 bed-sized quilts, and over 15 baby quilts. She has several quilts in progress. She enjoys the piecing process mostly, and the majority of her quilts are hand quilted.

Ms. Smith is currently a member of AQS, and belongs to the Village Quilters Guild of Lake Forest/Lake Bluff.

Nell D. Smith, Odessa, Texas

Nell is a quilting teacher at Odessa College (15 years), for quilt guilds, shops, and privately. A quilt appraiser certified by AQS, and a master needlework judge certified by the Embroiderers' Guild of America and chairman of the EGA Judges Certification Program. She serves as co-chairman of the textiles division of the Permian Basin Fair in Odessa, Texas. Her work has been shown locally, regionally, and nationally. She is a collector of antique garments. She has a B.S. degree in home economics from the University of North Texas. Married to Glenn R. Smith and has two grown children.

Rose Ann Snyder, Gautier, Mississippi

Rose Ann Schumacher Snyder was born February 18, 1947, in Kansas. She currently lives in Gautier, MS. She learned to sew in high school so taking up quilting was a natural. She started quilting in 1977. She prefers the traditional patchwork patterns and hand quilting. She has taught others to quilt in order to make new friends and keep the art alive. She enjoys entering contests, fairs, and displaying work. She also likes to demonstrate for the public. She placed honorable mention in the Mountain Mist contest in Houston in October 1983, with a whole cloth quilt called, "Quilted Counterpane."

Miriam K. Sokoloff, Brookline, Massachusetts

Born July 31, 1946 in Boston. Graduate of Simmons College, Hebrew College. Married with three daughters. Began quilting in 1981. Special interest in Judaic quilting. Israeli stamps and

illuminated Hebrew manuscripts have inspired some of her quilts. Also enjoys creating landscape quilts, both hand appliquéd and machine strip pieced. From 1983 to 1991, chaired a project of Stained Glass appliqué wallhangings (6 panels, each 4' x 7') for the Young Israel of Brookline Synagogue; synagogue and wallhangings destroyed by electrical fire 1/17/94. Member of Quilter's Connection in Arlington, MA, the Pomegranate Guild of Judaic Needlework, and AQS.

Audrey Truscott Somers, Deland, Florida

Audrey Truscott Somers was born in Hamilton, Ontario, Canada, on July 14, 1929, and moved to Florida with her husband and two very small children in 1957.

I'm a quilting beginner in spite of my 67 years and not anyone of great credentials – only a wife, mother of four boys, grandmother of two boys and two girls, and a retired secretary and medical records technician; fulfilling a long-time ambition to make a quilt. My mother was not a quilter but as a child we always had quilts on our beds.

My first attempt was a queen-size LeMoyne Star for our oldest son and his wife. I hand pieced and quilted it which took me two years. I'm now working on a queen-size sampler for another son and his wife, and hopefully will live long enough to make quilts for all of our children, grandchildren, and myself. Have also completed one over-sized crib quilt – machine pieced and quilted. At the moment, in addition to the sampler, am also working on what was to be a crib quilt, but has ended up being a twin-bed size – machine pieced and hand quilting. There are so many lovely old patterns I can hardly wait to finish what I'm doing now to start another. I do so enjoy the piecing and quilting, it gives such a relaxed, homey, contented feeling. My husband asks, "What do you do with all that material?" (can't pass by a fabric shop). He says quilting is a lot of work but to me it's fun and very satisfying.

Piece 'N Patch Quilters, Deland, Florida, is a quilting group I belong to. We meet twice a month. They are a wonderful group of ladies who I enjoy so much and they have taught me so much. The traditional patterns are my favorites, but I like to add my own color schemes and ideas to them so they have a little bit of me and not an exact copy. I'm not into competition or displaying yet and may never be. Seeing my quilt completed and enjoyed by others is enough compensation for now.

I visited the MAQS in Paducah, KY, last summer and was in awe of the displays. Such beautiful colors, designs, and workmanship was unbelievable.

Anne Veazie Sonner, Walnut, California

Quiltmaker and editor of quilting books for AQS. Anne learned to sew from her mother, and her aunt inspired her to love color and approach creative projects with a "why not?" attitude. Anne started quilting as therapy and a creative outlet. Quilting later became a great way to meet friends and now is a part-time job as well. Her professional background is in social work (abused children) and publications (quilting and plumbing). She is married to a wonderful man who gave her her first pieces of fabric for Christmas 1983, and she is the mother of a darling baby boy.

One of her quilts was juried into the 1990 AQS show and she has won several prizes in local shows and the L.A. County Fair.

Judy Speezak, Brooklyn, New York

Judy Speezak was born in Chicago in 1954. She has been a New York City resident since 1977. A self-taught artist, she dabbled in many different media before she began making quilts in 1985.

Speezak makes traditional-style patchwork quilts. Her work has won awards, and has been shown in numerous national exhibitions and publications. She collects early 20th century cottons, feed sacks, and elephant-image cotton fabrics, often incorporating them in her quilts.

Speezak teaches beginning and intermediate quiltmaking classes, and workshops in special techniques. She is a member of the Manhattan Quilters Guild (NYC), Empire Quilters (NYC), and the Quilters Guild of Brooklyn.

Patricia Spencer, Park City, Illinois

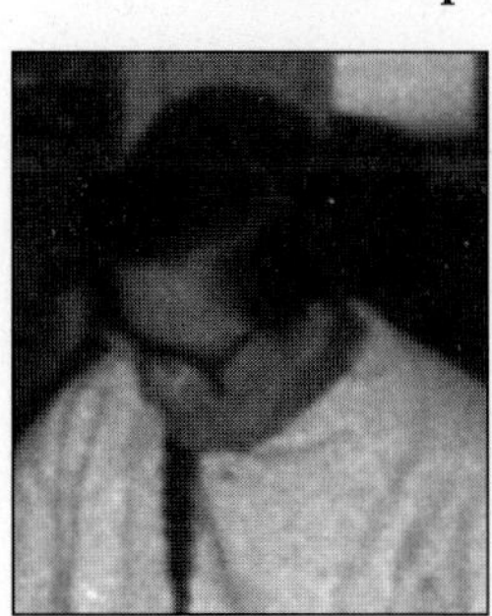

Learned to quilt 15 years ago, I like to make big quilts. In the picture I am adding my own piece work to an old, small quilt.

Aneta W. Sperber, Bloomington, Indiana

Aneta W. Sperber has added quiltmaking to a lifelong career in photography. The technology to support the permanent transfer of photographic images to fabric has made this combination possible. She has exhibited her photographs in numerous one person and group shows, and also her photographic quilts in quilt shows throughout the country. Her quilts are personal statements which often combine traditional quiltmaking approaches, photographs on fabric, and text.

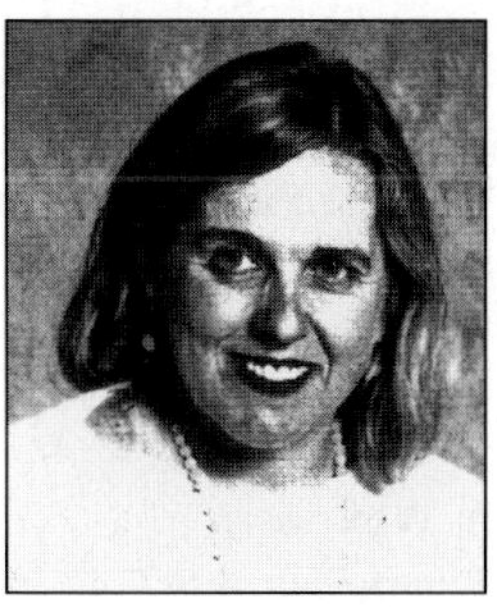

She taught photography for over 20 years, and has been lecturing about photography and quiltmaking for five years. She lectures about the history of photo-representational imagery on fabric and gives workshops in designing photo quilt projects.

She founded photoTextiles to give other quilters an opportunity to use high quality fabric transfers of photographs in their quilting projects. She lives in Bloomington, IN, with her husband, Murray Sperber, and daughter, Gigi.

Trudy Springer, Purcellville, Virginia

Designed Waterford Quilters Guild group quilt Taj Reflections, 1990. Learned to sew from grandmother. Began collecting quilt patterns in 1950's and began designing rugs and needlepoint in 1973. Switched completely to quilting after joining guild in 1988. Fascinated by textiles needlecrafts of many countries visited during working years; expanding my personal history through histories of women and their quilts. Now participate in exchanges, challenges, raffle quilts, guild leadership, newsletter publication, expanding book and fabric collections! Love the designing and piecing and am still struggling with my quilting stitch. Born in Wyoming, grew up in Nebraska and California; since world travels now live in Purcellville, VA.

Helen Squire, Paducah, Kentucky

Since 1973 I have been a quilt shop owner, mail-order source for quilting supplies, a teacher, lecturer, designer, consultant, and author. Perhaps best known as the *Dear Helen, Can You Tell Me?* columnist for *Lady's Circle Patchwork Quilts* magazine, I have recently retired after 20 years and relocated from NY – NJ to Kentucky where I am Director of Sales & Marketing for the American Quilter's Society. My quilting design series of AQS pattern books continues to grow. The newest release, *Helen's Guide to Quilting in the 21st Century*, joins *Dear Helen, Ask Helen*, and *Show Me Helen* as popular choices for patterns. Nothing gives me more pleasure than attending a quilt show or convention and seeing my patterns used in a quilt, especially in award-winning quilts.

Bonnie Stahl, Milwaukee, Wisconsin

My love for quilts started in my childhood from watching my grandmother quilt. I was fortunate to have her help me start a quilt when I was 10 years old. It took me a long time but I did finish that quilt and stitched on it my maiden name along with my married name and the years 1953 – 1985. Since then I have been hooked on the best pastime ever! At the AQS show, I was delighted to find a quilt in that pattern and learn the name of it since I had been searching all these years in vain.

All of my quilts have been machine quilted and all but one have been given as gifts. It is so rewarding to see my mom who is in her 80s and does not sew, enjoying the quilts I have made her.

Susan Standley, Tucson, Arizona

Susan is a member of Log Cabin Quilters in the Arizona Quilting Guild. She is a collector of half completed projects. Since meeting with the "Never a Dull Needle" group, which includes Melody David-Baker, Terri Johnson, and their children, she has finished more projects than she has started. She has even finished an Aunt Jemima doll she started 5 years ago! Susan was first introduced to quilts by her grandmother, Althea Metcalfe, but really created the first quilt of her own when she was a college student 15 years ago.

Susan was born September 13, 1960, in San Diego, California. She lives in Tucson, Arizona, with her husband, Bob Standley, and son, Robbie who is 4 years old. Baby number 2 is due in late August, 1995.

Carole Steiner, Santa Maria, California

I have loved playing with fabrics since childhood, and that love evolved into making quilts. I am fascinated with traditional patterns, and enjoy giving them different settings along with adding appliqué to achieve a more up-to-date look. I really like to do hand quilting, so I leave plenty of open space for quilting designs. After much encouragement from my friends, I began entering some quilts into shows, and to my amazement, they were winning awards. My quilts have won awards at the local, state, national, and international levels, with my most

memorable being the prestigious Gingher Award at the 1995 AQS show. That surprise truly knocked me off my feet! Quiltmaking is a "feel good" craft that has no limitations. It reaches all audiences, all cultures, and brings people of the world together through a common bond.

Clare Guill Steinfeld, Cordova, Tennessee

I was born in Union City, TN, and moved to Memphis in 1972. I have three children and four grandchildren and have been quilting since 1970. I was organizer and served as first president of the Memphis Cotton Patchers Quilt Guild in 1985. In 1986 I was 3rd prize winner in Better Homes & Gardens Club small quilting projects contest. In 1989 I won 4th place in a miniature quilt contest sponsored by "The Guest Room" (VA) and was among the top 25 in the *Creative Quilting Magazine* contest with my quilt shown on their Jan. 1989 cover. I have been a consistent ribbon winner and won Best of Show awards at the Mid-South Fair in Memphis, TN.

Eda E. Steinman, Monroe, New York

Born in New York City, I was raised in upstate New York. I attended The Fashion Institute of Technology in NYC, where I studied advertising design and photography. My interests include computers, gardening, and researching the history of my 200-year-old farmhouse that I share with my husband and two cats. I have been making quilts of original and traditional design since 1979, professionally since 1984. My work has been exhibited in juried shows across the United States and was published in the book *Award-Winning Quilts and Their Makers, Vol. IV*, and I have contributed articles to *Quilting International* and *Traditional Quilter* magazines. I teach machine quilting techniques, and am on staff at Quilting-in-the-Valley, a biennial quilting seminar in Warwick, NY. As a member of The Warwick Valley Quilter's Guild, I have served as vice president and program director. My quilt, "In My Father's House," is on loan to the Museum of the American Quilter's Society in Paducah, KY, from 1993 to 1996, and my quilt "Inventing Fire" received 2nd place in the Wall Quilt/Professional category at the 1993 AQS show.

Carol-Ann Stentiford, Harwinton, Connecticut

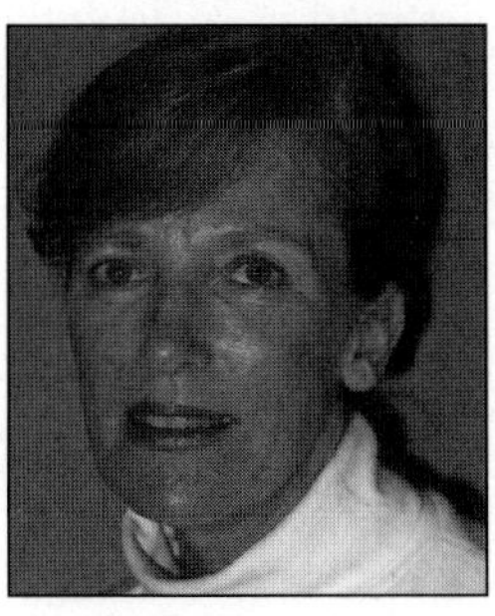

Carol-Ann Stentiford was born in Torrington, CT. She graduated from Fones Dental Hygiene School and has been in the dental field ever since. She now resides in Harwinton, Connecticut.

While Carol-Ann still enjoys demanding pursuits, a 1981 automobile accident forced a change in her activities. Being a true Gemini, she became interested in both quilting and basket making. One of her first quilts was made for her husband. It included 19 cross-stitch birds, and won first prize in the New England Craft Adventure.

Over the years the design classes in quilting and basket weaving enhanced each other. Her style was primarily traditional in both arts. She represented and demonstrated for several historical societies, had invitational gallery showings, and was featured in several periodicals and books. Many of her works are in private collections.

Recent events have caused yet another change. Her new work, now includes the use of silk, and is contemporary and free-form.

Marcia Stevens, Brainerd, Minnesota

After my first feeble attempt at quilting in 1975, I realized that I needed help. Through community education classes, workshops, and a quilt club, my expertise in piecing and hand quilting improved and I became addicted to this art form. In 1984, disillusioned with office employment, I decided to start a quilting business.

I purchased my first commercial quilting machine and Little Pine Studio became a reality. Over 2,500 quilts later, I feel that my experience with the management and creation of design ideas emulating hand quilting placed me at the forefront of commercial machine quilting. In 1993 I began teaching my style and techniques to other machine quilters in my studio and across the country.

I teach individuals how to maximize the capabilities of their commercial quilting machines through intensive one-day workshops. At the 1995 AQS show, a friend and I entered a quilt, "Minnesota Winter," in the group category and it placed third in the competition. To the best of our knowledge it is the first commercial machine quilted entrant to have won national recognition.

Barbara A. Stewart, Jupiter, Florida

Collector, designer, quiltmaker. I'll begin with my grandmother, Leslie May King, prime needleworker. She lived with my family for years. Her room had wondrous stashes of fascinating bits of various sorts of needlework. Way back in 1950 Gram King gave me a box of seven cut and partially sewn quilts saying that since I was the only one of the girls who sewed she would entrust their finishing to me. I'm still working on them, but those seven different designs eventually piqued my interest in color, design, pattern, and fabric to the extent that quilting is about the only sewing I do today. I've carried my quilts from Ohio to California and now to Florida. I am happy to know that my daughter, Linda Lewis, and granddaughter, Allegra, carry on the tradition today in Hawaii. I've only recently started to enter competitions and am currently a finalist at Paducah in the miniature category.

Gail Stewart, Overland Park, Kansas

I made my first doll quilt at age eight and have sewn ever since. A symposium I attended inspired me to design a quilt using the skills I learned. I have published patterns, given lectures and programs, appraised, judged, and taught classes in Missouri, Kansas, Minnesota, Nebraska, and Florida. I belong to many quilt guilds and have initiated miniature quilt auctions for charity at various quilt shows. Awards for my quilts include best of show, viewer's choice, quilter's choice, and many first prize ribbons. My quilts have been juried into the New England Quilt Museum, the Kansas Historical Museum, and published in *Quilt Art Engagement Calendar*. I continue to love all aspects of quiltmaking and strive to keep the art alive by sharing.

Marie Monteith Sturmer, Traverse City, Michigan

Stencil quiltmaker, author, stencil designer, teacher. Quilts in permanent collections with Museum of American Quilter's Society, Paducah, KY, and American Folk Art Museum, NYC.

Rose Sundling, Glendive, Montana

A member of the Sacred Heart Quilter's Group.

Egle B. Sundstrom, Forest Park, Illinois

Born February 1, 1939, in Lithuania, educated in Australia and the USA, and currently residing in Forest Park, IL. Egle comes from an artistic family, her mother, Elena, was an opera singer; her father, Antanas, was an artist and art historian. Egle started painting and singing as a child and continued those studies at university. She has given 4 solo recitals, sang in numerous concerts, and 16 years with the Lithuanian Opera Company. She served on its board for 14 years. Her love of needlework and sewing recently led to quilting. Since 1990 she has made 27 quilts, and currently has 37 quilts and wearables in progress. Fabric has filled her home and threatens to push her out the door. Egle won best of show, first place, and two second place ribbons in 1994. Her quilt, "Arabian Nights," was accepted at AQS in Paducah, KY, in 1995. This was the first year she entered this show. Egle's favorite technique is hand appliqué. She loves working with many fabrics and colors and designing quilts. She also loves quilting – by hand or machine and embellishing her quilts and garments. Recently she started to teach quilting. She is a member of 4 quilting guilds, on the board of SCQG, and a member of AQS, NQA, and IQI. Egle works as administrative assistant to the president and C.E.O. of Tootsietoy.

Holly Sweet, Cary, North Carolina

Teacher, designer, quiltmaker. Holly Wilson Sweet was born April 24, 1942, in Detroit, MI, and graduated from Indiana University at Bloomington in 1964. She currently resides with her husband and son in Cary, NC.

She began quilting in 1985, and teaching quilting classes in rural Indiana in 1987 under the name of the Stitchin' School. She belongs to AQS and Capital Quilter's Guild in Raleigh, NC. She enjoys designing and piecing scrap quilts and hopes to begin teaching again in her North Carolina home.

Lita Claytor Swindle, Tampa, Florida

Born in Christmasville (Carroll County), Tennessee, October 26, 1934. I began early quilting with my mother, Faye Elinor Claytor, and experimenting with quilting on my own. I have continually quilted since then and have exhibited at the National Quilting Association, Quilter's Workshop of Tampa Bay, Florida State Fair, and Hillsborough County Fair. I have taught basic and intermediate classes in Tampa and surrounding areas and I demonstrated quilting at Old MacDonald's Farm, Florida State Fair, from 1973 through 1990 and at quilt shows of Quilter's Workshop. Traditional designs, materials, and execution have been my major means of expression while trying to communicate to others my sense of the richness of the art.

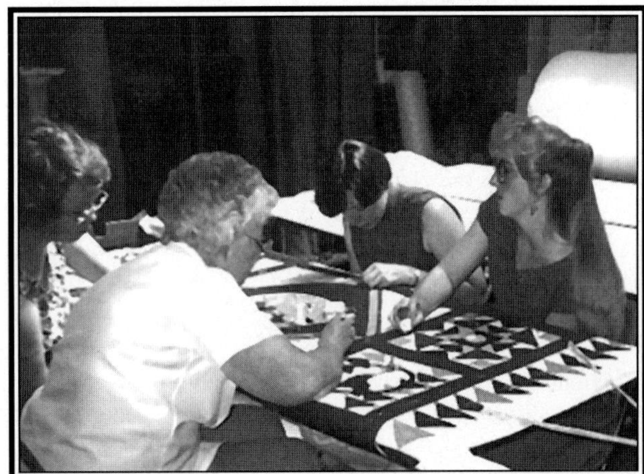

Members of Siskiyou Country Quilters Guild work on a wall-hanging.
Ann Hall, Bessie Short, Susan Reynolds, Melissa Hall.
(photo courtesy of Idabel Crowell, Montague, CA)

Willa Baranowski, Orchard Park, NY, talks about Penny Squares at the All Star Review, AQS Quilt Show, Paducah, KY.

Sue Campbell, Hyannus, MA, works on location shoot for Quilter's Palette television program.

Virginia Resnik, Rochester, VT, guides her commercial quilting machine.

Members of the Naples Quilt Guild, Naples, FL, display the Best of the Miniature quilts.
Left to right: Gail Stewart, Doris Janus, Joan Kirk, Ina Verschoaf, Robin Campbell-Morris

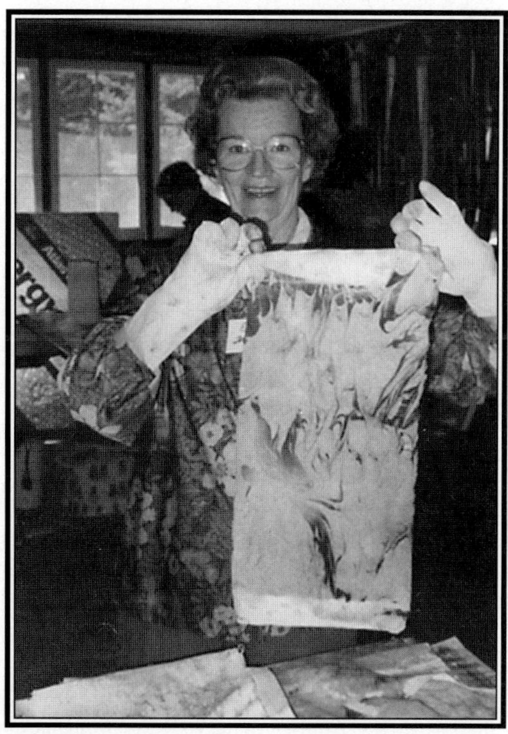

Elsa White, Mountainside, NJ, proudly displays her marbled fabric.

Diane Estrumse Taylor, Kennesaw, Georgia

Quiltmaker. Diane Grace Estrumse Taylor was born December 31, 1942, in San Antonio, TX. Because her father was in the Air Force, she has lived in many places around the USA, as well as in Japan and Hawaii. She graduated from Sprayberry High School in Marietta, GA, in 1961. She attended Wesleyan College in Macon, GA, for two years and then graduated from the University of Georgia in 1965, with a BFA degree in art education. She is a member of the Delta Zeta Sorority and was a Phi Kappa Phi honor graduate. A former elementary and high school art teacher, she taught at the Warner Robbins AFB school in Warner Robbins, GA, and at Dykes High School in Atlanta, GA. Diane, her husband, Hubert, and her daughter Stephanie live in Kennesaw, GA.

Diane began quilting in January 1991, when she took an appliqué class from Wanda Hizer at the Stars and Squares Quilt Company shop in Marietta, GA. Since then she has taken many other quilting classes in various locations, which has resulted in many UFO's as well as finished quilts. Giving them to relatives is a great joy.

Presently she is a member of AQS, the GA Quilt Council, the Allatoona Quilters' Guild in Acworth, GA, and the Southern Hearts Quilters' Guild in Kennesaw, GA. She has been the official photographer and assistant librarian for the Allatoona Guild. She organized a benevolent quilting project for the Kennesaw police department this past winter. For this project, 24 child size quilts were made by the Southern Hearts Quilters and donated to the police department to be given to children in accident or emergency situations. Other quilts she has helped to piece and quilt have been given to battered women's shelters.

Most recently she won first place for her miniature Pineapple quilt, "Confetti Celebration" at the Fall Convention of the Georgia Quilt Council, 1994. It was selected as the "People's Choice" in the paper foundation category.

Diane made a very special quilt for the "Georgia Quilt Project, Inc." It is in an 1800's pattern called "Chimneys and Cornerstones" done in antique shades of red, green, and cream. It was on display at the Atlanta History Center from January through April of 1996, and published in a full-color catalog with all the other Olympic quilts. It was presented, along with 399 others, made by GA quilters, at the opening ceremonies of the Summer Olympics – 1996 in Atlanta, GA.

Elsie Taylor, Treynor, Iowa

I was first exposed to quilting when about ten years old, back in the Depression era of the 1930's. Learning to hand sew quilt squares and carpet rags before graduating to the treadle sewing machine. 4-H Club followed with numerous sewing awards including blue ribbon at National 4-H style review in Chicago, 1938.

Classes at Iowa State University, Iowa Western Community College, and Joslyn Art Museum as well as weaving workshops filled my spare time while helping run a 400 acre Iowa farm and raising two sons. Helped start an Art Association in Council Bluffs and a Coop Art Gallery in Omaha, NE. Sold art work, including many woven wallhangings through the Coop Gallery and the Des Moines Art Center.

After husband and I retired from farm in 1980, I returned to my first love, quilts. Had never really left the love of fabric as it was expressed in the many woven and fabric constructed art pieces made for corporate offices in SW Iowa and Nebraska.

In recent years following the old motto of my mother's, "Bloom where you are planted," I have been teaching quilted vest and jacket techniques. Currently preparing a program for the American Cancer Society, "Making Memories with Images on Fabric." This will be a part of the Cancer and the Arts program for the Methodist Hospital in Omaha. A thirty year survivor of cancer, I am attempting to leave something of myself for my family and my community. Children, grandchildren, nieces, and nephews have been recipients of my quilts.

Helen Dobbin Taylor, Medford, Massachusetts

Quilter, collector. Born in Natick, MA, in 1914. Graduated from Girls' Latin School in Boston 1932, and from Tufts University 1936 with a degree in chemistry. Married and have 3 children and 3 grandchildren. I started quilting in 1978 with a crib quilt for my first grandchild. My main interest is traditional quilts

and I have made 13 bed-size quilts and many wallhangings and miniatures. I am a member of AQS, New England Quilter's Guild, Thursday Morning Quilters, and Quilter's Connection. I was involved with the treasury of QC for several years and have had 2 quilts in their show every year. Makes comfort quilts for AIDS babies and battered women.

Joyce Lovell Tennery, Oak Ridge, Tennessee

Joyce Lovell Tennery was born Jan. 22, 1939, in Dupo, IL, graduated from Illinois State University. Joyce and her husband reside in Oak Ridge, TN, where she has a fiber studio.

She began quiltmaking by learning to appliqué as a teenager. She and her two daughters have made quilts together. Currently, she travels across the country judging quilt shows and teaching quiltmaking and has taught for AQS, NC Quilt Symposium, NQA, Appalachian Quilting Party, VA Quilt Consortium, and Quiltfest. She is a certified judge and is qualified to judge master quilts. Joyce has served on boards of Smoky Mt. Quilters, NQA, and TN Valley.

Color and design are Joyce's favorite part of quiltmaking. Her quilts are in the Opryland Hotel, MAQS in Paducah, Methodist Hospital, and other private collections.

Ruth Webb Thacker, Corpus Christi, Texas

In late 1988 I joined the Coastal Bend Quilt & Needlework Guild. That has been a wonderful experience working with a group of lovely people who share the same interest. I am a traditional quilter and love piecing and appliqué. I have won 1st place on a handmade and hand-quilted, "Passing of Time," quilt in our quilt show March 1995. I also won 1st place and judge's choice in appliqué, "Rapsody of the Sea," an original design in the same show. I am formerly of Oklahoma City, OK, and now live in Corpus Christi, TX.

Ruth Theis, Glendive, Montana

A new quilter with Sacred Heart Quilter's Group; am learning the art of quilting and enjoying it.

Helen Kearney Thobhani, Littleton, Colorado

Quiltmaker. Helen Kearney Thobhani was born June 11, 1943, in

Raleigh, North Carolina. She currently lives in Littleton, Colorado, where she works as senior chemist in the transportation field. Helen's interest in quiltmaking materialized in 1989, when an uncle asked her to repair a "Britches" quilt made by her paternal grandmother, Susan Dunston Kearney. Helen was given her first quilt, a graduation present, by her maternal grandmother, Helen Young Morning.

Helen is the founding president of Rocky Mountain WaShonaji, a guild of African American women in the Denver metropolitan area. She is a member of Arapahoe County Quilters, the Colorado Quilting Council, and has donated small quilts for fundraisers and children in shelters.

Diana K. Thompson, Douglas, Michigan

I started to quilt because there was a need. My husband was away in the Navy – money was short. I was 22 and hooked in 1972. I taught myself how to machine and hand piece, hand appliqué, hand quilt, and draft my patterns. At first, it was hard to give my quilts away. But as I learned, more people put out their hands for a quilt. Before a quilt was off the frame it was asked for. I rarely keep a quilt for myself. I made 30 quilts, a few mini quilts, and several baby and wallhangings. I entered three contests and won one. I have taught two people to quilt, my mother at 74, and my daughter at 16. I believe in passing knowledge on. I like it the most, when I have a needle in my hand, stitching pieces together, quilting a design. Then, best of all giving it away. Oh, the surprise!

Bonnie Jean Thornton, Yachats, Oregon

Designer, quiltmaker, artist. Bonnie Jean Thornton was born Nov. 28, 1938, in Everett, WA. She and her husband, John, have retired to Yachats, OR, where she has built a studio to continue quilting.

Bonnie's quilts are original designs often inspired by her environment, experiences of travel, and living in several areas in the U.S. While in the Seattle area, she was a member and served as secretary for the Contemporary Quilt Association.

Her quilts have been included in many national shows and have won prizes. One of her quilts is included in the collection of the Museum of American Folk Art and many are in private collections. She was honored as the selected artist for Mastercraft

Exhibit Artsplash 1992 in Redmond, WA.

Loma Viola Darling Tippin, Waterford, Michigan

The first quilt I made was from a wedding quilt top Grandma Mizer made us in the Ocean Waves pattern. That was in 1950. My second quilt was made with penny blocks embroidered by my husband's great-great-grandmother in 1893 for her granddaughter's 16th birthday. I started taking classes in 1974.

I made a Road to California quilt in yellows and golds, and sewed the pieces in the car on the way to that state. I got 175 autographs of stars on the blocks: Mickey Rooney, Roy Clark, Walter Pigeon, Mae West, and Glen Ford all signed.

In 1976 I made a Bicentennial quilt to honor our 200th year. President Ford was in Michigan that year, and Governor Milliken's wife helped me get his and Betty Ford's signatures. I appliquéd his autograph on the central portion of the quilt, and then decided I should also honor the First Ladies. The "First Ladies" quilt, with autographs from every one since Bess Truman (1945), won 1st place in my category and best of show at the 1976 Americana Show in California. The *L.A.Times* featured it on the cover of its Sunday magazine issue.

In 1981, I organized the Crazy Quilters of Clare County (now 52 members). I am also a member of the Mt. Pleasant Guild, the Michigan Quilt Network, and the Polk Patchers in Florida. I took all the classes I could, and have taught classes in beginning and advanced quilting. I have also taught in California and Florida. My quilting philosophy has been to help anyone with problem areas anyplace, anytime; never be an old dog that can't learn new tricks; learn and share; try new areas, new techniques – to stretch myself; strive to do perfect work (seldom is it perfect, but it will be close!); never criticize other quilters' stitches; and have a good time.

My great-grandmother, grandmother, mother, and two sisters were all quilters. Between 1974 and 1994, I made 29 full-sized quilts, 45 wall quilts, and 55 mini quilts or clothing pieces, including the "Sally Rand" quilt.

Barbara Jean Toohig, McLean, Virginia

Member of the National Quilting Assoc., American Quilter's Society, Embroiderers Guild of America, Council of American Embroiderers, McLean Quilters Unlimited.

I have loved needlework since my grandmother taught me to make yo yo quilts many decades ago. Now, most interested in

viewing quilts, attending workshops, and presenting programs on needle arts, especially molas. I have a nice collection of tourist molas, trade molas, and art molas.

Most fun and exciting was being one of small group of women to visit and study stitching with the Cuna Indians in the San Blas Islands. The matrilineal society is fascinating. Most rewarding was to be asked to embellish a liturgical vestment for a Jamaican ordination. Our small group of four women had gone to help set up a sewing workroom to enable the women to develop marketable skills.

Eileen Jahnke Trestain, Phoenix, Arizona

I began quilting with instruction from my grandmother, Jessie Stowers Hertel. I grew up in Middleville, Michigan, near Grand Rapids. My family still resides nearby. In 1984, I married, and moved to Dallas, TX. David Trestain is my wonderful husband, and we have one child, Tricia. In 1994, we again moved, this time to Phoenix, Arizona.

I am a quilted textile appraiser, certified by AQS. I design patterns for dimensional appliqué, have written articles for magazines, and am preparing a book on antique fabrics for AQS. I love to travel and teach on the subject of antique quilts and fabrics, and on appliqué techniques.

In 1987 – 1989, I was asked to work on a research project for the Heritage Farmstead in Collin County, TX, and we documented quilts in that county during that time. After moving to Phoenix, I was asked to chair a new program for the Arizona Quilters Guild, to hire national level speakers for AQG. I am the president of the charter board of Phoenix Area Quilters Association.

Jenny Tripp, North Brookfield, Massachusetts

12-year-old home schooler, the middle child. My hobbies are reading and quilting.

Student since 1992, participating in designing projects to sew and quilt for my home and for town functions. 1st and 2nd place ribbons from Hardwick Country Fair for my hand-sewn and quilted projects.

Kathy Tsark, Honolulu, Hawaii

Author, collector, designer, quiltmaker, publisher, researcher, judge, and teacher. Editor of *Hawaiian Quilt Research Project Newsletter*.

Hawaii born and raised, Kathy Tsark became interested in Hawaiian quilting in 1972. By 1980, she designed and published a line of quilting patterns and kits and marketed them through the mail by writing a quarterly newsletter about Hawaiian quilting. This endeavor was a part-time business for 12 years. After 15 years, the *Hawaiian Stitchery Newsletter* is still in print. Also, the past several years, she has been the editor of the *Hawaiian Quilt Research Project Newsletter*, a non-profit organization.

In 1993, Tsark opened Kwilts 'n Koa, The All Hawaiian Shoppe, in Kaimuki on the island of Oahu. Three years old, Kwilts 'n Koa specializes in Hawaiian quilting, teaching classes, and selling supplies and various Hawaiian gifts. Tsark, together with Tsark's 27-year-old son, Robert, who also is an expert quilter, and her niece LeAnn, an expert quilter in her own right, make up the team that runs the store 5 days a week. Kathy loves to spend her time making and designing quilts. She has made many quilts which combine Hawaiian quilting techniques with patchwork and always has six or so quilts in progress. She also enjoys making quilted clothing and is interested in producing patterns for such items.

Holice Turnbow, Shepherdstown, West Virginia

Designer, author, teacher, and quiltmaker. I have been quilting since the early 1970's and conduct workshops and lectures in many techniques of quilting with emphasis on the development and use of quilting designs – specifically whole-cloth designs. Serve as quilting consultant to Spartex, Inc., for which I design or adapt whole cloth designs for screen printing. I have researched and developed a series of whole cloth designs based on quilts in the collection of the Smithsonian Institution. I also serve as quilting consultant to Benartex Fabrics providing advice and assistance on current trends of designs wanted by quilters. I design and write instructions for a series of fast and easy crib quilts for *Quilt Craft* magazine. I have appeared on five PBS shows with Kaye Wood and a 13 part series, *Heirlooms by Design*. I am co-curator of The Hoffman Challenge with Betty Boyink. Certified quilt judge and teacher by the National Quilting Association.

Worked with the US Postal Service and the Department of Cultural and History of the State of West Virginia in first day ceremonies to introduce a postage stamp commemorating quiltmaking.

Nadine A. Turner, Porterville, California

Teacher, collector, and quiltmaker. Having been raised with a family of quilters, this has always been a part of my life. After retirement I started teaching quilting in my home and then the city of Porterville's Parks and Leisure Department was looking for a quilting teacher and I was hired. I continued in this position for about six years. In 1984, I was the founding president of the Porterville Quilters that has grown from 12 original members to group of over 70. Through the years I have held many offices and chairmanships. Many of my quilts have won awards at fairs and quilt shows. Even at the age of 85, I still remain active and my love for quilting is eternal. I enjoy seeing my students go on to become proficient quilters and award winners.

Indiana quilt group making serious decisions and having fun, too.
Left to right: Marti Lowery, Trudy Schmidt, Karen Hasler, Lorane Mason,
& Carol Kubiski.

Some of the Cannonville, Utah, Relief Society members quilting on a current project.
Left to right: Kay Dunham, Glenna Fletcher, Anita Fletcher & LaVera Moss.

Trisha G. Underwood, Woodstock, Connecticut

Born March 17, 1958, in Worcester, MA. Grew up in Waltham, MA. Married my husband September 17, 1986, in Colorado while traveling across the country.

Started quilting in 1988 after becoming pregnant with my first child and completed a baby crib quilt six months after she was born.

I have made four wallhangings, quilted a Christmas tree skirt, and quilted Christmas stockings since. I have three young children so I try to stick to small projects.

I like to do appliqué most but also enjoy piecing and hand quilting. I won 42 Grandmother's Fan blocks from the Woodstock Hill Quilters. We each made two blocks. I am now putting them together to make my first bed size quilt; a king size.

I belong to two local quilt groups as well as AQS and the NEQG. I love to go to quilt shows, as well as take quilting classes.

Barbara Vallone, Racine, Wisconsin

Barbara Albeck Vallone was born June 24, 1938, in Racine, WI, where she still lives with her husband, Charles.

She teaches quilting classes at Wustum Museum; she started two local quilt groups, Rainbow and Prism Quilters; she organizes several workshops for local quilters, including quilting bees to make baby quilts for children of abused or homeless women.

In 1988 she developed a Quilt Discovery Project for the Racine Historical Museum which documented 667 quilts in Racine County. Many of these quilts are displayed at Preservation Racine's annual Tour of Historic Places in featured homes. She is coordinating the quilt display for downtown Racine's Avenue of Quilts, begun January 1994.

Meiny Vermaas-van der Heide, Tempe, Arizona

Making quilts since 1982, I view each of my studio art quilts as a challenge that satisfies my hunger for beauty, color, form, and

texture. Born in 1956 in the Netherlands, they reflect my Dutch heritage crossing boundaries through innovative use of traditional American patchwork. Inspiration from the work of Dutch painters, like Piet Mondriaan and Vincent van Gogh combined with the color of flowers reminiscent of Holland, can be experienced in respectively the "Homage to Mondriaan," the "Piece for Peace," the "Celebration of Life," the "Lines," and the "Fields of Color" series. After living in Arizona for 8 years, the colors and visual textures of the Sonoran Desert and the almost "Classic European" heritage of Modernism as found in the style, blend together in the "Southwest" and the "Reflection" series.

At the same time I want to share emotions in my quilts, whether religious, personal, or universal; therefore almost all are labeled as "Green Quilts" or "Earth Quilts." For me the "Green Quilt" label stands for environmental concern brought in a positive way, open-ended. Earth Quilts are my acknowledgement that environmental issues cannot be seen without questioning "war and peace," economic and social issues as well.

My widely published work has been shown in numerous exhibitions on both sides of the Atlantic. Most notable international juried exhibitions in the fiber field: Needle Expressions '92, Visions '92, Europa Quilts '93, Quilt National '93, and Visions '94, where among others Paul J. Smith, former Director of the American Craft Museum, and Michael Monroe, former Director of the Smithsonian Institution's Renwick Gallery of American Craft, served as jurors.

She is a juried member of Arizona Designer Craftsmen, the regional representative to the Studio Art Quilt Association Arizona, as well as a member of the Patchwork Professionals in the Netherlands and the European Textile Network. She is also a member of the American Craft Council, the Surface Design Association, the AIQA, AQS, and the NQA. She has curated the "Focus on Quilts" exhibit, currently in the 1992 – 1996 Traveling Exhibition Program sponsored by the Arizona Commission on the Arts.

Having made more than 50 "Green Quilts" and 60 "Earth Quilts" to date, I have been honored to participate in 12 environmental "Green Quilt/Earth Quilt" theme exhibitions, as well as having several solo exhibitions. In 1995 my work was shown in three solo exhibitions with an environmental "Green Quilt/Earth Quilt" theme within four months: "Introduction to Green Quilts," Rutland, VT; "Earth Quilts-Green Quilts," New York; NY; and as a featured artist in "Fabric of Legacies," Fort Collins, CO. My quilts are my voice, therefore I am willing to loan my quilts for exhibitions just to spread their message.

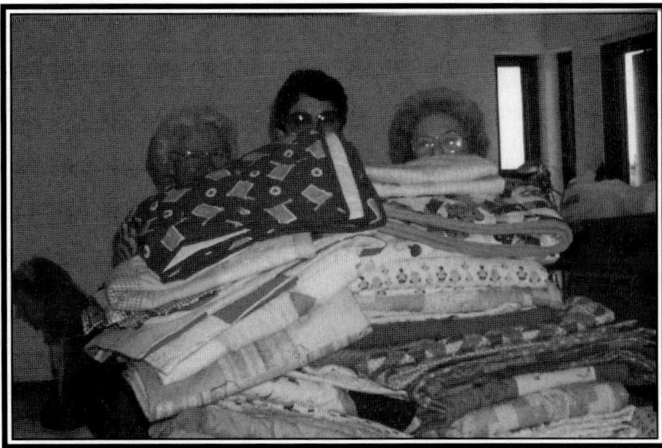
Coastal Quilt and Needlework Guild, Corpus Christi, Texas.
Left to right: Vivian Visali, Toni Lambert, and Cornelia Morgan.

Kristina Volker, Pleasanton, California

Designer, quiltmaker, writer, and editor. I came to the U.S. (New York) in 1952. My family tradition contains no quiltmaking, but my mother taught me to embroider and sew by hand. After a liberal arts degree, 8-year teaching career, and starting a family, I "discovered" quiltmaking, and my husband and sons have actively participated in and encouraged my development. A member of East Bay Heritage Quilters (Berkeley, California) since 1980, I have gone on not only to make my own and group quilts but to teach, write, edit, design, repair, and study them. I named and twice co-chaired my guild's VOICES IN CLOTH show and have served on many boards. For 14 years, I have enjoyed the weekly stimulus and support of my local minigroup, the Four Winds. I continue to take classes, travel, and support local and national groups and events; these keep my own juices flowing.

From commission and restoration work, writing, organization, and volunteer time, through seminars, workshops, classes, and conferences over 15 years in California, I have loved every minute – especially the people!

Quilting at a guild meeting.
Left to right: Dorenda Collins, Iris Marble, H. Miller, Leo McClain.

Mary Emma Allen quilting with 4-year-old granddaughter, Kara Lynn Mastin, Plymouth, NH.

Carol Wagner, Roseville, Minnesota

Carol Wagner was born in Milwaukee, Wisconsin, graduated from the University of Wisconsin-Milwaukee. She and her husband currently reside in Minnesota. She began quilting in 1975 and teaching adult community education classes in 1983. Carol has taught at AQS, Houston Quilt Festival, NQA, and to guilds across the country. She designs, appliqués, and hand quilts all of her quilts and thinks the hardest part is transferring her mental image to fabric. Her Statue Liberty quilt was Minnesota's winning entry in the Great American Quilt Festival in New York City, and her quilts have won awards in shows across the country.

Carol is the author of *Adapting Architectural Details for Quilts* and *New Patterns from Old Architecture* published by AQS. She has designed for Oxmoor House needlework books and written for *American Quilter*, *Quilting Today*, and *Quilt World*. She is a member of AQS, NQA, AIQA, and Minnesota Quilters.

Cherita Page Walker, Zeigler, Illinois

Cherita Page Walker was born in 1925, in Elizabethtown, IL. She grew up in Detroit, MI, graduated from high school in Detroit, attended SIU in Carbondale, IL.

Her mother, Mary Frances Gustin Page, taught her how to quilt at the age of 12. She has made 50 quilts, has no special quilt, loves them all.

Has made full-size and baby quilts, for own use, and grandchildren. Her quilts are registered with the State of IL, her "Engagement Ring Quilt" can be found in a book published by the State of IL, *History From the Heart: Quilt Paths Across Illinois*. Her name can be found in the Quilters' Walk in Paducah, KY. Belongs to AQS. Her quilts have been displayed at Du Quoin State Fair of Illinois, and on State of IL Quilt Tour in 1994.

Beth Frisbie Wallace, Francestown, New Hampshire

Fiber artist, quiltmaker, teacher, and designer. Beth's work is

distinguished by original designs and a rich variety of fabrics. Her wearable art has been shown in "Craftwear" at Annual League of NH Craftsmen's Fair and Sharon Arts Center. Beth's wallhangings have won ribbons at Vermont Quilt Festival and been juried into N.E. Quilters' Guild "Images," League of NH Craftsmen Annual Show, "Small Quilt Art Exhibition" and "Living with Crafts" at League of NH Craftsmen's Fair. Her pieces are in private collections such as CMC Hospital, Manchester, NH. Beth teaches diverse topics including basic skills, color, and original designs to quilters of all levels.

Juried into League of NH Craftsmen, 1991. Designed Christmas ornament for White House collection, 1993.

Faith S. Wallace, Wilmington, North Carolina

Designer and quiltmaker (hobby/amateur). Art major and educator. My interest in quilting and sewing began with my grandmother and mother. From them I learned to sew but not to quilt. In high school I won the Crisco Award for my skills as a seamstress. After graduation I pursued a career in graphic arts. Later, when I married I put my efforts towards helping my husband in his business. My hectic pace came to a halt in the late '80's as I had an auto accident. It was then I began to renew my love of quilting through reading and making baby quilts for gifts. Quilting became therapy during that difficult time. This lead me to search out classes to see the process and meet other quilters. At present I have returned to school, working on a visual arts degree. Fabric art in the form of quilting, will hold a special place for me as an art educator.

Judy Anne Walter, New York, New York

Judy Anne Walter was born August 7, 1951, in Cleveland, Ohio. Although she has spent most of her life in Chicago and the Midwest, she currently resides in Woodside, Queens, New York.

Judy began making quilts when she was in high school out of her dressmaking scraps. Today her geometric quilts containing vivid hand-dyed fabrics have been shown throughout the United States in group and juried shows including "The Quilt Movement" at the Dairy Barn (Athens, OH) and "Personal Landscapes" which toured nationally for two years. She has shown

her work in Chicago in three one-woman shows, in invitational shows at the Textile Art Centre, and in an exhibit for the Chicago Cubs at Marianne Desan Gallery.

Her work has received numerous awards, including a Judge's Special Merit Award at the 1986 American Quilter's Society Show. Judy's work is included in the collections of Compaq Computer Corporation (Houston, TX), Loyola University Medical Center (Maywood, IL), Highland Park Medical Associates (Highland Park, IL), Schiff Hardin and Waite (Chicago, IL), as well as in private collections. Her work has appeared in *Quilter's Newsletter, American Quilter, Lady's Circle Patchwork Quilts, Quilting USA, Patchwork Quilt Tshushin, Quiltworld,* and *Quiltworld Omnibook.* Her wearable art was included in the 1985, 1986, and the 10th Anniversary Superstar Fashion Shows sponsored by Fairfield Processing Corporation.

Judy has been teaching fiberarts since 1980. She has been on the teaching faculty for many conferences including Sievers School of Fiberarts (1991, 1990), North Carolina Quilt Symposium (1994, 1992), Minnesota Quilt Symposium (1993), The Big Tree Conference (1991), American Quilter's Society 1989 Conference, Quilting by-the-Lake (1989, 1987), and has taught for numerous quilt guilds and art centers. Judy was named "1986 Teacher of the Year" by *Professional Quilter Magazine.* She has had arts residencies at Artpark (Lewiston, NY; 1987), Quilting by-the-Lake (Cazenovia, NY; 1989), and as an Artist-in-Education (1989 – 1991) through the Illinois Arts Council. Judy is the author of *Creating Color: A Dyer's Handbook*, published in 1990 by Cooler by the Lake Publications.

Judy Alsip Ward, Corbin, Kentucky

Born January 4, 1900, in Whitley County, KY. Currently resides in Corbin, KY. She has been a quilter since childhood, making more quilts than she remembers. One year she grew cotton, corded it enough for one quilt, a Dalhia. She dyed feed sacks and sashed it. The Dalhia was recently shown in Cincinnati, OH, and took an honorable mention with articles in newspapers. It's a Depression quilt, made in early forties.

Through the years her quilts have been shown at fairs and shows. She makes tops today but no longer quilts. Christmas 1993 she gave her three children and six grandchildren a quilt each, recently made, all are full and queen size. All patterns are favorites used; at 95 she yet sews and promotes needlework.

Katherine Stubbs Ward, Riviera Beach, Florida

Quiltmaker, teacher, designer, judge, author. Katherine Stubbs Ward was born October 17, 1943, in Bradenton, Florida. She graduated from Manatee H.S. in 1961, received a BS degree in fashion merchandising in 1965, and a Masters in social work in 1974 from Florida State University, Tallahassee.

Kathy began quilting in 1982, and teaching at a local quilt shop in 1984. She now teaches locally and nationally, including NQA, N.C. Quilt Symposium, and AQS. Kathy received teacher's certification from NQA in 1989. She completed the NQA judge's course and has been involved in judging on local, regional, and national levels. Kathy is a founding member and past president of Palm Beach County Quilters' Guild and a member also of Gold Coast Quilters' Guild, NQA, S.E. Florida Art Quilters, and a charter member of AQS. She has served on the board of local guilds and NQA.

The sewing machine is Kathy's favorite sewing tool, and she especially loves designing garments and quilts that have texturing and special machine techniques. She has received awards locally and nationally for her garments and quilts.

Meg Warner, York, Pennsylvania

Meg Metzler Warner was born March 4, 1947, in Chicago, IL. She grew up in Nappanee, IN, and graduated from Manchester College, N. Manchester, IN, in 1970. Since 1973, Meg and her husband, Bill, have lived in York, PA. Meg was introduced to quilting by her late mother-in-law, Alice May Warner, and made her first quilt in 1978. Since 1984 she has concentrated on designing and making original contemporary quilts.

Meg has had quilts juried into the "Flights of Imagination" shows at the Artworks at Doneckers in Ephrata, PA; the "Quilters Heritage Celebration" in Lancaster, PA; and the AQS show in Paducah, KY. She was invited to participate in the Pilgrim/Roy Quilt Challenge in 1994, and her quilts are in many private collections.

Judi Warren, Maumee, Ohio

Since 1981, Judi has presented lectures and workshops to quiltmakers in the U.S., Canada, Switzerland, and Japan. Her quilts have been in six Quilt National exhibitions, in galleries and juried shows throughout the world, and are in private collections in America, Japan, and Australia. Judi's book, *Fabric Postcards* was published by AQS in 1994. She has written articles for *American Quilter* and *Quilts Japan* magazines and is represented in *88 Leaders of the Quilt World Today* (Nihon Vogue).

With an art education background, and an MFA degree, Judi introduces color and design vocabulary in popular quiltmaking workshops that emphasize exploration and discovery, and encourage students to express personal themes and content in their quilts.

Larry Warrick, Seattle, Washington

Larry learned to quilt at age 14. He is self taught and owes some of his experience to his aunt. Larry's work is all hand done. He has done patchwork, appliqué, some embroidery, but enjoys quilting the best.

Larry teaches quiltmaking at three community colleges in the state of Washington. He has won over 50 state ribbons at the Western Washington State Fair and also has won a National ribbon in 1989 in the NQA Show.

He has been published in many newspapers, been in the *Quilter's Newsletter Magazine*, and published in the 1991 edition of *Great American Quilts*.

Mary Ann Wasick, West Allis, Wisconsin

Born in 1946, in Milwaukee. I began quilting around 1980 specializing in clothing embellishments on collars and vests, many of which I designed. I am influenced by Victorian crazy quilting and appreciate the embroidery techniques. I cherish my collection of antique doilies, handkerchiefs, thimbles, and sewing tools.

I exhibited vests, a doll, wallhangings, and soft sculpture pieces at the Waukesha Technical College and West Allis City Hall Gallery. Won a viewer's choice award for quilted outfit – "Home Town." I won most creative award at the Honey Bee Quilt Guild (1994) membership challenge show. I directed the documentation of the quilt collection at the West Allis Historical Society's Museum for the Wisconsin Quilt History Project.

I have had several book reviews on quilting and crafts published in *Library Journal* and *Kliatt Paperback Books for Young Adults*.

Patricia Sims Watson, Canadian, Texas

Patricia Sims Watson, a fifth generation Texan, born in the hill country during the Depression, entire schooling in Marble Falls, now living in Canadian in the Texas Panhandle. My working career was a secretary.

My mother quilted and my grandmother pieced quilts on her treadle machine. I began quilting 13 years ago in Oklahoma and later in Gillette, Wyoming. I learned to knit and crochet at age 35, and have made over 200 afghans; to needlepoint 20 years ago and to do counted cross-stitch 10 years ago.

The traditional pieced patterns are my favorites, especially the Log Cabin, and I like scrap quilts. I machine quilt, in the ditch, most of the quilts I give away. I also combine hand and machine quilting on many. Of the 60 or more quilts I have made I have kept only a few. I have ideas for dozens more.

Mary Ann Waxler, Mapleton, North Dakota

Mary Ann Odegard Waxler was born Dec. 11, 1928, in Fargo, ND. She and husband, George, reside on a farm near Mapleton, ND, where they have lived for 47 years. Mary Ann became interested in quilting about the same time the Quilters' Guild of North Dakota was organized in 1980. She is a charter member and past president of that organization and enjoys being involved in all activities of the guild.

When she began quilting she made several bed-size quilts but has gradually reduced her expectations to more realistic proportions. Currently she is more apt to experiment with original designs or try new quilting techniques or styles on smaller projects such as; wall quilts or baby quilts. She particularly enjoys hand piecing and hand quilting, but also frequently uses the sewing machine and rotary cutter to save time.

She enjoys teaching quilting classes and drawing "Suzy Quilter" cartoons or writing articles for the guild newsletter.

Bernice M. Wayman, Redlands, California

Quiltmaker. My great-grandmother taught me to pull a needle and thread through cloth at the tender age of 2 on a farm in Iowa. I discovered the art of quiltmaking in southern California some 40 years later. Although a sewing machine is my preference for piecing and quilting, I also enjoy quilting by hand which would make my great-grandmother proud. In my career I have worked extensively with computers and am now using my home computer to create original quilt designs. My goals include both teaching my craft to beginning quilters and writing about quilting. My first quilt, which I made for my sister, won a ribbon at NQA's California Gold Rush in 1995, at Riverside, CA.

Kathy Weaver, Highland Park, Illinois

Designer. My involvement with quilting is linked to my concern with society's inequities. In my political art quilts I use the soft, nurturing quilt medium as a means to entreat the viewer to study the message of the work. Lush textures, rich diversity of materials, intense colors, and drawn, painted, and photo-silk-screened surfaces provide additional enticement to uncover layers of information in the pieces. The ease and delight one feels upon experiencing the surface is in contrast to the stark, devastating images portrayed. This contrast serves to unsettle the observer's emotions and to mirror the condition of society. The incongruities and unfair consequences of life resulting from one's economic or political situation are reiterated in the quilts.

Memorable quilting experiences: Paper/Fiber XVIII Judge's Award, Artforms '95 Eli Lilly Award of Distinction, projects with children of Onward Neighborhood House.

Lynn Biddulph Weber, Long Beach, California

I was born in Mount Clemens, Michigan, and now live in Long Beach, California. I am married to Franz K. Weber, lighting designer, and have two stepchildren, Leeana and Brent. I am a charter member of Quilters by the Sea, started in Long Beach in 1993. I love making big quilts and with my projects and fabric collection am slowly taking over all the rooms of my house. I also do Hardanger embroidery and have won several ribbons, including a blue ribbon. Have shown three quilts in the county fair. Although no awards have yet been received, I am hoping this will be my year!

Ramonda V. Weckerle, Roseburg, Oregon

My quilting adventure began 20 years ago, when I saw an adult education class offered by Quilting (San Diego, CA). That was about the time someone discovered, in a hardware store, the rotary cutter. I was fortunate to be near the Eleanor Burns facility "Quilt in a Day," and was introduced to fast patch piecing. This definitely planted and reinforced the now embedded quilting seed. The Navy transferred my husband to Guam and so the seed went with me. Upon our return, I found new and refreshing

ideas had been discovered in the quilting field. I have done just about the entire spectrum of quilting and have finally found my niche. Curation and documentation with the Douglas County Museums Quilt Research Group (group composed of Judy Byrd, Irene Zenev, and myself). I enjoy the experience of theory and development, and execution of an idea. In particular – "The Square Root of Two."

I am an AQS member and have entered many times and attended the second annual show. I enjoy lecturing about the history of quilting. I teach sparingly and show my quilts. I prepare and conduct exhibitions, contests, and shows for quilting in our area. One of my most unusual projects was designing and creating a stage quilt for the play: *Quilter's in Six Weeks*. Member of the Chula Vista Quilters Guild, CA; Umpqua Valley Quilters Guild, OR; and founded the Imperial Beach Library's Thursday Morning Quilters, CA.

Saundra L. Weed, Westland, Michigan

Author, artist, and designer. Saundra specializes in 3-D "quilted paintings" that combine both her art background and fashion design skills. A graduate of the National School of Dress Design, she also creates quilted clothing and jewelry. Saundra is an active member of the Greater Ann Arbor Quilt Guild and the Quilt Guild of Metro Detroit in the Michigan area. "I only belong to organizations that use their skills to provide a community service," says Ms. Weed. The GAAQG supplies over 275 quilts a year to "Safe House," as well as clothing and other items. Ms. Weed added "quilts were created with love to add comfort to the home. It is important to me that we continue to share that love and comfort with others."

Saundra Weed, author of *Dollars Sales and Sense*, a complete business system for artists, craftsmen, and creative sewers, is a well known writer and lecturer in the sewing community. Her sewing, quilting, and "How to" articles appear regularly in such national publications as *Wearable Crafts* magazine and *Observer Eccentric Newspaper's* Specialty Publications. *Creative Sewing as a Business*, her new book is designed to help creative sewers to accurately assess and price their art quilts, and start their own home based sewing business.

Lorre Marie Weidlich, Austin, Texas

Lorre Marie Weidlich was born on December 31, 1950, in

Photo by Evergreen Studios.

Cincinnati, Ohio. She first developed an interest in stitchery of all kinds, including quilting, during her college years at the University of Michigan in Ann Arbor, MI.

From Michigan she moved to Austin, TX, to attend the graduate folklore program at the University of Texas. There she pursued quilting as a scholarly interest, culminating in a dissertation about the current quilt revival.

Today she divides her time between teaching, judging, and lecturing, and doing research into the culture of the quilt world. She has published in both scholarly and popular periodicals, and has won numerous awards for her quilted works.

Janell Hansen Weinberger, Sun Prairie, Wisconsin

Janell Hansen Weinberger was born September 17, 1965 in Waupaca, WI. She graduated from Sun Prairie High School in 1993 and still lives in Sun Prairie, WI. She and her husband, David, have three children. Janell visited her first quilt class at age 5 and now teaches quilt classes for adult education. She started winning ribbons at quilt shows and 4-H fairs at age 13. Her original design quilts have appeared in *Quilt Art* calendars in 1994 and 1997. *Quilting Today Magazine* published her work in issue #32. She has a series of English piecing patterns for sale in many quilt shops and continues to create pieces for publication. Janell is the entry chairman for the Prairie Heritage Quilt Show, Sun Prairie, and has done some quilt judging. She is teaching her daughter, Jessi, to piece her first quilt.

Helen Weinman, Centerville, Massachusetts

Teacher, shop owner, designer, and quiltmaker. Helen Weinman was born September 9, 1948, in New York City, attended Syracuse University and Pace University, and currently resides on Cape Cod, MA.

Helen Weinman is a teacher, lecturer, quiltmaker, and shop owner of "Heartbeat Quilts" in Hyannis, MA. She started quilting in 1986, taught her first class in 1987, quitting her full-time job as a paralegal to pursue a career as a quilt professional.

She has conducted Quilt Camp weekends in Ogunquit, Maine, and on Cape Cod for the past six years and has earned a reputation for being a strong motivator inspiring students with prolific quiltmaking and creative fabric choices. Workshops are in fast

piecing techniques, machine quilting, and fabric selection.

Helen's quilts have been featured in several issues of *Traditional Quilter* magazine and Carol Doak's books, *Easy Paper Pieced Keepsake Quilts* and *Mix and Match Paper Foundation Quilts*. Her success is due to her sense of humor, positive attitude, honesty, and hard work. In her free time, Helen enjoys playing tennis, gourmet cooking, and making homemade jam. Founder and organizer of Quiltcamp™, since 1987, area coordinator of ABC Quilts.

Susan K. Whatley, Oriental, North Carolina

Susan K. Whatley was born Nov. 25, 1935, in Burlington, NC; graduated from Oak Ridge (TN) High School in 1954; and received her BS and MS degrees in engineering science and mechanics from the University of Tennessee in 1976 and 1979, respectively. She and her husband, Marvin E., currently reside in Oriental, NC, where they moved after cruising aboard their sailboat for 5 years following retirement from Oak Ridge National Laboratory.

Both Susan's mother and grandmother quilted all the bedding used in her youth and her mother gave her a quilt to start housekeeping. As her children married, she commissioned quilts for the first two from Alison Arnold in Oak Ridge, TN, but when she asked Alison to make a third quilt, Alison signed her up for a quilting class instead. She took her first sampler class in 1986 while working as an engineer but did not finish it until 1988.

She is currently a member of the Crystal Coast Quilter's Guild, AQS, and the NQA.

Deborah White, Hansville, Washington

I am a wife and mother of two teenagers and a one year old. I began quilting about 13 years ago as a sanity keeper when I was a stay-at-home mom. It worked, it gave me something to look forward to everyday.

Now, I am a miniature quilt artist. I design, teach, lecture, and I love to enter competitions; it drives me to accomplish things I would otherwise not attempt. I have placed first in several national competitions, Miniatures From the Heart, Columbus Heritage, and Quilters Unlimited Showcase; but one of my biggest thrills was second place at the AQS show.

Some of my best friends and memories have come from my involvement with quilting. Whether it is hanging a quilt show, going to a retreat, or just roaming the countryside for antiques, when I think of quilting I think of my buds.

Elsa K. White, Mountainside, New Jersey

Born in Elizabeth, NJ, on April 13, 1924. Before starting kindergarten, my Danish grandmother taught me to crochet, knit, and sew. My first exposure to quilting was a visit to my husband's home in Kentucky (1945). The quilts on canopied beds were exquisite. The fine handwork took my breath away. I started my first quilt – a baby quilt, and later, wedding quilts for my children.

My interest has never waned. I attended many classes and seminars over the years, to observe new techniques. In 1973, I was invited to teach two classes at the Newark Museum (NJ), the Short Hills Arboretum (NJ) followed by several adult schools, at one time conducting eight 2½ hour classes per week. Twenty-two years later I still enjoy my classes and the warm friendships which have developed. Member of Garden State Quilters, New Hampshire League of Craftsman, and T & T Quilter's Group. I have conducted two quilt shows from my students. Judged several local shows. Quilting instructor for 23 years and quiltmaker for 48 years. My class at Newark Museum, NJ, made Bicentennial quilt (now in their collection). Won honorable mention in *Quilter's Newsletter* contest. Two classes made a quilt and sold it for $3,500 and donated proceeds to a hospital.

Marlene Cronk White, Webster, New York

Traditional quiltmaker. Member of Genesee Valley Quilt Club, Webster Quilt Guild, Irondequoit Quilt Guild, and various national organizations. Taught basic quilt classes and demonstrations. President GVQC 1974 – 1975 and 1995 – 1996. Chairman GVQC 1995 Quilt Show. Chairman of GVQC quilt raffle.

Margaret Whitesides, Brighton, Tennessee

Margaret Cates Whitesides was born August 3, 1917. She and her husband, Mandell, live near Brighton, TN. At about age 10 her mother taught her to quilt. But she seriously started making quilts in 1983. Margaret and several other members of a senior citizens group at Holly Grove Church began making quilts as a money-making project for the group.

Also she has made several quilts for her grandchildren. Double Wedding Ring and Log Cabin are two patterns she has used. Also her most prized one is an appliquéd rose quilt she made for her daughter-in law.

Katy J. Daugherty Widger, Edgewood, New Mexico

Katy J. Daugherty Widger, born February 17, 1954, Carlsbad, New Mexico. Married to Ken R. Widger, 1981. Art major, San Juan College, Farmington, New Mexico, 1987 – 1989. Author: *Color Wheel Fabric Dyeing*, 1991; *Print Your Own Fabric*, 1995. Finalist AQS Show 1991, 1993, 1994. Juror's Award of Merit – Quilt National '95. Published in quilting books and magazines: *American Quilter*; *Quilter's Newsletter Magazine*; *Fiber Arts Design Book Five*, Lark Books, 1995.

I began quilting in 1984 inspired by a Victorian crazy quilt made by grandmothers. Since 1988, I have created the surface design on all fabric used in my quilts, utilizing hand-carved stamps and hand-dyeing techniques.

Most of my works are abstract representations of my personal response to the landscape and sky of my native New Mexico, reflecting my deeply held belief that "God's eternal Deity and power are clearly perceived in the things that He has created."

Marguerite Wiebusch, Burlington, Indiana

A quilting enthusiast since 1964, doing extensive quilt photography, collecting research materials, and quilting friends.

Self-published three books of original quilting patterns; *Feathers & Other Fancies*, *More Feathers & Other Fancies*, and *Some More Fancies, Etc.*

A 24-year member of NQA, and NQA certified judge since 1983. A charter member of AQS and MAQS, fortunate to have attended every AQS show and always white glove. For four years, chairman of documentation of the Indiana Quilt Registry Project, and co-authored *Quilts of Indiana* published 1991 by IU Press.

I serve on the Indiana State Quilt Guild Board of Directors and belong to four quilting groups and the Marie Webster Quilters Hall of Fame. My special interests are research, wallhangings, and miniatures.

Both my husband, Richard, and I value the many friends we have made all over the U.S. in my pursuit of quilts but the surprise Friendship Quilt: "A Collection of Red Barns," presented to me in October 1992 by some special friends will always be a cherished memory. To our delight the quilt was juried into the 1995 AQS show.

Rhea Wiens, Fresno, California

Rhea Wiens was born on August 11 in Blackfoot, Idaho. She lives in Fresno, California, with her husband, John.

She is credited with being a charter member of several quilting groups and quilting bees and has started several groups in California and Washington. She has taught 4-H girls, church groups, and has involved friends in making quilts for nursing homes, the veterans hospital, the community hospital's less fortunate newborn babies, and the police patrol cars.

Currently she is teaching quilting classes for the Fresno Adult School and for several fabric stores. She finishes quilts for others with the professional quilting machine purchased several years ago when she began her quilting business. She encourages friends and students to join the San Joaquin Valley Quilters' Guild of which she is a member. She is a member of the Quilts and Company Group and a participant in several round robin quilting groups.

Betty Wilkins, Mt. Pleasant, Pennsylvania

Betty Newell Wilkins was born Aug. 23, 1922. She learned to quilt from her grandmother and mother, when she was about 12 years old. When she began to quilt they used oil lamps for light. Quilting is how they filled the long winter evenings. When there were no quilts to quilt they cut patches for the next quilt.

Most of the quilts Betty does are for friends or people referred to her by friends. She has quilted wallhangings and baby quilts, but most of the quilts she does now are queen or king size. She has quilted mostly pieced quilts; Lonestar, Flower Garden, Trip Around the World, but no real fancy quilts. In 12 years she quilted 72 quilts, some of those she quilted with colored thread.

Beth Ann Williams, Grand Rapids, Michigan

Collector, designer, quiltmaker. When Beth started quilting in 1992, she had only very limited sewing experience. She had been diagnosed with a very grave illness, with an uncertain prognosis, and was concerned about leaving a legacy for her two children.

Although she has never taken a class, workshop, or formal lesson, she hesitates to say she is self taught, as she has studied literally hundreds of books and magazines in the course of learning the art. Three years and over 30 projects later, she has progressed rapidly, exploring quilts as a way to express herself artistically in traditional patterns, colorwash, and appliqué in which she is exploring Celtic patterns. With the prognosis much more positive, she looks forward to a long career.

First public showing was part of a juried exhibition of Irish art in conjunction with a local "Taste of Ireland" festival in Rockford, MI. Response was positive, she has received invitations for further exhibitions in the Grand Rapids area as part of the local Irish and Irish-American community.

Beverly Mannisto Williams, Cadillac, Michigan

Quilt designer, quiltmaker, and bobbin lace maker. Born Dec. 2, 1942, in Grand Rapids, MI, and living most of my life in Cadillac, MI. Having married young to Chad Williams and raising three sons with little means of purchasing gifts for love ones, learned to make them myself. After years of creating "disposable items," I took the time to make a quilt as a 25th wedding anniversary gift to myself. That whole-cloth quilt with a handmade bobbin lace edge lead to many national awards, the NQA Master Quilter's Guild, NQA Best of Show, and AQS Gingher Workmanship Award. When releasing this quilt to reside at the MAQS I felt I had raised another child and the time came to share it with others. I have made garments for the Fairfield Fashion Show and Sulky of America. I continue to create quilts and lace, work part time, show grandchildren the joys of creativity, and teach quilting and bobbin lace on occasion.

Mary Lou Williams, Tempe, Arizona

Teacher, quiltmaker. Mary Lou Williams was born Sept. 2, 1939, in Meadville, PA. She has a B.A. in home economics from Goshen College and an M.S. in home ec. ed. from Texas Women's University. Mary Lou and her husband, Ron, live in Tempe, Arizona.

Her mother taught her to quilt at age 14, but she really began quilting seriously in 1977, while teaching at Glendale Community College in Arizona.

She is currently active in Arizona Quilters Guild, having served as publicity chair in 1993 – 94, and as chairwoman of a local chapter from 1990 to 1992. She is at present teaching in AQG's Traveling Teacher program for the fourth year.

Her love in addition to making quilts is to share her knowledge and encourage others.

Linda L. Winter, Holdrege, Nebraska

Quiltmaker, collector, teacher, lecturer, and designer. Linda Esslinger Winter was born March 2, 1947, in Oxford, Nebraska; graduated from Arapahoe High School in 1965; and attended School of Practical Nursing, Kearny, Nebraska. Linda and her husband live in Holdrege, Nebraska.

Observing her mother and grandmother as they quilted, Linda started her first quilt at the age of seven. She not only enjoys quilting but also preserving our quilt heritage.

Remembering those feedsacks from childhood and a stack of feedsacks purchased at her great-aunt's sale started her in research of the Depression era quilts. She also enjoys working with new fabric as well as vintage fabrics.

Linda is currently a member of her local and state guild, AQS, Feedsack Club, and Colorado Quilting Council. I have won ribbons at the local fair as well as at the state fair. Also at several quilt shows on several of my quilts. One quilt published by Oxmoor House.

Joen Wolfrom, Fox Island, Washington

National/international teacher and lecturer, quiltmaker, and textile artist. Enjoys gardening, cooking, reading, and relaxing in nature. First career: elementary school teacher.

Author of *Landscapes & Illusions, The Magical Effects of Color,* and *The Visual Dance – Creating Spectacular Quilts.* Developed techniques for strip-pieced landscapes, Log Cabin, and free-flowing curved designs. Currently interested in color and design exploration in both traditional and contemporary quilts.

Commissioned pieces in United States, Canada, United Kingdom, Europe, and Japan. Enjoys meeting, sharing, working with quilters, and making new friends during teaching engagements in U.S. and other countries.

Margaret Wood, Phoenix, Arizona

Award-winner Margaret Wood, began sewing at age 9 and helped her mother make quilts at age 12. Her adult quilting started in

1977 at age 27. She has won awards and shown in Phoenix, Santa Fe, LA, San Francisco, New Orleans, and other cities.

Arizona born and raised, Ms. Wood has a BA in elementary education and a Master's in library science. In 1981 she wrote a book titled *Native American Fashion* and started a clothing business with the same name. In 1991 she changed the focus of her work to quilts with clothing as a sideline.

A Navajo/Seminole Indian, all her quilt themes reflect Indian myth, design, and symbolism. She makes wallhangings and full-size art quilts. Methods include machine piecing, hand and machine appliqué, hand and machine quilting.

Tina B. Woodall, Winchester, Virginia

Tina B. Woodall was born August 8, 1959, in Winfield, KS. She currently resides in Winchester, VA, with her husband and their three children. They are expecting another child soon.

Tina has been quilting since 1990. To date she has made 30 quilts. Her favorite part of the process is hand quilting, although hand piecing comes in a close second.

She loves traditional designs, most notably Texas Star, Kansas Twister, and Grandmother's Flower Garden. Her sisters, Amy Lindberg and Jenny Hubbard, also quilt.

Marlene Brown Woodfield, LaPorte, Indiana

Marlene Brown Woodfield was born March 29, 1936, in Lafayette, IN. She and her husband, Ted, live in LaPorte Co, IN. After her graduation from Purdue University, she taught pre-school for 26 years before retiring to pursue her hobby of quilting.

Marlene enjoys making quilts requiring a large number of fabrics to get the texture and shading. She is currently teaching multifabric facial imagery and how to make pictorial multifabric (charm) quilts along with several other classes.

She has won numerous awards and has a wall quilt included in the MAQS permanent collection. She is a member of Dunes Country Quilters, Michigan City, IN; String-A-Long Quilt Guild, Valparaiso, IN; Indiana State Quilt Guild; AQS; NQA; and AIQA.

Sarah Hildreth Woodring, Charlotte, North Carolina
Quiltmaker, designer, historian, collector, and teacher. One of the founders of Charlotte Quilters Guild and have held many offices. President of NC Quilt Symposium.

Area coordinator for NC Quilt Project. Seventy-five documentation days throughout the state recorded more than 10,000 quilts. Book was published.

Guest curator at History Museum for quilt exhibit. Numerous awards and many commissions.

Norma Jean Woods, Paragould, Arkansas

Norma is 55 years old, a housewife, and pattern designer. Mother of three grown children and the grandmother of six. Being one of 11 children, quiltmaking was necessary to keep our beds supplied with enough covers to stay warm during cold winter months. I began helping my mother piece string quilts at age nine. We made string quilts because there was absolutely no waste of fabric.

We would cut squares of paper from the catalog and sew strips across the squares overlapping the layers to form straight seams. We then cut away the excess fabric that extended beyond the paper square to have a completed block. We saved all the cutaways for more blocks.

Being very creative and talented with needlework, my mother taught me to strip the tops together and quilt them on a frame that hung from the ceiling. We used chalk and string to mark fan designs on the top for quilting lines.

During the following years my love for sewing continued to grow. I learned to coordinate colors and follow sewing patterns in home economics.

After my first marriage in 1957, I went to work in a factory making clothing. We had three children and sewing for them was my favorite pastime.

In 1976 my husband became ill with cancer. It was necessary to quit working to be with him when he had chemotherapy. Because we needed my income I purchased industrial sewing machines and opened a custom sewing business at home.

In 1978 we went to Arkansas State Fair and I saw a hand guided quilting machine being demonstrated. My love for sewing combined with God-given talent to draw, sparked my imagination. I daydreamed about how I could create different quilting designs

with that machine for a year before I got up enough courage to invest in one.

I opened the custom quilting business in January 1980 in Hoxie, AR, known as Norma's Quilt Shop and began creating designs right away to use on the machine. Anything I could draw in a continuous line I could stitch on the layers of a quilt. It was fantastic.

Quiltmaking was experiencing a revival because of the energy shortage and women were joining the work force in great numbers. My business was successful partly because finding time to make the tops was possible but quilting them was too time consuming for working women.

The popularity of my designs grew and the company where I purchased my machine offered to sell patterns as a complement to their product. The first patterns were hand copied, but, it was only a short time before a copier became necessary. I now have 125 different patterns, 65 copyright designs available. My designs are sold world-wide and the business has grown to the point that I was forced to discontinue the custom quilting service. I now make quilts by custom order only and for my own pleasure.

Girl Scouts in Sandy, OR, getting ready to quilt.
Front: Gelsey Muggli, Dominique Berge. Second row: Caitlyn Terrell, Andi Daugherty, Dominica Russell, Savannah Smith, Julianne Smith, Amy Daugherty, Shayla Smith, Karen Dysart. Back row: Glorianne Muggli.

Blanche Young, Westminster, California

Author, quiltmaker, teacher. Blanche Young has had a life-long romance with fabric and sewing machines. Blanche made her first quilt at the age of 13 and admits that she has yet to tire of it. Skilled in all types of sewing, she began her teaching career with classes on clothing construction. Quilt classes replaced these in the early 1970's.

Blanche's ability to modify and streamline the sewing techniques for several favorite quilt designs led to publishing of several landmark books. She is well-known throughout the quilting world, for her quilts with their exciting and unusual color combinations as well as her enthusiasm and humor. She has been a featured teacher at many major quilt conferences and shows. A prolific quiltmaker, she makes dozens of quilts each year and has generously donated more than 50 quilts to different organizations for fund-raising purposes. When she isn't making quilts in her studio at her home in Westminster, California, or traveling to teach, she finds time to visit her seven children and 18 grandchildren.

Pat Young, Laguna Hills, California

Active in Beach Cities Quilter's Guild, this published teacher still finds time to quilt for her new grandson, Kyle. A quilter of 15 years and teacher for six years, she has won several awards from county fairs and local quilt guilds for her watercolor, crazy quilting, and broderie perse techniques. She loves presenting her "trunk show" and teaching quilt guilds the latest types in quilting.

Rosemary Youngs, Walker, Michigan

My name is Rosemary Youngs and I am a busy mother of four children as well as a preschool teacher. I am also a very traditional quilter and I love to design my own patterns. I love the whimsical quilts of the 1930's and the red and green quilts of the 1800's. I have collected a nice selection of reproduction fabrics as well as authentic fabrics that I found at estate sales. The most important thing about quilting is sharing and I don't just mean patterns and fabric. I meet with five special women every Wednesday to quilt, we share our lives, we laugh as well as cry together. The friendships we have formed are very special.

I have started entering my quilts in shows, including Paducah. The awards have been a nice surprise but the thought through sharing that I might inspire someone to quilt is much more important!

Karen E. Zalewski, Lewisville, Texas

I made my first quilt in 1975 as a gift for my parents. I've been teaching quilting since 1976. I've had two magazine articles published and one pattern published in a magazine. I'm writing a book and starting a pattern business. I have a quilting machine and do quilting for people.

My most memorable experience was my first winner. I saw the contest advertised while on vacation in New Mexico. When I returned from that vacation I learned we were relocating to North Carolina. I designed the quilt on the trip to NC. My first grandchild was born at the same time. So as soon as we moved in we were off to Minnesota to see him. I bought the fabric in Minnesota. The quilt "Southwest Sunset" earned me an honorable mention for color.

Maggine Zentner, Glendive, Montana

A member of the Sacred Heart Quilter's Group; am one of the two sewers who puts together all the patchwork quilts, and finishes off the quilts. Also do much quilting on my own for gifts to family/friends.

J. Richard Becker Jr., perusing through an album of quilts made for church women. Richard uses this treadle model G Singer for most of his quilting.

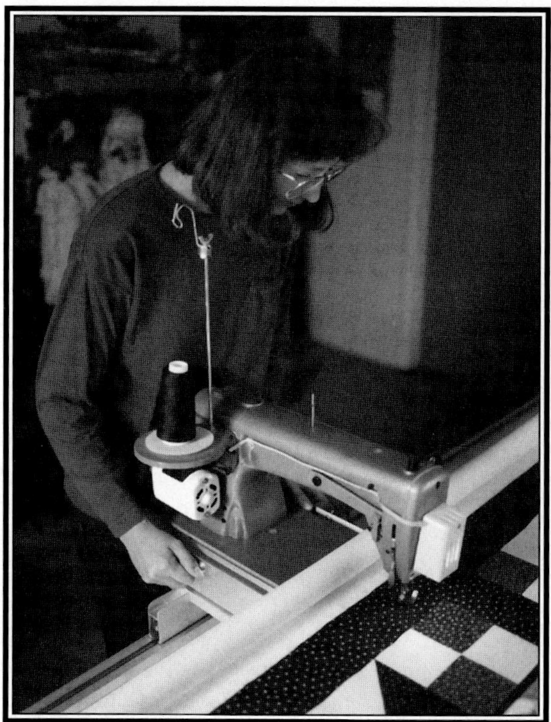

Theresa Bowden Fleming working on her commercial sewing machine.

Quilting in Harmony '95.
Catherine Greenwood, Judy Kaiser, Jackie Woosley, Rose Vanness, Bettye Sheppard.

ACQG	Angela City Quilt Guild		IRQN	Illinois Regional Quilters Network
AIQA	American International Quilt Association		ISQG	Indiana State Quilt Guild
AOL	America On Line		KHQS	Kentucky Heritage Quilt Society
APNQ	Association of Pacific Northwest Quilters		MAQS	Museum of the American Quilter's Society
AQG	Arizona Quilters Guild		MBA	Master of Business Administration
AQS	American Quilter's Society		MEd	Master of Education
AQSG	American Quilt Study Group		MQN	Michigan Quilting Network
ASN	American School of Needlework		MS	Master of Science
BA	Bachelor of Arts		MSQG	Mississippi State Quilt Guild
BFA	Bachelor of Fine Arts		MVQG	Mississippi Valley Quilter's Guild
BCQG	Big Creek Quilt Guild		NEA	National Endowment of the Arts
BS	Bachelor of Science		NEQG	New England Quilters Guild
CBQ & NG	Coastal Bend Quilt & Needlework Guild		NOW	National Organization of Women
CCQG	Capitol City Quilt Guild		NQA	The National Quilting Association
CQA	Canadian Quilters Association		PAAQT	Professional Association of Appraisers of Quilted Textiles
CQC	Colorado Quilting Council			
CQSG	Canadian Quilt Study Group		PIQF	Pacific International Quilt Festival
CQSP	Connecticut Quilt Search Project		QBL	Quilting by the Lake
ECQA	Eastcoast Quilters Alliance		QNM	*Quilter's Newsletter Magazine*
EGA	Embroiderer's Guild of America		QRS	Quilt Restoration Society
F.A.C.E.T.	Chicago-based art critique group		QSDS	Quilt Surface Design Symposium
FRCQ	Front Range Contemporary Quilters		RNQG	Rhododendron Needlers Quilt Guild
GAAQG	Greater Ann Arbor Quilt Guild		SAQA	Studio Art Quilt Associates
GHQG	Greater Hartford Quilt Guild		SCQG	Salt Creek Quilter's Guild
GSQA	Gulf States Quilting Association		SFVQA	San Fernando Valley Quilt Association
GVQC	Genesee Valley Quilt Guild		SPQG	Southtowns Piecemakers Quilting Guild
IQI	Illinois Quilters Inc.		SUNY	State University of New York
IQG	Iowa Quilters Guild		SVQG	Simi Valley Quilt Guild
IQN	Industrial Quilters Network		TAFTA	The Australia Forum for Textile Arts
IMIA	International Medical Informatics Assoc.		WGQG	West Georgia Quilter's Guild

The Class Act Quilting Beelette, Indianapolis, IN, makes quilts for charity. Left to right: Pat Hamby, Beverly Brewington, Judy Hill, Kay Banister, Suann Handschy, Dallas Reed, Libby Swarm, Carolyn Shay, Sandra Charles, Lynda Doyle.

Left to right seated: Ruby Churchill, Lee Johnson, Ruth Thacker. Left to right standing: Ruby Zunker, Helen McKinzie, Becky Selph, Ella Jo Allen, Janice Bryant, Shirley Jones, Helen Dickman, Viola Keck. (photo by Kathleen K. Qualia)

AQS Books on Quilts

This is only a partial listing of the books on quilts that are available from the American Quilter's Society. AQS books are known the world over for their timely topics, clear writing, beautiful color photographs, and accurate illustrations and patterns. Most of the following books are available from your local bookseller, quilt shop, or public library. If you are unable to locate certain titles in your area, you may order by mail from the AMERICAN QUILTER'S SOCIETY, P.O. Box 3290, Paducah, KY 42002-3290. Customers with Visa or MasterCard may phone in orders from 7:00–4:00 CST, Monday–Friday, Toll Free 1-800-626-5420. Add $2.00 for postage for the first book ordered and $0.40 for each additional book. Include item number, title, and price when ordering. Allow 14 to 21 days for delivery.